l o g o m a c h i a

# Logo

# machia

THE CONFLICT

OF

THE FACULTIES

*Edited by Richard Rand*

*University of Nebraska Press: Lincoln & London*

The paper in this book meets the minimum require-
ments of American National Standard for Information
Sciences – Permanence of Paper for Printed Library
Materials, ANSI Z39.48-1984

Library of Congress Cataloging in Publication Data
Logomachia: the conflict of the faculties / edited by
Richard Rand.   p. cm.
Papers originally presented at a symposium on the
topic of Kant's Der Streit der Fakultäten. It was spon-
sored by the English Department of the University of
Alabama in 1987.
ISBN 0-8032-3884-3 (cl.)   ISBN 0-8032-8940-5 (pbk.)
1. Education, Higher – Philosophy – Congresses.
2. Education, Higher – United States – Philosophy –
Congresses.   3. Philosophy – Congresses.
4. Academic freedom – Congresses.   5. Philosophy
and religion – Congresses   6. Law – Philosophy –
Congresses.   7. Medicine – Philosophy – Congresses.
8. Kant, Immanuel, 1724-1804. Streit der Fakultäten.
I. Rand, Richard A. (Richard Aldrich).
LB2322.2.L64   1992   378'.001-dc20   92-6977   CIP

Text in Adobe Minion, designed by Robert Slimbach,
typeset by Keystone Typesetting, Inc. The paper is
Glatfelter 55 lb. Natural. Book design by R. Eckersley.

# CONTENTS

These papers were read at a symposium sponsored by the English Department of the University of Alabama in 1987, 'Our Academic Contract:
*The Conflict of the Faculties* in America.' As indicated by the title, the
symposium took for its topic Immanuel Kant's *Der Streit der Fakultäten*
(1798).[1] Some papers deal directly with that essay, others indirectly,
working out of it, against it, around it, or away from it. ❧ The impetus
for this symposium came from a similar event held at Columbia University in April 1980, celebrating the centennial of Columbia's Graduate
School. More precisely, it came from a lecture delivered there by Jacques
Derrida entitled 'Mochlos; or, The Conflict of the Faculties.'[2] Included
here as an indispensable point of reference, 'Mochlos' made a singularly
powerful impression, calling attention to Kant's essay (a work unknown
even to many specialists in Kant studies), proposing a compellingly deconstructive reading of that work, and taking it as a point of departure
for further thoughts on the institution of the university. ❧ In *The Conflict of the Faculties,* Kant spells out the blueprint for the modern research university, assigning, within that blueprint, a site for those who
would pursue the work of 'reason' – the 'philosophical' faculty that con-
fers the Ph.D. degree, as distinguished from the faculties of law, medicine, and theology. Kant develops a juridical basis for the resolution of
intra-university conflicts, and of conflicts between the university and the
state, with the state serving at once as the professor's patron and censor.
Kant's essay, in point of fact, is an occasional exercise, written after the
occasion of censorship befalling his own publications in Prussia during
the 1790s. Seizing the moment of censorship, and working that moment
as a lever of opportunity (*mochlos* is a Greek word for 'lever'), Kant presents his own schematic proposal for the protection of academic freedom. His blueprint caught on with his fellow philosophers (among

them Wilhelm von Humboldt, who drew up the plan for the University of Berlin in 1810), becoming a success so canonical that, when American universities adopted it at the end of the century (Columbia was one of the first to do so), a subtle and intricate invention had turned, so to speak, into a self-evident machine somewhat unmindful of its own inaugural circumstances. ❧ How, in a context where charters are cherished (the Declaration of Independence comes to mind), could *The Conflict of the Faculties* have remained so utterly ignored? It is as if, to borrow a Kantian distinction, 'historical' knowledge had been forsaken for an (assumed) acquisition of 'rational knowledge.' Derrida's 'Mochlos' itself does not address the problem; rather, it advances an argument that Kant's essay, in the very premises of its scheme, may have foreclosed its own transformation into effective political freedom. In Derrida's reading, Kant builds his edifice (and his essay) upon a metaphysical determination of language, one which holds that language can only happen either as action ('performance' in an executive sense) or as description ('constative' speculation). Kant, who is seen to promote this binary opposition of concept and deed, theory and decree, appears to contrive a division of labor in which the philosopher confines his public language to utterances of a constative mode, and resigns to the sovereign the performative language of command. The commonplace of the university as an 'ivory tower' finds its support in such a reading – all the more a 'tower' insofar as philosophers, for Kant, preside over the academy somewhat as the sovereign presides without. Philosophers, the 'lower faculty,' preside in the sense that they are held to judge, insofar as it is rationally possible to do so, the truth-value of matters concerning the 'higher faculties' of theology, law, and medicine. Where the higher faculties are seen as a bureaucratic extension of the state, the lower faculty is charged with judging the theoretical validity of the given law, medical procedure, or ecclesiastical statute; the higher faculties ought not to inhibit the publication of those judgments, and Kant holds the state itself responsible for keeping all intramural jurisdictions separate and distinct. (Kant's inversive nomenclature is ironic: 'The reason why this faculty, despite its great prerogative (freedom), is called the lower faculty lies in human nature: for a man who can give commands, even though he is someone else's humble servant, is considered more distinguished than a free man who has no one under his command.')[3] ❧ Hinging, as 'Mochlos' construes it, on an untenable or unreal concept of language, giving rise to many a parasitic effect, Kant's blueprint could not, and did not, merely *happen*. In the United States, indeed, the earliest research professors of philosophy (those with Ph.D.'s who also taught the subject known as 'philosophy') were primarily theologians: for example, George Sylvester Morris, a diligent reader of Kant and Hegel who organized the (Ph.D.) philosophy department at Johns Hopkins (Royce, James, Peirce, and Dewey were his colleagues and pupils), was above all a dogmatic Protestant from the Calvinist milieu of Vermont. In his paper 'University Education' (delivered in 1883, published in 1886), Morris imagines, without directly mentioning Kant, a scheme that duplicates the blueprint of *The Conflict of the Faculties*, except that he grounds his conception of 'truth' on a verse from Paul's Second Epistle to the Corinthians ('Our sufficiency is of God').[4] For Morris, in fact, the mission of the lower faculty was identical to that of a higher (theological) faculty. Morris's disciple Dewey, himself by origin a dogmatic Vermont Protestant and also a somewhat impatient reader of Kant, pursued, throughout his lower faculty career, the kind of power politics supposedly reserved for the higher faculty: his dealings with Nicholas Murray Butler and his rupture with Charles Beard, during the troubles of 1915 at Columbia, cast a hollow light on the ongoing political realities of academic freedom as a lower faculty prerogative.[5] After retrieving *The Conflict of the Faculties*, and letting it withdraw into the shadows of its deconstruction, 'Mochlos' closes with an opening onto the future, marking a call for responsibility at once 'older' and 'younger' than the one announced in Kant's 'juridico-egological form' and its 'ideal of decidability.' Such a new responsibility, arising from the 'beyond' of the university's future (much as the university itself 'commenced' with an extra-juridical, extra-curricular event of foundation), can only take the form of a 'negotiation-with' – with, among other things, the legacy itself of Kant. Derrida proposes a politics of the negotiating party, with every work negotiating even as it states a premise or a theory. 'Mochlos' does not offer a blueprint; at the most, it offers an imperative to negotiate the 'monstrous' future. The future is something we cannot know – hence a 'monster' to be saluted with a measure of fear – and one that might 'march forth' from the title itself of 'Mochlos.' The future is for negotiating: the unthinkable (the monster) is itself a rudder, a lever, and also a point, the pressure point of intersection in a leveraging movement, as of a pair of scissors or a nutcracker, in the movement known as 'decussation' (after the Latin *decem*, or 'ten,' from the Roman numeral X, a graphic equivalent for the Greek letter χ, as found, for example, in the word μοχλος). This movement, which is not to be confused with the process of economic circulation called a 'chiasmus,' is succinctly described by Sir Thomas Browne in *The Garden of Cyrus* (1658):

*Physicians are not without the use of this decussation in severall operations, in ligatures and union of dissolved continuities. Mechanicks make use hereof in forcipall Organs, and Instruments of Incision; wherein who can but magnifie the power of decussation, inservient to contrary ends, solution and consolidation, union, and division, illustrable from* Aristotle *in the old* Nucifragium *or Nutcracker, and the Instruments of Evulsion, compression or incision; which consisting of two* Vectes *or armes, converted towards each other, the innitency and stresse being made upon the* hypomochlion *or fulciment in the decussation, the greater compression is made by the union of two impulsors.*[6]

❧ ❧

The thought behind the Alabama symposium was in part a recuperative one – to reintroduce Kant's essay to an American readership ('Mochlos,' moreover, is published here for the first time in English). But how to proceed without effacing the actual remoteness of Kant and his topics? Referring to the Columbia centenary, 'Mochlos' notes that commemorative exercises in academia tend to occur either as birthday parties ('commemorative aesthetics' is the actual phrase), or as anatomy lessons where speakers explore, with transparent objectivity, a textual presence open to public view. But it also mentions a third option, the possibility of a deconstructive encounter, re-elaborating its matter into an 'entirely new problematic.' A protocol was therefore proposed that would let the essays of Kant and Derrida go out to the various speakers and respondents before, during, and after the time of symposium:[7] to let the two essays 'read' the invited speakers, with essays and speakers warring, settling, reporting, thinking, constating, figuring, founding, promising – such was the aim of the proposal. Kant himself may be said to have set the topics for these papers: thus Alan Bass, a psychoanalyst, speaks of Kant and medicine through the figure of Freud; Timothy Bahti also draws on medicine to ponder a problem of balance in literary studies today; Robert Young pursues the traces of Jeremy Bentham across the political conflicts of the British university scene; Christie McDonald and

Peggy Kamuf explore the work of Kant's contemporaries in France (Condillac, Mirabeau, Diderot, Condorcet), proposing their own critique of the academy; and John Llewelyn engages in a reading of Martin Heidegger, whose *Rektoratsrede* itself figures in 'Mochlos' (Derrida himself discussed Heidegger at the symposium, reading a selection from *Of Spirit;* in an interview, at the end of this volume, he develops some further thoughts on this work and other topics). ❧ In closing, I would like to express my thanks to those participants – Werner Hamacher, Carol Jacobs, David Farrell Krell, J. Hillis Miller, Naomi Schor, and David Sperling – whose essays, due to problems of timing, have not been included in this volume. Their contributions to the symposium were essential to its success, and have by now appeared in other publications. ❧ Thanks as well to Lindsay Waters and to the Harvard University Press for permission to publish 'Mochlos' in translation; to Salli Davis and James Yarbrough, of the College of Arts and Sciences at the University of Alabama, for a generous subvention toward the publication of this volume; to Christal Bell, Winifred Cobb, J. P. Hermann, Thomas Keenan, Eleanor Tubbs, Toby Whitman, and Amy Wygant for their many practical contributions to its development; and, above all, to Jacques Derrida for his patience and support throughout an endless process of editing, translating, and proofreading.

NOTES

1. Immanuel Kant, *The Conflict of the Faculties/Der Streit der Fakultäten,* trans. Mary J. Gregor (New York: Abaris Books, 1979).

2. Jacques Derrida, 'Mochlos; ou, le conflit des facultés,' *Philosophie* 2 (April 1984), 21–53.

3. Kant, *The Conflict of the Faculties,* p.29.

4. George Sylvester Morris, *University Education* (Ann Arbor, Mich.: n.p., 1886).

5. Gary Bullert, *The Politics of John Dewey* (Buffalo, N.Y.: Prometheus Bks., 1983), p.55.

6. *The Prose of Sir Thomas Browne,* ed. Norman J. Endicott (New York: Anchor Books, 1967), p.305.

7. I would like, as a matter of record, to state the connection between this symposium and the events surrounding the discovery of Paul de Man's war-

time writings. The symposium was organized over a period of two years, beginning in September 1985. In September 1987, three weeks before the event (8–10 October), Jacques Derrida reported the discovery of the wartime writings, and proposed that the symposium furnish a forum for an airing of the facts. After the first day of symposium papers (8 October), we announced the findings to the other participants, distributing photocopies of the articles on hand, and scheduling a discussion for the evening of 10 October, after the close of the symposium. Papers appearing in this volume are not connected to those discussions, which gave rise, for their part, to the two volumes brought out in 1989 by the University of Nebraska Press; none of these papers was revised in the light of those disclosures.

# 1

Mochlos;

or, The Conflict of the Faculties

*by Jacques Derrida*

Translated by

Richard Rand and

Amy Wygant

If we could say *we* (but have I not already said it?), we might perhaps ask ourselves: where are we? And who are we in the university where apparently we are? *What* do we represent? *Whom* do we represent? Are we responsible? For what and to whom?[1] If there is a university responsibility, it at least begins with the moment when a need to hear these questions, to take them upon oneself and respond, is imposed. This imperative for responding is the initial form and minimal requirement of responsibility. One can always not respond and refuse the summons, the call to responsibility. One can even do so without necessarily keeping silent. But the structure of this appeal to responsibility is such – so anterior to any possible response, so independent, so dissymetrical in its coming from the other within us – that even a nonresponse is charged a priori with responsibility. ᷤ And so I proceed: what represents university responsibility? This question presumes that one understands the meaning of 'university,' 'responsibility' – at least if these two concepts are still separable. ᷤ The university, what an idea! ᷤ It is a relatively recent idea. We have yet to escape it, and it is already being reduced to its own archive, to the archive of its archives, without our having quite understood what had happened with it. ᷤ Almost two centuries ago Kant was responding, and was responding in terms of responsibility. The university, what an idea, I was just wondering. This is not a bad idea, says Kant, opening *The Conflict of the Faculties (Der Streit der Fakultäten,* 1798). And, with his well-known humor, abridging a more laborious and tortuous story, he pretends to treat this idea as a find, as a happy solution that would have passed through the head of a very imaginative person, as the invention, in sum, of a fairly rational device that some ingenious operator would have sent to the state for a patent. And, in the West, the state would have adopted the concept of this very ingenious machine. And the machine would have marched along. Not without conflict, not without contradiction but, perhaps, simply, due to the conflict and the rhythm of its contradictions. ❧ Here is the opening of this short work that I wanted to invite to our commemoration, with that sense of vague disquiet that arises when, responding to the honor of an invitation from friends, one brings along, as an afterthought, some parasite with a weak command of table manners. But for this symposium, finally, it is not Socrates, it is Kant, and he says:

*It was not a bad idea* [kein übeler Einfall], *whoever first conceived and proposed a public means for treating the sum of knowledge (and properly the heads who devote themselves to it* [eigentlich die derselben gewid-meten Köpfe]*), in a quasi* industrial *manner* [gleichsam fabrikenmässig], *with a division of labor* [durch Vertheilung der Arbeiten] *where, for so many fields as there may be of knowledge, so many public teachers* [öf-fentliche Lehrer] *would be allotted, professors being as trustees* [als Depos-iteure], *forming together a kind of common scientific entity* [eine Art von gelehrtem gemeinen Wesen], *called a university (or high school* [hohe Schule]*), and having autonomy (for only scholars* [Gelehrte] *can pass judgment on scholars as such); and, thanks to its faculties (various small societies where university teachers are ranged, in keeping with the variety of the main branches of knowledge), the university would be authorized* [berechtigt: *Kant is being precise, the university receives its legitimate au-thorization from a power which is not its own]* to admit, on the one hand, *student-apprentices from the lower schools aspiring to its level, and to grant, on the other hand – after prior examination, and on its own author-ity* [aus eigner Macht, *from its own power] – to teachers who are 'free' (not drawn from the members themselves) and called 'Doctors,' a universally recognized rank (conferring upon them a degree) – in short,* creating [creiren] *them.*[2]

Kant underlines the word 'creating': a university is thus *authorized* to have the autonomous power of *creating* titles. ❧ The style of this decla-ration is not merely one of a certain fiction of origin: the happy idea of the university, one fine day, at some date, passing through someone's head, with something like the fictive possibility of an anniversary – this is what Kant seems to be evoking here. Indeed, further on in his text, af-ter dropping the rhetoric of an introduction, it is his first move to set aside the hypothesis of a somewhat random find, of an empirical, even an imaginative, origin to the university. Certain artificial institutions, he goes on to say, have as their foundation an idea of reason. And the university is an 'artificial' *(künstliche)* institution of this kind. Kant begins by recalling this fact for those who would like to forget it, believing in the naturalness of the place and the habitat. The very idea of government is founded on reason, and nothing in this respect depends on chance. Says he,

> For this reason it must be said that the organizing of a university, with respect to its classes and faculties, was not just a matter of chance, but that the government, without showing any special wisdom or precocious knowledge for doing so, was, from a particular need that it felt (for influencing the people through various teachings), able to fasten a priori *upon a principle of division that harmonizes happily* [glücklich] *with the principle currently in force.*

And Kant is well aware that he is in the process of justifying, in terms of reason, what was a de facto organization determined by the government of his day, as if by accident its king were a philosopher. Of this he is evidently aware, since he promptly excuses himself in a tone, as it were, of denial: 'But I will not, for all that, speak in its favor as if it had no fault.'[3] ❧ Within the introductory fiction, Kant had multiplied his rhetorical precautions, or rather he had somehow guaranteed the analogical statements with, so to speak, a real analogy: the university is analogous to society, to the social system it represents as one of its parts; and the teaching body represents, in one form or another, the goal and function of the social body – of, for example, the industrial society which will receive, in less than ten years' time, the great model of the University of Berlin; this, even now, remains the most imposing reference for what has been left us of the concept of the university. Here, then, is the series of analogies: within the university, one would treat knowledge a little *like* an industry *(gleichsam fabrikenmässig)*; the professors would be *as* trustees *(als Depositeure)*; together they would form a kind of essence or collective scholarly entity which would have its own autonomy *(eine Art von gelehrtem gemeinen Wesen . . . , die ihre Autonomie hätte)*. As for this autonomy, fiction and hypothesis are more prudent still. In itself, autonomy is doubtless justified by the axiom stating that scholars alone can judge other scholars, a tautology that may be thought of as linked to the essence of knowledge as knowledge of knowledge. When, however, the issue is one of creating public titles of competence, or of legitimating knowledge, or of producing the public effects of this ideal autonomy, then, at that point, the university is no longer authorized by itself. It is authorized (*berechtigt*) by a non-university agency – here, by the state – and according to criteria no longer necessarily or finally those of scientific competence, but those of a certain performativity. The autonomy of scientific evaluation may be absolute and unconditioned, but the political effects of its legitimation, even supposing that one could in all rigor distinguish them, are nonetheless controlled, measured, and overseen by a power outside the university. Regarding this power, university autonomy is in a situation of heteronomy, an autonomy conferred and limited, a representation of autonomy – in the double sense of a representation by delegation and a theatrical representation. In fact the university as a whole is responsible to a non-university agency. ❧ Kant knew something of this. And if he did not know it a priori, experience recently taught him a lesson. The King of Prussia had just recalled him to order. A letter from Friedrich Wilhelm reproached him for abusing his philosophy by deforming and debasing certain dogmas in *Religion within the Limits of Mere Reason*. Among us, perhaps, in 1980, there may be some who dream of receiving such a letter, a letter from a prince or sovereign at least letting us locate the law in a body and assign censorship to a simple mechanism within a determined, unique, punctual, monarchical place. For those who dream of so reassuring a localization, I shall therefore provide the pleasure of citing a sentence unimaginable today from the pen of a Carter, Brezhnev, Giscard or Pinochet, or even, perhaps, from that of an ayatollah. The King of Prussia reproaches the philosopher for having behaved in a manner impardonable, literally 'irresponsible' *(unverantwortlich)*. This irresponsibility Friedrich Wilhelm analyzes and divides into two. The accused appears before two juridical agencies. He bears, in the first place, his inner responsibility and personal duty as a teacher of the young. But he is also answerable to the father of the land, to a sovereign *(Landesvater)* whose intentions are known to him and ought to define the law. These two responsibilities are not juxtaposed, but are instead subordinated within the same system:

*You must recognize how irresponsibly* [wie unverantwortlich] *you thus act against your duty as a teacher of the young* [als Lehrer der Jugend] *and against our sovereign purposes* [landesväterliche Absichten] *which you know well. Of you we require a most scrupulous account* [*literally, an assuming of your responsibility,* Verantwortung] *and henceforth expect, so as to avoid our intense displeasure, that you would henceforth lapse no longer into such error, but rather would, as befits your duty, put your prestige and talent to the better use of better realizing our sovereign purpose; contrariwise, upon measures unfailingly disagreeable, you, persisting in your disobedience, would attend.*[4]

Kant cites this letter and justifies himself at length, in the Preface and finally beyond the Preface to *The Conflict of the Faculties.* Whatever one thinks of his system of justification, the nostalgia that some of us may feel in the face of this situation perhaps derives from this value of responsibility: it was thought at one time that responsibility was there, at least, for the taking – for something, and before some determinable someone. One could at least pretend to know whom one was addressing, and where to situate power; a debate on the topics of teaching, knowledge and philosophy could at least be posed in terms of responsibility. The agencies invoked – the state, the sovereign, the people, knowledge, action, truth, the university – held a place in discourse that was guaranteed, decidable, and, in every sense of this word, 'representable'; and a common code could guarantee, at least on faith, a minimum of translatability for any possible discourse in such a context. ℱ Could we say as much today? Could we understand ourselves, so as to debate about the responsibility proper to the university? I am not asking myself whether we could produce or simply spell out a consensus on this subject. I am asking myself beforehand if we could say 'we' and debate together, in a common language, about the general forms of responsibility in this area. Of this I am not sure, and herein lies a being-ill doubtless more grave than a malady or a crisis. We may all experience this to a more or less vivid degree, and through a pathos that can vary on the surface. But we lack the categories for analyzing this being-ill. Historical codes (and, a fortiori, historical datings, references to technical events or to spectacular politics, to the great unrest, for example, of '68), philosophical, hermeneutic, and political codes, etc., or even, perhaps, as performing instruments of decidability, codes in general – all seem powerless here. It is an im-pertinence of the code, which can go hand in hand with the greatest power, that lies, perhaps, at the source of this being-ill. For if a code guaranteed a problematic, then we in the university would feel better about ourselves, whatever the discord of the positions held, or the contradictions of the forces present. But we feel bad about ourselves, who would dare to say otherwise? And those who feel good about themselves are perhaps hiding something, from others or from themselves.

❧ Celebrating the anniversary of a university's founding, if one ignores the secondary gains that attend such commemorations, should suppose a confirmation, the renewing of a commitment, and, more deeply, the self-legitimation, the self-affirmation of the university. ❧ I just uttered the word 'self-affirmation.' Regarding the university, we hear it at once as translation and reference. This is the title of Heidegger's sadly celebrated discourse upon taking charge of the Rectorate at the University of Freiburg-im-Breisgau on 27 May 1933, *The Self-Affirmation of the German University (Die Selbstbehauptung der Deutschen Universität)*. If I dare to convoke here this great ghost and sinister event, it is not merely because, in doing so, I can avail myself of a pretext here for paying homage to Columbia University, for the welcome it managed to extend to intellectuals and professors emigrating from Nazi Germany. It is also because, however one judges it in terms of political circumstances (necessarily a very complex evaluation, one that I shall not attempt at this time), Heidegger's discourse on the self-affirmation of the German university undoubtedly represents, in the tradition of the *Conflict of the Faculties* and the great philosophical texts concerning the University of Berlin (Schelling, Fichte, Schleiermacher, Humboldt, Hegel), the last great discourse in which the Western university tries to ponder its essence and its destination in terms of responsibility, with a stable reference to the one idea of knowledge, technology, the state and the nation, up to the very limit at which a memorial gathering of thought makes a sudden sign toward the entirely-other of a terrifying future. Unable though I am to justify this hypothesis here, it seems to me that Heidegger, after this discourse, eventually goes beyond the limits of this still very classical concept of the university, one that guided him in *What Is Metaphysics?* (1929); or at least that the enclosure of the university – as a common place and powerful contract with the state, with the public, with knowledge, with metaphysics and technology – will seem to him less and less capable of matching a more essential responsibility, one which, before having to answer for knowledge, power, or something or other determinate, or to respond as a being or determinate object in the face of a determinate subject, must first respond *to* being, *from* the call of being, and must ponder this coresponsibility. But, once again, essential as it may seem to me, I cannot explore this path today. I shall try, shall we say, to keep a constant, if oblique and indirect, link with its necessity. ❧ When one pronounces the word 'responsibility' today in the university, one no longer knows for sure with what concept one can still regulate it. One hesitates at least between three hypotheses.

1. One can treat responsibility as a theme precisely academic. One would exhume this archived *topos*, whose code would no longer be our own, along the lines of a celebration, a birthday. In the course of a school exercise, one might, as a historian or philologist, embroider the topic with flowers of rhetoric, paying tribute to a secular institution which, though not entirely of its own time, would, for all that, not have aged, in a word, altogether badly. Within this hypothesis, that of commemorative aestheticism and all it supposes of luxury, pleasure and despair, one would still suppose that events of the past century, and especially of the most recent postwar era, would have ruined the very axiomatics of a discourse on responsibility – or, rather, of the discourse *of* responsibility. Given a certain techno-political structure of knowledge, the status, function and destination of the university would no longer stem from the juridical or ethico-political language of responsibility. No longer would a *subject*, individual or corporate, be summoned in its responsibility.

2. A second hypothesis, that of a tradition to reaffirm: one would then recall that more than a century ago, at the moment when Columbia's Graduate School was founded, the question of knowing for what, and to whom, a professor, a faculty, etc., is responsible, was posed within a philosophical, ethical, juridical, and political problematic, within a system of implicit evaluations, within an axiomatics, in sum, that survives essentially intact. One could posit secondary adaptations as a way to account for transformations occurring within the interval.

3. Keeping its value and meaning, the notion of responsibility would have to be re-elaborated within an entirely novel problematic. In the ties of the university to society, in the production, structure, archivization and transmission of knowledges and technology (of knowledges as technologies), in the political stakes of knowledge, in the very idea of knowledge and truth, lies the advent of something entirely other. To respond, what to respond about, and to whom, is a question perhaps more lively and legitimate than ever. But the 'what' and the 'who' would have to be thought entirely otherwise. And (a more interesting corollary, this) they could, from out of such an otherness, lead us to wonder what once they might have been, that 'who' and that 'what.'

Would these three hypotheses exhaust, in principle, all possibilities of a typical questioning about university responsibility? I am not sure of this, nothing in this domain seems to me assured. Everything seems to me obscure, enigmatic, menaced at once and menacing, in a place where danger today is concentrated the most. The Western university is a very recent *constructum* or artifact, and we already sense that its model is *finished:* marked by finitude, just as, at the instauration of its current model, between *The Conflict of the Faculties* (1798) and the foundation of the University of Berlin (10 October 1810, at the close of the mission entrusted to Humboldt), it was thought to be ruled by an idea of reason, by a certain link, in other words, with infinity. Following this model, at least in its essential features, every great Western university was, between 1800 and about 1850, in some sense re-instituted. Between that moment and the founding of Columbia's Graduate School, the time elapsed was less than between the last war and the present day. It is as if, with a minor delay, we were celebrating tonight the birthday of modern universities in general. Whether involving an anniversary or a university, all this turns, as they say in French, very fast. ᛦ For me, there arose the idea of reopening with you *The Conflict of the Faculties* because the *fatum* of responsibility seems inscribed there at the origin, on the very eve of the modern university, in its pre-inaugural discourse. It is inscribed there in language receiving from Kant its first great illustration, its first conceptual formalization of major rigor and consequence. There, at our disposal, we find a kind of dictionary and grammar (structural, generative, and dialectical) for the most contradictory discourses we might develop about – and, up to a point, within – the university. I do not call this a Code, precisely because the *The Conflict of the Faculties* situates the Code and a written Code *(Gesetzbuch)*[5] within a tightly circumscribed and determined part of the university, within the faculties called 'higher' – essentially instruments of the government (the faculties of theology, law and medicine). If *The Conflict of the Faculties* is not a code, it is a powerful effort at formalization and discursive economy in terms, precisely, of formal law. Here, again, Kantian thought tries to attain to pure legitimation, to purity of law, to reason as the court of last resort. The equivalence between reason and justice as 'law,' as 'right,' finds its most impressive presentation here. ᛦ For us, however, most often and in a manner still dominant, the discourse of responsibility makes an appeal, in a mode we find tautological, to a pure ethicojuridical agency, to pure practical reason, to a pure idea of the law, and correlatively to the *decision* of a pure egological subject, of a consciousness, of an intention that has to respond, in decidable terms, from and before the law. On this I do insist: it is thus for us most often and most prevailingly, though the bond is not indissoluble for all eternity. It is not natural, it has a history. One can doubtless imagine dissolving responsibility's value by relativizing, secondarizing or deriving the effect of subjectivity, consciousness or intentionality; one can doubtless decenter the subject, as is easily said, without retesting the bond between, on the one hand, responsibility, and, on the other, freedom of subjective consciousness or purity of intentionality. This happens all the time and is not altogether interesting, since nothing in the prior axiomatics is changed: one denies the axiomatics *en bloc* and keeps it going as a survivor, with minor adjustments *de rigueur* and daily compromises lacking in rigor. So coping, so operating at top speed, one accounts and becomes accountable for nothing: not for what happens, not for the reasons to continue assuming responsibilities without a concept. ❧ Conversely, would it not be more interesting, though difficult and perhaps impossible, to think of responsibility – a summons, that is, requiring a response – as no longer passing, in the last instance, through an ego, an 'I think,' an in-tention, a subject, an ideal of decidability? Would it not be more 'responsible' to try pondering the ground, in the history of the West, on which the juridico-egological values of responsibility were determined, attained, imposed? There is perhaps a fund here of 'responsibility' which is at once 'older' and – to the extent it is conceived anew, through what some would call a crisis of responsibility in its juridico-egological form and its ideal of decidability – is *yet to come,* or, if you prefer, 'younger.' Here, perhaps, would be a chance for the task of thinking what will have been, up to this point, the representation of university responsibility, of what it is and might become, in the wake of upheavals no longer to be concealed from ourselves, even if we still have trouble analyzing them. Is a new type of university responsibility possible? Under what conditions? I know nothing about this, though I know that the very form of my question still constitutes a classical protocol, of a type precisely Kantian: in posing thus my question I continue to act as a guardian and trustee responsible for traditional responsibility. Kant in effect tells us the conditions under which a rational university will, according to him, have been possible. Reading him today, I perceive his assurance and his necessity much as one might admire the rigor of a plan or structure through the breaches of an uninhabitable edifice, unable to decide whether it is in ruins or simply never existed, having only ever been able to shelter the discourse of its non-accomplishment. This is the uncertainty with which I read Kant, but I shall spare you further considerations of the pathos of this uncertainty, the intermittent despair, the laborious or ironic distress, the daily contradictions, the desire to challenge and militate on several fronts at once, so as to save *and* to risk, etc. From the depths of this uncertainty I still believe in the task of another discourse on university responsibility. Not in the renewal of the contract in its old or barely renovated forms; but since, concerning entirely other forms, I know nothing clear, coherent or decidable, or whether such forms will ever be, or whether the university as such has a future, I continue to believe in the interest of light in this domain – and of a discourse attaining, tomorrow, to the novelty of the problem. This problem is a task, it remains for us a *given-to*, to what I do not know, to doing or thinking, one might have once said. I say so not just as a member of the university. It is uncertain that the university itself, from within, from its idea, is equal to this task or this debt; and this is the problem, the breach in the university's system, in the internal coherence of its concept. For there may be no possible inside to the university, and no internal coherence to its concept. And so I mention this task both as a university person taking care not to deny his membership (since the one coherent attitude, for someone refusing commitment on this point, would amount, in the first place, to resigning), and as a non-member sensitive to the very fact that, nowadays, the university as such cannot reflect, or represent itself, or change into one of its own representations as one of its possible objects. With a view to this other responsibility, I shall hazard a contribution that is modest, preliminary, and above all in keeping with the time at our disposal here, which no one in decency should exceed. With this economy and these rhetorical constraints taken into account, I set myself the following rule: to try to translate *The Conflict of the Faculties* in part, and under the heading of an introductory or paradigmatic essay, so as to recognize its points of untranslatability, by which I mean anything that no longer reaches us and remains outside the usage of our era. I shall try to analyze those untranslatable nodes; and the benefits that I anticipate – if not in the course of this brief effort, then at least in the systematic pursuit of this kind of reading – will be an

inventory not merely of what was and no longer is, or of certain contradictions, laws of conflicts, or antinomies of university reason, but of
what, as well, may exceed this dialectical rationality itself; and the untranslatability we experience may signal an incapacity, perhaps, of the
university to comprehend itself in the purity of its inside, or to translate
and transmit its proper meaning. And this, perhaps, from its origin. 🐾
Will it suffice today to speak of contradiction in the university? Is it not
the first interest of the Kantian text to recognize a conflict at the university's very interior? Kant foresees its inevitable recurrence, a necessity
somehow transcendental and constitutive. He classes the different types
and places of contradiction, the rules of their return, the forms of their
legality or illegality. For he wishes at all costs to *state the law,* and to discern, to decide between legal conflicts and between illegal conflicts that
would set into opposition the faculties of the university. Kant's principal
concern is legitimate for someone intending to make the right decisions:
it is to trace the rigorous limits of a system called 'university.' No discourse would be rigorous here if one did not begin by defining the unity
of the university system, in other words the frontier between its inside
and its outside. Kant wishes to analyze conflicts *proper* to the university,
those arising between the different parts of the university's body and its
power, here meaning, namely, the faculties. He wants to describe the
process of these *internal* contradictions, but also to class, to hierarchize,
to arbitrate. But even before proposing a general division of the teaching
body, and before recognizing the two major classes of faculties, higher
and lower, that can confront each other, Kant encounters a prior, if not a
pre-prior, difficulty, one that we today would sense even more keenly
than he. As one might expect, this difficulty involves the definition of a
certain outside maintaining with its inside a link of resemblance, participation and parasitism that can produce an abuse of power, an excess
that is properly political. An exteriority, therefore, within the resemblance. It can take three forms. Only one of these seems dangerous to
Kant. The first is the organization of specialized scholars into academies
or societies. These 'workshops' do not belong to the university, Kant is
content to mention them. He does not envisage any collaboration, any
concurrence, any conflict between the university and these scientific societies. And yet these do not, as do the private amateurs that he mentions in the same passage, represent a state of nature in science. These
institutions, which are also among the effects of reason, play an essential

role in society. Nowadays, however – and this is a first limit to the translation of the Kantian text in our politico-epistemological space – there can be very serious competition and border-conflicts between non-university centers of research and university faculties claiming at once to be doing research and transmitting knowledge, to be producing and re-producing knowledge. These issues are no longer isolated or circumscribed when they involve the politics of scientific research, including all socio-technical strategies (military, medical or other, with such limits and categories losing all pertinence nowadays) and all information technology at the intra- or interstate level, etc. A whole field is largely open to the analysis of this university 'outside' that Kant calls 'academic.' In the days of Kant, this 'outside' could be confined to the margin of the university. This is no longer so certain or simple. Today, in any case, the university is what has become the margin. Certain departments of the university at least have been reduced to that condition. The state no longer entrusts certain investigations to a university that cannot accept the structures or control the techno-political stakes. When regions of knowledge can no longer give rise to the training and evaluation properly belonging to a university, then the whole architectonics of *The Conflict of the Faculties* finds itself menaced, and with it a model regulated by the happy concord between royal power and pure reason. The *representation* of this model remains almost identical throughout the West, but the link to power, and to the investigations it programs in research academies and institutes, differs widely between states, regimes and national traditions. These differences are marked by interventions on the part of the state and of public or private capital. They cannot fail to reverberate in the researchers' practice and style. Certain objects and types of research escape the university. Sometimes, as in certain Eastern countries, the university is totally confined to the pursuit of reproducible teaching. The state deprives it of the right to do research, reserved for academies without teachers. This arises most often from calculations of techno-political profitability as figured by the state, or by national (or international), state (or trans-state) capitalist powers, as one might imagine happening with the storage of information or the constitution of data banks, where the university member has to surrender any representation as a 'guardian' or 'trustee' of knowledge. Certainly such representation *once constituted* the very mission of the university. But with the library no longer being the ideal type of archive, the university no longer remains the center of knowledge, and can no longer provide its subjects with a representation of that center. And since the university, either for reasons of structure or from its attachment to old representations, cannot avail itself of certain kinds of research, or operate within them, or transmit them, it feels menaced in certain places around its own body; menaced by the development of the sciences, or, a fortiori, by questions *from* science and *on* science; menaced by what it sees as a devouring margin. A singular and unjust menace, it being the constitutive faith of the university that the idea of science is at the basis itself of the university. As such, how could that idea menace the university in its technical development, to the point where no one can any longer separate knowledge from power, reason from performativity, metaphysics from technical mastery? The university is a (finished) product, I would almost call it the child of an inseparable couple, metaphysics and technology. At the least, the university furnished the space or the topological configuration for such an offspring. It is a paradox that, at the moment when such offspring overflows the places assigned it, and the university becomes small and old, its 'idea' reigns everywhere, more and better than ever. Menaced, as I said a moment ago, by a devouring margin, since non-university research associations, public, official or otherwise, can also form pockets within the university campus. Certain members of the university can play a part there, irritating the insides of the teaching body like parasites. In tracing the system of the pure limits of the university, Kant wants to track any possible parasiting. He wants the power to exclude it – legitimately, legally. Now the possibility of such parasiting appears wherever there is language, which is also to say a public domain, publication, publicity. Wishing to control parasiting, if not to exclude it, is to misunderstand, at a certain point, the structure of language acts. (If, therefore, as I note in passing, analyses of a deconstructive type have so often had the style of theories of 'parasitism,' it is that they too, directly or indirectly, involve university legitimation.)[6] 🍂 We are still on the threshold of *The Conflict of the Faculties*. Kant has more trouble keeping a second category on the outside. But in naming it, he seems very conscious this time of political stakes. It has to do with the 'lettered' class: *die Litteraten (Studirte)*. These are not scholars in the proper sense (*eigentliche Gelehrte*), but trained in the universities, they become government agents, diplomatic aides, instruments of power (*Instrumente der Regierung*). To a large extent, they have often forgotten what they are thought to have learned. The state accords them a function and power to its own ends, not to the ends of science: 'Not,' says Kant, 'for the great good of the sciences.' To these former students he gives the name of 'businessmen, or technicians of learning' *(Geschäftsleute oder Werkkundige der Gelehrsamkeit)*. Their influence on the public is official and legal *(aufs Publicum gesetzlichen Einfluss haben)*. They represent the state and maintain redoubtable power. In the examples cited by Kant, it seems that these businessmen of knowledge have been taught by the three faculties called 'higher' (theology, law, medicine). They are ecclesiastics, magistrates and doctors, who are not educated by the philosophy faculty. Nowadays, to be sure, in a class so defined of businessmen or technicians of knowledge, we would have to inscribe a massively larger variety and number of agents – on the outside, on the border, in university places. They are every responsible figure in the public or private administration of the university, every 'decision-maker' in matters of budgets and the allocation or distribution of resources (bureaucrats in a ministry, 'trustees,' etc.), every administrator of publications and archivization, every editor, journalist, etc. Is it not, nowadays, for reasons involving the structure of knowledge, especially impossible to distinguish rigorously between scholars and technicians of science, just as it is to trace, between knowledge and power, the limit within whose shelter Kant sought to preserve the university edifice? We shall return to this question. It is always, in fact, as a matter of 'influence over the general public' that Kant elaborates his problem. Businessmen of science are redoubtable for having an immediate tie to the general public, which is composed, not of the ignorant, as the term is often rendered in translation, but, as Kant crudely says, of 'idiots' *(Idioten)*. In fact, since the university is thought to lack any power of its own, it is to the government that Kant appeals to keep this class of businessmen in line *(in Ordnung)*, since they can at any time usurp the right to judge, a right belonging to the faculties. Kant asks of governmental power that it create, on its own, conditions for counter-power, that it ensure its own limitation and guarantee to the university, which is lacking in power, the exercise of its free judgment in deciding the true and the false. The government and the forces it represents, or that represent it (civil society), should create a law limiting their own influence, submitting statements of a constative type (those claiming to tell the truth), or indeed of a 'practical' type (insofar as implying a free judgment), to the jurisdiction of university competence, and to something within it, we shall see, which is finally most free and responsible in respect to the truth: the philosophy faculty. The principle of this demand may seem exorbitant or elementary – one or the other, one as well as the other – and it already had, under Friedrich Wilhelm, no chance of being applied, and not for reasons of empirical organization alone, which thereafter could only become aggravated. One would have to imagine today a control exercised by university competence (and, in the last instance, by philosophical competence) over every declaration coming from bureaucrats or subjects representing power directly or indirectly, the dominating forces of the country as well as the forces dominated, insofar as they aspire to power and contribute to political or ideological debate. Nothing would escape it – not a single position adopted in a newspaper or book, on radio or television, in the public pursuit of a career, in the technical administration of knowledge, in every stage between the research known as 'basic' and its civil, police, medical, military, etc., 'applications,' in the world of students and non-university teaching (instructors at elementary or high school, of whom Kant, in this very place, has, strangely, nothing to say), among all 'decision-makers' in matters of bureaucracy and university accounting, etc. In short, no one would have the authority to use his or her knowledge *publicly* without being subject, by law, to the control of the faculties, 'to the censorship of the faculties,' as Kant literally says. This system has the appearance and would have the reality of a most odious tyranny if (1) the power of judging and deciding here were not defined by a respectful and responsible service to *truth*, and if (2) it had not been stripped, in principle and structure, of all executive power, all means of coercion. Its power of decision is theoretical and discursive, and limited to the theoretical part of the discursive. The university is there *to tell the truth*, to judge and to criticize in the most rigorous sense of the term, namely to discern and decide between the true and the false; and when it is also entitled to decide between the just and the unjust, the moral and the immoral, this is so insofar as reason and freedom of judgment are implicated there as well. Kant, in fact, presents this requirement as a condition for struggles against all 'despotisms,' beginning with the one that could give control inside the university to those direct representatives of the government that members of the higher faculties are (theology, law, medicine). One could play endlessly at translating this matrix, this model, combining its elements into different types of modern society. One could also therefore legitimately entertain the most contradictory of evaluations. Kant defines a university that is as much a safeguard for the most totalitarian of social forms as a place for the most intransigently liberal resistance to any abuse of power, resistance that can be judged in turns as most rigorous or most impotent. In effect, its power is confined to a power-to-think-and-judge, a power-to-say, though not necessarily to say *in public,* since this would involve an *action,* an executive power denied the university. How is the combination of such contradictory evaluations possible for a model that is one and the same? What must be such a model, to lend itself thus to this? I can only sketch out an answer here to this enormous question. Presuppositions in the Kantian delimitation could be glimpsed from the very start, but today they have become massively apparent. Kant needs, as he says, to trace, between a responsibility concerning truth and a responsibility concerning action, a linear frontier, an indivisible and rigorously uncrossable line. To do so he has to submit language to a particular treatment. Language is an element common to both spheres of responsibility, and one that deprives us of any rigorous distinction between the two spaces that Kant at all costs wanted to dissociate. It is an element that opens a passage to all parasiting and simulacra. In a way, Kant speaks only of language in *The Conflict of the Faculties,* and it is between two languages, between one of truth and one of action, between one of theoretical statements and one of performatives (mostly of commands) that he wishes to trace the line of demarcation. Kant speaks only of language when he speaks about the 'manifestation of truth,' or 'influence over the people,' or the interpretation of sacred texts in theological terms, or, conversely, in philosophical terms, etc. And yet he continually effaces something in language that scrambles the limits which a criticist critique claims to assign to the faculties, to the interior of the faculties, and, as will be seen, between the university's inside and its outside. Kant's effort – such is the scope of a properly philosophical project and the need for a judgment capable of deciding – tries to limit the effects of confusion, simulacrum, parasiting, equivocality and undecidability produced by language. In this sense, the philosophical demand is best represented by an information technology which, while appearing nowadays to escape the control of the university – in Kantian terms, of philosophy – is its product and its most faithful representative. This is only apparently paradoxical, and it is in facing the law of this apparent paradox that an ultimate respon-

sibility would be, if such a thing were possible, there for the taking today. The force of parasiting inhabits natural language beforehand, and is
common to both the university and its outside. An element of publicity,
the necessarily public character of discourse, especially in the form of
the archive, designates an unavoidable *locus* of equivocation that Kant
would like to reduce. Whence the temptation to transform, into a reserved, intra-university and quasi-private language, the discourse, precisely, of universal value which is that of philosophy. If a universal
language is not to risk equivocation, it has, at the least, not to be published, popularized or divulged to the general public, which would necessarily corrupt it. In his response to the King of Prussia, Kant defends
himself thus:

*As a* teacher of the people *I have, in my writings, and particularly in the
book* On Religion Within the Limits, etc., *contravened none of the supreme and* sovereign *purposes known to me, in other words I have done no
harm to the public religion of the land; this is already clear from the fact
that the book does not pertain thereto in any way, being, for the public, an
unintelligible and closed book, a mere debate between faculty scholars, of
which the public takes no notice; the faculties themselves, to be sure, remain, to the best of their science and conscience, free to judge it publicly; it
is only the appointed public teachers (in schools and from the pulpit) who,
by any outcome of such debates as the country's authority may sanction for
public utterance, are bound.*[7]

It is, then, the *publication* of knowledge, rather than knowledge itself,
which is submitted to authority. Reducing publication so as to save a rigorous discourse, i.e. a rational, universal and unequivocal discourse, in
science and in conscience – this is a double bind, a demand in contradiction with itself, intrinsically in conflict with itself, as if, *within* the
Kantian text, it were already not translatable from itself into itself. This
contradictory demand was not satisfied in the time of Kant. How could
it be today, when the fields of publication, archivation and media-
processing expand as strikingly as have, at the other end of the spectrum, the overcoding and hyperformalization of languages? Where is the
beginning of publication? ❧ There is seriously and essentially still more.
The pure concept of the university is constructed by Kant on the possibility and necessity of a language purely theoretical, inspired solely by
an interest in truth, with a structure that one today would call purely

constative. This ideal is undoubtedly guaranteed, in the Kantian proposal as such, by pure practical reason, by prescriptive utterances, by the
postulate of freedom on the one hand, and, on the other, by virtue of a
de facto political authority supposed in principle to let itself be guided
by reason. But this in no way keeps the performative structure from
being excluded, in principle, from the language whereby Kant regulates
both the concept of the university and what within it is purely autonomous, namely, as will be seen, the 'lower' faculty, the faculty of philosophy. I let myself be guided by this notion of performativity, not because
it strikes me as being sufficiently clear or elaborated, but because it sig-
nals an essential topic of the debate with which we are engaged. In
speaking of performativity, I think as much of the performativity, or
output, of a technical system, a place where knowledge and power are no
longer distinguished, as of the Austinian notion of a language act not
confined to stating, describing, or saying that which is, but capable of
producing or transforming, into itself alone, under certain conditions,
the situation of which it speaks: the founding, for example, of a Graduate School – not today, when we can constate it, but a century ago,
within a very determined context. Interesting and interested debates that
are being developed more and more around an interpretation of the
performative power of language seem linked, in at least a subterranean
way, to urgent politico-institutional stakes. These debates are being developed equally in departments of literature, linguistics and philosophy;
and in themselves, in the form of their interpretative statements, they
are neither simply theoretico-constative nor simply performative. This is
so because the performative is not *one:* there are various performatives
and there are antagonistic or parasitical attempts to interpret the performative power of language, to police it and use it, to invest it perfor-
matively. And philosophy and politics – not only general politics but
also a politics of teaching and knowledge, a political concept of the university community – are engaged there every time, whether or not one is
conscious of the fact. A very symptomatic form nowadays of the political implication that has always been at work, at all times, in every university gesture and utterance. I am speaking not just of those acts for
which we have to take a politico-administrative responsibility: requests
for funding and their awards, the organization of teaching and research,
the granting of degrees, and, especially, the enormous mass of evaluations, implicit or declared, to which we commit ourselves, each bearing

its own axiomatics and political effects (the dream, here, of a formidable study, more than sociological, of the archive of these evaluations, including, for example, the publication of every dossier, jury report and letter of recommendation, and the spectrum analysis, dia- and synchronic, of all codes in conflict there, intersecting, contradicting and overdetermining one another in the twisting and mobile strategy of interests great and small). No, I do not think only about this, but more precisely as well about the concept of a scientific community and a university that ought to be legible in every sentence of a course or seminar, in every act of writing, reading or interpretation. For example – but one could vary examples to infinity – the interpretation of a theorem, poem, philosopheme or theologeme is only produced by simultaneously proposing an institutional model, either by consolidating an existing one that enables the interpretation, or by constituting a new model to accord with it. Declared or clandestine, such a proposal calls for the politics of an interpretative community gathered around the text, and indeed of a global society, a civil society with or without a state, a veritable regime enabling the inscription of that community. I shall go further: every text, every element of a corpus reproduces or bequeathes, in a prescriptive or normative mode, one of several injunctions: come together according to this or that rule, this or that scenography, this or that topography of minds and bodies, and form this or that type of institution so as to read me and write about me, organize this or that type of exchange or hierarchy to interpret me, evaluate me, preserve me, translate me, inherit from me, make me live on *(überleben* or *fortleben* in the sense that Benjamin gives to those words in *Die Aufgabe des Übersetzers).* Or inversely: if you interpret me (in the sense of deciperment or performative transformation), you shall have to assume one or another institutional form. But it holds for every text that such an injunction gives rise to undecidability and the double bind, both opens and closes, that is, upon an overdetermination that cannot be mastered. This is the law of the text in general – not confined to what one calls (up from) written works in libraries or computer programs – a law that I cannot demonstrate here but must presuppose. Moreover, the interpreter is never subjected passively to this injunction, and his own performance will in its turn construct one or several models of community. And different ones for the same interpreter – from one moment to the next, from one work to the next, from one situation or strategic evaluation to the next. Those responsibilities are his. It is hard to speak generally on the subject of what for, or before whom, they are taken. They involve the content and form of a new contract every time. When, for example, I read some sentence from a given text in a seminar (a reply by Socrates, a fragment from *Capital* or *Finnegans Wake*, a paragraph from *The Conflict of the Faculties*), I do not fulfill a prior contract, I can also write, and prepare for signature, a new contract with an institution, between an institution and the dominant forces of society. And this operation, as with any negotiation (pre-contractual, in other words continually transforming a prior contract), is the moment for every imaginable ruse and strategic ploy. I do not know if there exists today a pure concept of *a* university responsibility, nor would I know, in any case, how to express, in this place or within the limits of this lecture, all the doubts I harbor on this subject. I do not know if an ethico-political code bequeathed by one or more traditions is viable for such a definition. But today the minimal and in any case the most interesting, most novel and strongest responsibility, for someone attached to a research or teaching institution, is perhaps to make this political implication, its system and its aporias as clear and thematic as possible. In speaking of clarity and thematization, even when those thematizations assume the most unexpected and convoluted pathways, I still appeal to the most classical of norms, but I doubt that anyone could omit to do so without, yet again, putting into question every thought of responsibility, as one may naturally always wish to do. By the clearest possible thematization I mean the following: that with students and the research community, in every operation we pursue together (a reading, an interpretation, the construction of a theoretical model, the rhetoric of an argumentation, the treatment of historical material, and even of mathematical formalization), we argue or acknowledge that an institutional concept is at play, a type of contract signed, an image of the ideal seminar constructed, a *socius* implied, repeated or displaced, invented, transformed, menaced or destroyed. An institution – this is not merely a few walls or some outer structures surrounding, protecting, guaranteeing or restricting the freedom of our work; it is also and already the structure of our interpretation. If, then, it lays claim to any consequence, what is hastily called deconstruction *as such* is never a technical set of discursive procedures, still less a new hermeneutic method operating on archives or utterances in the shelter of a given and stable institution; it is also, and at the least, the taking of a position, in

work itself, toward the politico-institutional structures that constitute
and regulate our practice, our competences, and our performances. Precisely because deconstruction has never been concerned with the contents alone of meaning, it must not be separable from this politico-
institutional problematic, and has to require a new questioning about
responsibility, an inquiry that should no longer necessarily rely on codes
inherited from politics or ethics. Which is why, though too political in
the eyes of some, deconstruction can seem demobilizing in the eyes of
those who recognize the political only with the help of prewar road
signs. Deconstruction is limited neither to a methodological reform that
would reassure the given organization, nor, inversely, to a parade of irresponsible or irresponsibilizing destruction, whose surest effect would be
to leave everything as is, consolidating the most immobile forces of the
university. It is from these premises that I interpret *The Conflict of the
Faculties*. I return to it now, though in truth I do not believe I ever left it.
&. Kant, then, wanted to make a line of demarcation pass between
thinkers in the university and businessmen of knowledge or agents of
government power, between the inside and the outside closest to the
university enclosure. But this line, Kant certainly has to recognize, not
only passes along the border and around the institution. It traverses the
faculties, and this is a place of conflict, of an unavoidable conflict. This
frontier is a front. In effect, by referring himself to a de facto organization which he seeks, in keeping with his usual line of argument, not to
transform but rather to analyze within its conditions of pure juridical
possibility, Kant distinguishes between two classes of faculty: three
higher faculties and a lower faculty. And without treating this enormous
problem, he hastens to specify that this division and its designations
(three higher faculties, one lower faculty) are the work of the government and not of the scientific corporation. Nonetheless he accepts it, he
seeks to justify it within his own philosophy and to endow this *factum*
with juridical guarantees and rational ideals. The faculties of theology,
law and medicine are called 'higher' because closer to government
power; and a traditional hierarchy holds that power should be higher
than non-power. It is true that Kant does not hide something later on;
his own political ideal tends to favor a certain reversal of this hierarchy:

*Thus we may indeed eventually see the last becoming first (the lower fac-
ulty becoming the higher faculty), not in the exercise of power [my emphasis, and Kant, even with this reversal, remains true to the absolute*

*distinction between knowledge and power] but in giving counsel [and counsel, as he sees it, is not power] to the authority (the government) holding it, which would thereby find, in the freedom of the philosophy faculty and the insight it yields, a better way to achieve its ends than the mere exercise of its own absolute authority.*

Kant's model here is less the philosopher-king of Plato than a certain practical wisdom of the British parliamentary monarchy, mentioned in a lengthy, amusing footnote to the 'General Division of the Faculties.'[8] ❧ Since this ideal reversal has not occurred, things being, that is, what they actually are, the higher faculties are those that train the agents of the government and anyone else with whose help the government brings off its 'strongest and most lasting influence' over the general public. And so the government controls and oversees those higher faculties that represent it directly, even if it does not itself teach. It sanctions doctrines, and can require that some be advanced and others withdrawn, whatever their truth may be. This makes up a part of the contract signed between the higher faculties and the government. If, be it said in passing, this sole Kantian criterion were kept (representing the interests of state power and of the forces sustaining it), would one be assured nowadays by a boundary between the higher faculties and the others? And could one limit the higher faculties, as before, to theology, law and medicine? Would one not find some trace of that interest or that representation of power within the lower faculty, of which Kant says that it should be absolutely independent of governmental commands? The lower (philosophical) faculty should be able, according to Kant, to teach freely whatever it wishes without conferring with anyone, letting itself be guided by its sole interest in the truth. And the government should arrest its own power, as Montesquieu would say, in the face of this freedom, should even guarantee it. And it should have an interest in doing so, since, says Kant with the fundamental optimism characterizing this discourse, without freedom truth cannot be manifested, and every government should take an interest in the manifesting of truth. The freedom of the lower faculty, though *absolute,* is a freedom of judgment and intra-university speech, a freedom to speak out on *that which is,* through judgments essentially theoretical. Only intra-university speech (theoretical, judicative, predicative, constative) is felt to recognize this absolute freedom. Members of the 'lower' faculty cannot and should not as such give orders *(Befehle geben).* In the last instance, the government keeps by

contract a right to control or censure any who would not, in their statements, be constative, or not, in a certain sense of this word, representa-
tional. Think of the subtleties in our current interpretations of non-
constative utterances, and the effect these would have on such a concept
of the university and its ties to civil society and state power! Imagine the
training that would have to be reserved for censors or government experts charged with verifying the purely constative structure of university
discourses. Those experts, where would they be trained? By what faculty? By the higher, or the lower? And who would decide? In any case,
and for essential reasons, we do not have at our disposal today the truth
about performative language, or any legitimate or teachable doctrine on
the subject. What follows from this? Every discussion on the subject of
*speech acts* (relations between acts of language and truth, acts of language and intention, 'serious' and 'non-serious,' 'fictive' and 'non-
fictive,' 'normal' and 'parasitic' language, philosophy and literature, linguistics and psychoanalysis, etc.) has politico-institutional stakes that we
should no longer hide from ourselves. These concern the power or non-
power of academic discourse, or of research-discourse in general. ◆ The
division between two classes of faculties must be pure, inaugural and
rigorous. Instituted by the government, it must still proceed from pure
reason. It does not permit, in principle, any confusion of boundary, any
parasitism. Whence the untiring, desperate, not to say 'heroic' effort by
Kant to mark off juridical frontiers: not only between the respective responsibilities of the two classes of faculties, but also between the types of
conflict that cannot fail to arise between them in a kind of antinomy of
university reason. Faculty class struggle will be inevitable, but juridism
will proceed to judge, discern and discriminate, in a manner decisive,
decidable and critical, between conflicts legal and illegal. ◆ A first frontier between classes of faculties reproduces the limit between action and
truth (a statement or proposition with truth-value). The lower faculty is
totally free where questions of truth are concerned. No power should
limit its freedom of judgment in this respect. It can doubtless conform
to practical doctrines as ordained by the government, but should never
hold them as true *because* dictated by power. This freedom of judgment
Kant takes to be the unconditioned condition of university autonomy,
and that unconditioned condition is nothing other than philosophy. Autonomy is philosophical reason insofar as it grants itself its own law,
namely the truth. Which is why the lower faculty is called the philoso-

phy faculty; and without a philosophy department in a university, there is no university. The concept of *universitas* is more than the philosophical concept of a research and teaching institution; it is the concept of philosophy itself, and is Reason, or rather the principle of reason *as an institution*. Kant speaks here not just of a faculty but of a 'department': if there is to be a university, 'some such department' of philosophy has to be 'founded' *(gestiftet)*. Though inferior in power, philosophy ought 'to control' *(controlliren)* all other faculties in matters arising from *truth*, which is of 'the first order,' just as *utility* in the service of government is of 'the second order.'[9] That the essence of the university, namely philosophy, should also occupy a particular place and a faculty within the university topology, or that philosophy in and of itself should represent a special competence – this poses a serious problem. It did not escape Schelling, for example, who objected to Kant about it in one of his *Vorlesungen über die Methode des akademischen Studiums* (1802). According to him, there cannot be a particular faculty (or, therefore, power, *Macht*) for philosophy: 'Something which is everything cannot, for that very reason, be anything in particular.'[10] ❧ It is a paradox of this university topology that the faculty bearing within itself the theoretical concept of the totality of university space should be assigned to a particular residence, and should be subject, within the same space, to the political authority of other faculties and the government they represent. In principle, this is conceivable and rational only to the degree that the government *ought* to be inspired by reason. And in that ideal case, there should be no conflicts. But there are, and not just contingent or factual oppositions. There are inevitable conflicts, and even conflicts that Kant calls 'legal.' How can this be? ❧ It stems, I believe, from the paradoxical structure of those limits. Though destined to separate power from knowledge and action from truth, they distinguish sets that are each time somehow in excess of themselves, covering each time the whole of which they should figure only a part or a sub-set. And so the whole forms an *invaginated pocket* on the inside of every part or sub-set. We recognized the difficulty of distinguishing the inside from the outside of the university, and then, on the inside, of distinguishing between the two classes of faculties. We are not done, however, with this intestine division and its folding partition on the inside of each space. The philosophy faculty is further divided into two 'departments': the *historical* sciences (history, geography, linguistics, humanities, etc.) and the *purely rational* sciences (pure mathematics, pure philosophy, the metaphysics of nature and morals); pure philosophy, on the inside of the so-called philosophy faculty, is therefore still just a part of the whole whose idea it nonetheless safeguards. But insofar as it is *historical*, it also covers the domain of the higher faculties. 'The faculty of philosophy,' writes Kant, 'can therefore require all disciplines to submit their truth to an examination.'[11] Due to this double overflowing, conflicts are inevitable. And they must also reappear inside each faculty, since the faculty of philosophy is itself divisible. But Kant also wishes to construct a limit between legal and illegal conflicts. An illegal conflict merely sets into opposition, and in public, various opinions, feelings, and particular inclinations. Though always involving influence over the public, such a conflict cannot give rise to juridical or rational arbitration. It primarily concerns a demand from the public, which, considering philosophy to be nonsense, prefers to approach the higher faculties or scientific bureaucrats in its demand for pleasures, short-cuts, or answers in the form of fortune-telling, magic or thaumaturgy. The people seek clever leaders *(kunstreiche Führer)*, 'demagogues.' And members of the higher faculties, such as theologians, can, just as well as the bureaucrats educated by those faculties, answer that demand. In the case of these illegal conflicts, the philosophy faculty as such is, according to Kant, absolutely impotent and without recourse. The solution can only come from beyond – this time, once again, from the government. And if the government does not intervene, if it takes, that is, the side of particular interests, then it condemns the faculty of philosophy, meaning the soul itself of the university, to death. This is what Kant calls the 'heroic' way – in the ironic sense of heroic medicine – which ends a crisis by means of death. Some might be tempted into a headlong recognition of the death of philosophy that others among us oppose in several Western countries, notably in France.[12] But things do not let themselves be taken so simply in this Kantian schema. The 'illegal' conflict is only of secondary interest to Kant: putting individual inclination and particular interests into play, it is pre-rational, quasi-natural, and extra-institutional. It is not properly a university conflict, whatever its gravity may be. Kant devotes longer analyses to the legal conflicts that properly arise from university reason. These conflicts surge inevitably from within, putting rights and responsibilities into play. The first examples that Kant gives – the ones that visibly preoccupy him the most – pertain to the sacred, to faith and revelation; it is the responsibility of the philosophy faculty 'to examine and judge publicly, with cool reason, the origin and content of a certain supposed basis of the doctrine, unintimidated by the sanctity of the object, for which one presumably feels something, having clearly decided *(entschlossen)* to relate this supposed feeling to a concept.'[13] Such a conflict (with, for example, the higher faculty of theology) reintroduces feeling or history into a context where reason alone should be; it still harbors within itself something natural, since it opposes reason to its outside. It is still a parasiting of the legal by the illegal. But Kant does not wish to recognize this, or in any case to declare it. He imagines instances of interior arbitration, with sentence and arrest pronounced by a judge of reason in view of a 'public presentation of the truth' *(öffentliche Darstellung der Wahrheit)*. This trial and this arbitration should remain interior to the university and should never be brought before an incompetent public that would change it back into an illegal conflict, and feed it to factions, to popular tribunes, notably to those that Kant calls *Neologists (Neologen)*, 'whose name, rightly detested, is nonetheless ill understood, when applied indiscriminately to all who propose innovations for doctrines and formulae (for why should the old ways always be taken as better?).'[14] It is because they *ought* by right to remain interior that these conflicts *ought* never to disturb the government, and they have to remain internal *for that reason:* never to disturb the government. ❧ And yet Kant is obliged to recognize that this conflict is interminable and therefore insoluble. It is a struggle that eventually destabilizes departmental regimes, constantly putting into question yet again the borders where Kant would constantly contain antagonism. Kant further refines upon this antagonism of the conflict of the faculties, saying that it 'is not a war' *(kein Krieg)*, proposing for it a solution that is properly parliamentary: the higher faculties would occupy, says he, the right bench of the parliament of science and would defend the statutes of the government. 'But in as free a system of government as must exist where truth is at issue, there must also be an opposition party (the left side), and that bench belongs to the philosophy faculty, for without its rigorous examinations and objections, the government would not be adequately informed about things that might be to its own advantage or detriment.' Thus, in conflicts concerning pure *practical* reason, the inquest and the *formal* charge of the trial would be confined to the philosophy faculty. But in matters of *content*, which touch on the most important questions for mankind, the preliminary hearing falls to the higher faculty, and particularly to the faculty of theology (see 'The Conclusion of Peace and Resolution of the Conflict of the Faculties').[15] And yet, despite this parliamentary juridism, Kant is obliged to admit that the conflict 'can never end,' and that the 'philosophy faculty is the one which ought to be permanently armed for this purpose.' The truth under its protection will always be threatened because 'the higher faculties will never renounce the desire to govern' or dominate *(Begierde zu herrschen).*[16] ⧫ I break off brusquely, the university is for closing, it is very late, too late for this Kantian discourse, which is perhaps what I meant to say. But know that the sequel, which I have not discussed, is most interesting and least formal, the most informal. It deals with the actual *content* of conflicts among theologians, jurists, doctors, and the technicians or bureaucrats they train. ⧫ You have wondered all along, I am sure, where, as we say nowadays, I was coming from, which side was mine in all these conflicts, (1) to the right of the boundary or (2) to its left, or (3) more probably, as various others would (rightly or wrongly) suppose, a tireless parasite moving in random agitation, passing over the boundary and back again, either seeking (no one would know for sure) to play a mediator treating of perpetual peace, or seeking to reignite the conflicts and wars of a university sick from the very outset with apocalypse and eschatology. These three hypotheses, whose responsibility I leave in your hands, all appeal to the system of limits proposed by *The Conflict of the Faculties,* and they all let themselves be constrained by it still. ⧫ Here it will have been my responsibility, whatever the consequences, to pose the question of the right to the law: what is the legitimacy of this juridico-rational and politico-juridical university system, etc.? The question of the right to the law, of the founding or foundation of the law, is not a juridical question. And a response cannot be either simply legal or simply illegal, simply theoretical or constative, simply practical or performative. It cannot take place either inside or outside the university bequeathed us by tradition. This response and reponsibility in regard to such a founding can only take place in terms of foundation. Now the foundation of a law is no more a juridical or legitimate matter than is the event of a university's founding a university or intra-university event. If there can be no pure concept of the university, if, within the university, there can be no pure or purely rational concept of the university, this – to speak somewhat elliptically, given the hour, and before the doors are shut or the meeting dismissed – is due very simply to the fact that the university is *founded*. An event of foundation can never be comprehended merely within the logic that it founds. The foundation of a law is not a juridical event. The origin of the principle of reason, which is also implicated in the origin of the university, is not rational. The foundation of a university institution is not a university event. An anniversary of the foundation may be, but not the founding itself. Though such a foundation may not be merely illegal, it also does not arise from the internal legality it institutes. And while nothing may seem more philosophical than the foundation of a philosophical institution, whether it involves a university, a school, or a department of philosophy, the foundation of the philosophical institution as such can never be *already strictly* philosophical. We are here in that place where the founding responsibility occurs by means of acts or performances – which are not just acts of language in the strict or narrow sense, and which, though evidently not constative utterances regulated by a certain determination of the truth, are also perhaps not simply linguistic performatives; this last opposition (constative/performative) still remains too closely programmed by the very philosophico-university law – in other words by reason – that is being opened to challenge here. Such a challenge would not belong to a philosophical setting merely, and would no longer be a theoretical question in the style of Socrates, Kant, Husserl or others. It would be inseparable from novel acts of foundation. We live in a world where the foundation of a new law – in particular a new university law – is necessary. To call it *necessary* is to say in this case *at one and the same time* that one has to take responsibility, a new kind of responsibility, and that this foundation is already well on the way, and irresistibly so, beyond any representation, any consciousness, any acts of individual subjects or corporate bodies, beyond any interfaculty or interdepartmental limits, beyond the limits between an institution and the political places of its inscription. Such a foundation cannot simply break with the tradition of an inherited law, or submit to the legality that it authorizes, even among those conflicts and forms of violence that always prepare for the instauration of a new law, or a new epoch of the law. Only within the epoch of the law is it possible to distinguish legal from illegal conflicts, and, above all, as Kant would wish, conflicts from war. ❧ How do we orient ourselves toward the foundation of a new law? This new foundation will negotiate a compromise with the traditional law. Traditional law should therefore provide, on its own foundational soil, a support for leaping to another place for founding, or, if you prefer another metaphor to that of the jumper planting a foot before leaping – of 'taking the call on one foot' *(prenant appel sur un pied)* as is said in French – then we might say that the difficulty will consist, as always, in determining the best lever, what the Greeks would call the best *mochlos*. A *mochlos* could be a wooden beam, a lever for displacing a boat, a wedge for opening or closing a door, something, in short, to lean on for forcing and displacing. When one asks how to be oriented in history, morality or politics, the most serious discords and decisions have to do less often with ends, it seems to me, than with levers. For example, the opposition of right and left, in this originally parliamentary sense, is perhaps largely, if not entirely, a conflict between several strategies of political *mochlos*. Kant serenely explains to us that, in a university as in a parliament, there ought to be a left (the philosophy faculty, or lower faculty: the left is down for the moment) and a right (the class of higher faculties representing the government). When I asked an instant ago how we should orient ourselves toward the foundation of a new law, I was citing, as you doubtless recognized, the title of another small work (1786) by Kant *(How to Be Oriented in Thinking? Was heisst: Sich im Denken orientieren?)*. This essay speaks, among other things, of the paradox of symmetrical objects as presented in yet another essay of 1768 *(Foundation for the Distinction of Positions in Space: Von dem ersten Grunde des Unterschiedes der Gegenden im Raume)*, namely, that the opposition of right and left does not arise from a conceptual or logical determination, but only from a sensory topology that has to be referred to the subjective position of the human body. This was evidently related to the definition and perception, ultimately specular, of the left and right sides. But if I quickly displace myself at this point from speculation to walking, then indeed, as Kant will have told us, the university will have to go on two feet, left and right, each foot having to support the other as it rises with each step to make the leap. It involves walking on two feet, two feet *with shoes*, since it turns on an institution, on a society and culture, not just on nature. This was already clear in what I recalled about the faculty parliament. But I find its confirmation in an entirely different context, and you will certainly want to forgive me this rather rapid and brutal leap; I am authorized by the memory of a discussion, held in this very place some two years ago with our eminent colleague, Professor Meyer Schapiro, on the subject of certain shoes in Van Gogh. This was concerned, in the first place, with the Heideggerian interpretation of that 1935 painting, and with knowing whether those two shoes made a pair, or two left shoes, or two right shoes, the elaboration of this question having always seemed to me one of greatest consequence. Treating of the conflict between the faculty of philosophy and the faculty of medicine, and after speaking about the power of the human soul to master its morbid feelings, after involving us in dietetics, his hypochondria, sleep and insomnia, Kant proceeds to offer the following confidence, to which I shall add, out of respect for your own sleep, not one word. I only underline the *mochlos* or *hypomochlium*:

*Since insomnia is a failing of weak old age, and since the left side is gener-ally weaker than the right, I felt, perhaps a year ago, one of those cramplike seizures and some very sensitive stimuli. . . . I had to . . . consult a doc-tor. . . . I soon had recourse to my Stoic remedy of fixing my thought forc-ibly on some neutral object . . . (for example, the name of Cicero, which contains many associated ideas . . . ).*[17]

And the allusion to a weakness of the left side calls for the following note:

*It is sometimes said that exercise and early training are the only factors that determine which side of a man's body will be stronger or weaker, where the use of his external members is concerned – whether in combat he will han-dle the sabre with his right arm or with his left, whether the rider standing in his stirrup will vault onto his horse from right to left or vice-versa, and so forth. But this assertion is quite incorrect. Experience teaches that if we have our shoe measurements taken from our left foot, and if the left shoe fits perfectly, then the right one will be too tight; and we can hardly lay the blame for this on our parents, for not having taught us better when we were children. The advantage of the right foot over the left can also be seen from the fact that, if we want to cross a deep ditch, we put our weight on the left foot and step over with the right; we otherwise run the risk of falling into the ditch. The fact that Prussian infantrymen are trained to start out with the left foot confirms, rather than refutes, this assertion; for they put this foot in front, as on a* hypomochlium, *in order to use the right side for the impetus of the attack, which they execute with the right foot against the left.*[18]

NOTES

1. Jacques Derrida's paper was delivered on 17 April 1980 at Columbia University, for the centenary of the founding of its Graduate School.

2. Immanuel Kant, *The Conflict of the Faculties/Der Streit der Fakultäten,* trans. Mary J. Gregor (New York: Abaris Books, 1979), p.23. Translation modified throughout.

3. Ibid.

4. Ibid., p.11.

5. Ibid., pp.36 ff.

6. See, for example, Jacques Derrida's *Of Grammatology,* trans. Gayatri Chakravorty Spivak (Baltimore: Johns Hopkins University Press, 1976), notably p.54; *Plato's Pharmacy* (in *Dissemination,* trans. Barbara Johnson (Chicago: University of Chicago Press, 1981), p.128; *Signature Event Context,* in *Margins of Philosophy,* trans. Alan Bass (Chicago: University of Chicago Press, 1982), and *Glas,* trans. John P. Leavey, Jr., and Richard Rand (Lincoln: University of Nebraska Press, 1987).

7. Kant, *The Conflict of the Faculties,* p.15.

8. Ibid., pp.59, 27.

9. 'Whereas the utility the higher faculties promise the government is of secondary importance. We can also grant the theology faculty's claim that the philosophy faculty is its handmaid (though a question remains, whether the servant is the mistress's torchbearer or trainbearer) *[ob diese ihrer gnädigen Frau die Fakel vorträgt oder die Schleppe nachträgt],* provided it is not driven away or silenced. For her very modesty – merely being free, and leaving others free, to find the truth for the benefit of all the sciences and to set it before the higher faculties to use as they will – must commend it to the government as above suspicion, indeed, as indispensable.' Second Section, 'The Concept and Division of the Lower Faculty,' ibid., p.45.

10. 'To the extent that the sciences obtain, through and in the state, an effectively objective existence, and to the extent that they become a power *[Macht],* the associations formed by each in particular are called faculties. As for their mutual relations – and a comment here is particularly necessary since Kant, in his work on *The Conflict of the Faculties,* strikes us as having treated the issue from an altogether unilateral point of view – it is clear that theology, as a science where the heart of philosophy is found to be objectified, should occupy the first and highest place; and to the extent that an ideal power *[Potenz]* is higher than a real one, it follows that the faculty of

law precedes the faculty of medicine. As for a faculty of philosophy, however, it is our thesis that there is not, nor can there be, any such thing, the proof lying in the simple fact that something which is everything cannot, for that very reason, be anything in particular.' Friedrich Schelling, *Vorlesungen über die Methode des akademischen Studiums* (Jena: University of Jena, 1802).

11. Kant, *The Conflict of the Faculties*, p.45.

12. See, for example, the works and struggles of GREPH (Groupe de Recherches sur l'Enseignement Philosophique) in *Qui a peur de la philosophie?* (Paris: Flammarion, 1977). See also *Les Etats généraux de la philosophie* (Paris: Flammarion, 1979).

13. Kant, *The Conflict of the Faculties*, p.55.

14. Ibid., p.57.

15. Ibid., pp.57–58. On matters of content, see p.111.

16. Ibid., p.55.

17. Ibid., p.193.

18. Ibid. Redundancy. Let us repeat here the name of Polyphemus. *Mochlos* is also the name for the 'wedge' or wooden lever that Ulysses – or the ruse of No One, *outis, Metis* – puts into the fire before driving it into the pupil of the Cyclops (*Odyssey* 9.375–88).

# 2

Institutions of Change:

Notes on Education in the Late Eighteenth Century

*by Christie McDonald*

Since the bicentennial of the French Revolution, education in America has become an issue of and for democracy in America: people scrutinize models that politicians set, as the news media delve into every possible detail of educators' lives and work; educators are reviewing the implications of everything they teach from the most apparently apolitical to the most explicitly political texts; institutions are questioning their role within society. ❧ In 1987, E. D. Hirsch's *Cultural Literacy: What Every American Needs to Know* was published, as was Allan Bloom's successful and disturbing book, *The Closing of the American Mind: How Higher Education has Failed Democracy and Impoverished the Souls of Today's Students.*[1] Both books address themselves, although in very different ways, to foundational questions of knowledge through the institutions of teaching. Hirsh deals with the problem of cultural literacy, 'national language and national culture' (the title of one of his chapters); he speaks of and to the American population – those who will achieve high school diplomas – about what should be expected of them. His goal is to establish a repertoire of basic knowledge that every American should possess. In contrast, Bloom's is, by his own admission, an unabashedly elitist view of education, written at a time when more Americans than ever are attending college. His critique took form in reaction to changes in attitude and in the curriculum brought about during the turbulent years of the 1960s, changes to which he could not or would not accommodate. For example, Bloom's outright refusal of feminism, the only political movement to have survived that period, indicates a reactionary turn in a thought process linking education and the decline of culture. Whereas in the 1950s a prevalent view held that the university was an ivory tower, removed from the world of politics and the interests of finance, the lessons of the decades since the 1960s have been quite different. With the politicization of the student body in the 1960s, and the subsequent analyses of the placement of investments by private universities, it has become clear that the university as an institution participates in the economics and politics of the society at large. The lesson has been learned: there is no haven anywhere, and administrators, students, and teachers alike must be mindful of pressures from without and within. However, in the closing pages of his book, Bloom outlines the kind of transparent community he would wish for in the university; it is an unreconstructed Rousseauistic dream where the simulacra of society and its inevitable evils cannot penetrate, where men (would women be there too? nothing is sure) live in friendship and in the truth of selfhood, of humanity. ◆ While Bloom pinpoints a crisis within the university as a crisis in reason, and defines reason as that which established modern nations, he blames cultural relativism (a term largely undefined) for what he sees as the disintegration in values. For Bloom, the legacy of an institution founded on reason and the imperative of free thinking remains in shadow form only, dethroned by what he calls political and theoretical democracy in contemporary America. ◆ Philosophy provides the key for Bloom. But which philosophy and whose? That is the question. Whereas high school students are taught the basics of philosophy in Europe, he argues, philosophy is a word whose indefinite relativism in America evacuates it of meaning: 'Everybody has a philosophy.' Bloom summarily discusses what he considers to be the failed attempt of literature departments within universities to fill a gap left by philosophy in America. He links this attempt to 'Deconstructionism,' and concludes with an attack: 'Everything has tended to soften the demands made on us by the tradition; this [deconstructionism] simply dissolves it. . . . This will not be the last attempt of its kind coming from the dispossessed humanities in their search for an imaginary empire, one that flatters popular democratic tastes.'[2] ◆ The point of reference for this conference is *The Conflict of the Faculties* by Immanuel Kant, and our focus is on the question of the university in a tradition. Kant codified a certain consensus emerging from eighteenth-century thinkers which put philosophy at the center of the disciplines, as a part within the whole. The mandate of philosophy was the understanding and questioning of that whole. In its turn, the university was a part of a larger whole – society – and one which by its function anticipated the whole. This paper deals with some of the reasons why the idea of philosophy as the discipline of reason, although it alone seemed to legitimate culture, may be traced back before Kant to the eighteenth century,[3] and how letters and philosophy became instruments of change during the prerevolutionary and revolutionary period. ৯ In the eighteenth century, politics and society were inseparable from the question of education and instruction. There was consensus about the goal of education: it was to further the progress and happiness of women, men, and country with the development of the intellectual faculties. What was at issue was the invention of a system of instruction without which the newly emerging society, the society envisaged by the revolutionaries of 1789 and those intellectuals who prepared their way, could not be realized. In its inaugural moments, the educational system in general and the university in particular presented the necessity of an order, a hierarchy, and the potential for questioning that order. The imperative of a change within society became coextensive with a change in education: how to create a new society and form new habits and *mores* that would endure. That was the pressing question. As the representatives of philosophy, culture, and the nation took charge of education and gradually replaced the figure of the sovereign leader, the theory and practice of passing on knowledge and power would change. Innovation in the concept of education would occur through analogy – to the mind, to knowledge, and to society. ৯ In his article 'Mochlos,' Jacques Derrida states that Kant guarantees his analogical statements by a 'real' analogy: that of the university to society, to the social system that it represents as one of its parts. That is, within the model of the university in early nineteenth-century Germany, science was likened to industry, and professors were treated as a group of autonomous guardians of the system. Derrida asks of Kantian thinking: what is the legitimacy of this juridico-rational and politico-juridical system of the university? Because the model for the university was based on an analogy to structures outside it, and because of an increasing sense of responsibility both to society and for the effects of science and technology, the self-autonomy of the university presented a conflict internal to itself. The question I wish to trace comes out of a series of educational projects created just before and in the flux preceding the French Revolution. If legitimacy of the institution depends upon analogy to society, how does this model operate when its very creation coincides with that of the educational project designed to stabilize it? In the two decades preceding the Revolution, thinkers had questioned the foundations of thinking and society. Now they were faced with the necessity of constituting a system within which thinking would not only question but implement social forms that were philosophically sound, making of them traditions to be carried on. ❧ I will look at the following three texts: *Introduction to the Course of Study for the Instruction of the Prince of Parma,* by Etienne Bonnot de Condillac; 'Plan for a University,' a text written by Denis Diderot for Catherine of Russia; and 'A Discourse on National Education' by Mirabeau, with some comment added from Mme de Staël. What is common to these discussions, as well as to the contemporary debate about education, is the attempt to bring the institutions of teaching in harmony with a vision of society based on reason and the freedom of reason to establish its own limits. The concept of responsibility to the individual, to society, and to progress would emerge as a consequence of the analogy out of which the institution was formed. ❧ *The Course of Study for the Instruction of the Prince of Parma* was written by Condillac in 1773 and published in 1775. This plan calls for a one-to-one relation between tutor and student because the course of study was destined for an individual of noble extraction. The questions raised in the introduction concern the basis for the educational process. Condillac outlines his project with clarity: based in psychology, the order of learning will be the same order as that of the natural progress of the human mind; ontogenesis follows phylogenesis in this ideal of pedagogy. The principle here is that the age of reason, the age at which one is capable of comprehending, is the moment when the child begins to observe. Thus, the 'true and only method of learning' is one that goes from the known to the unknown. One begins with what the child knows, and goes on from there.[4] In the process, the tutor will move from element to element as if he too were making discoveries. ❧ The principle of pedagogy lies in analysis of how comprehension in the individual operates to generate habits of the mind. One must teach the student to understand his or her mind in order to stimulate a desire to know. All the rest should follow. Condillac advocates a form of education that produces reflection rather than rote memory work. The only drawback he envisages for a student disposed toward such reflective thinking is that education then creates more problems than it solves, putting obstacles in the way of the development and progress of the faculty of reason. What this means is that education does not simply provide knowledge. Rather, it provides the means to gain knowledge. Although there is inequality among individuals – some are limited by their talents, others advance – what one teaches is *how to think.*[5] This, however, requires comprehension of what constitutes thinking *itself.* ❧ For Condillac, judgment is formed either by habit or reflection, or a combination of the two. All the habits of the body are judgments of habit; they work toward self-preservation. For certain actions, reflection requires too much time – returning a punch, for example. Ideas may be linked in two ways in the mental habits one acquires: if they are associated and come all at once, the mind may have difficulty in observing them in a linear fashion. If, on the other hand, they are related in a sequence, then they may be perceived in succession, as one element evokes others. When these associations become familiar, they turn into habits that the mind forms and obeys without further reflection. ❧ At a certain level, associations must be at once automatic and shared. The problem is to show how any particular association relates to a general concept without reducing the uniqueness of the response. Although the role of education is to develop a common pool of knowledge, the question is whether associations must become reflex in order to allow communication between people within the same society. In other words, how does one arrive at a shared system of association and still allow for the reflection of individual thought? ❧ The relationship that thought establishes among ideas is the principle upon which memory is based. The capacity to combine thoughts is thus the only means of thought. Just as the body seems to act by instinct when it obeys its habits, so thought occurs by inspiration when it adheres to chains of ideas; the same process also forms taste. Thinking is the result of bringing together several ideas; these relations are then retained as models no longer questioned or examined, and according to which aesthetic judgments are made. Now judgments can either be good or bad. Locke maintained that madness came from the association of ideas, from certain false judgments according to which the habits of judgment are contracted. What determines the truth or falsity of the judgment is reflection at the moment that precedes inception of these habits. Since for Condillac the association of ideas constitutes the fundamental operation of the mind, the basis of education will be instruction in how to contract only good habits of thinking. ❧ Condillac's rule of thumb in conceptualizing education for the individual required a return to origins: to retrace the way in which the varying peoples themselves had begun. Observation helps the Prince to understand that societies share different associations and create customs at varying rates of progress. According to Condillac's account of the development of society, when people reached the stage where they had assured themselves subsistence, they then began to look for the pleasures of life. This marked the beginning of the fine arts. Taste improved because the mind turned from the necessities of existence to the objects of leisure and beauty – reasoning now applied to all kinds of objects. Then speculation began, and with it came the philosophers and poets.[6] The phylogenetic order moved from the harsh necessities of life to questions of taste, and on to abstract or speculative thinking. Implicit within this mythic history is the idea that progress (of the mind and society) is always progress for the better, a general assumption of the Enlightenment. So ontogeny follows phylogeny in this scheme. History indicates the way to teach, the order in which tutors themselves should present the fields of study. A Prince learns to govern by understanding history as a course in moral and legislative instruction[7] by observing those who precede him, judging from past events what will or will not be effective for the future. As the Prince gains in knowledge, he must discover for himself the necessity for general principles as well as the rules themselves. In this way, *the child – not the teacher – will appear to have created the arts and sciences all over again.* In Condillac's plan, the tutor provides the setting for the student to invent him or herself by retracing the origins of society. It is a performative act with a determined outcome: the student will *invent* his or her place on the hierarchy. This is a view of education consonant with the values of the *ancien régime:* instruction *must vary* with the level of the person in society: at the lowest level, little education is required; at higher levels more knowledge and education become necessary. This view holds that not everyone is equal; *education is for the few.* Even though learning is considered to be a social and political act, in its beginning as in its end, no sociopolitical reform is envisaged here. Condillac's project differs in this respect from those of Diderot and Mirabeau. Diderot wrote the 'Plan d'une université' in 1776 for Catherine II of Russia, to whom he gave his library and for whom he served as librarian. In this text, Diderot states unequivocally that the goal of public instruction should always be to enlighten men (and women) and make them virtuous. Without instruction, a nation might be strong, but it would always be barbaric; an enlightened nation required enlightened public education. This ideal comes neither from force nor interest, but virtue. There can be no virtue without justice, no justice without enlightenment.[8] The creation of a university should be projected in its entirety from an initial plan. Be-

cause public and private interest are often at odds, because nothing re-
sists reason more obstinately than inveterate abuses, public education
must not be created piecemeal, with fragments organized by agents of
differing interests. Instead, it must be created as a totality with the long-
term interest of the empire in view. No matter what the financial means
at any given moment, Diderot cautions the Empress not to leave the
overall organization to posterity. ❧ Diderot informs Catherine that the
time is right for creating a university. The human mind has thrown off
its shackles: the futility of scholastic studies is recognized; the craze for
systematic thinking diminished. No longer is it a question of being an
Aristotelian, a Cartesian, a Malebranchian, or a Leibnizian. The desire
and taste for 'true science' reigns everywhere, and knowledge has
reached a high degree of perfection. In Russia, the absence of traditional
institutions works to the advantage of innovative thinking and new
knowledge. In that respect, Catherine's position is free of the traditional
obstacles and the Russian situation can be considered superior to that of
the French: before her lie wide-open spaces in which to build.[9] ❧ What
is Diderot's definition of a university and public education in general? It
is an institution whose doors are open indiscriminately to all the children of a nation, an institution where the teachers, remunerated by the
state, teach the basic knowledge of all the sciences. In this open admis-
sions policy, with equal opportunity,[10] Diderot suggests that it is more
than possible that a genius may come from a simple rather than a pala-
tial dwelling. (Diderot even questions whether one can educate a genius
at all; the system has fulfilled its responsibility, he maintains, if it has not
stifled him or her.) The explicit goal of public education, however, must
be *general* education for the *general* level of students: the 'natural' aver-
age, rather than the very brilliant or the very slow, determines the pace.
❧ Diderot proposes a system opposed both to the individual instruction prescribed by Condillac and to the elite education described by
Bloom. In his view, education is not designed to make the student pro-
found. Rather it initiates the student into the knowledge without which
he or she would be ill-prepared for life, without which, that is, he or she
might be disgraced under certain conditions: ignorance of the law in a
magistrate, for example, would be as destructive as an ignorance of the
language is shameful.[11] ❧ Just as Diderot, as editor in chief of the *Encyclopedia*, had been concerned with the order of knowledge, so he is concerned here with the order of studies in the university. The two cannot

be dissociated, and similar images describe both, evoking a system of knowledge in which there must be first principles, general notions, and axioms. A course in 'universal science' is like a *grand avenue,* he states, at whose entrance a number of subjects all shout at once: 'Instruction, instruction! We know nothing; let them teach us.'[12] In the article 'Encyclopedia,' a text designed to account for and be within the totality of the *Encyclopedia,* Diderot compares first principles to avenues; the avenues lead to smaller streets, the specialized regions of knowledge. As the students stream onto the avenue, not all are capable of going all the way. As they move along, the numbers diminish: some will stop early on; others further along; some will go far. One moves from the first step, which is the most useful to the greatest number, to the last which is least useful to the smallest number. So the integration of knowledge follows an itinerary from general to specialized forms, passing from easy to difficult material. The teaching of general principles forms the cornerstone of the educational structure. In Diderot's terms, setting the first rock well in place assures a forever unmovable edifice. ❧ Diderot divides knowledge into two classes: essential, or primitive knowledge, and knowledge of convenience. The first belongs to all levels of society and must be acquired early; the second belongs to the state or the profession that one has chosen. The first is elementary knowledge, the second is knowledge in depth. This distinction defines the difference between the transmission of fundamental knowledge at the undergraduate level and the teaching of specialized knowledge at the graduate level. Yet even in the elementary stages of this process, not everyone has the same needs: the day worker requires less education than the manufacturer, who requires less than the merchant, who requires less than the military man, who requires less than the magistrate or religious person; all of these require less than the statesman. ❧ In the case of the poet, no object escapes his (or her) range. Diderot wonders whether one can be a great poet with less than total knowledge of the classical and modern languages; history, physics, and geography; of the political and social forces that bind society together (religions, the customs of nations, of one's own nation, and the passions, vices, virtues, and moral character of individuals). Because poets must be so very learned, there can be very few. At the same time, Diderot warns that it is dangerous to produce too many rhetoricians, priests, monks, philosophers, jurists, or doctors. Some are too dangerous; others spend their lives thinking and so remain indifferent to the true happiness of society. Diderot concludes this argument by stating that there should be more philosophers than doctors; more doctors than lawyers; more lawyers than orators; and almost no poets. ໖ Diderot classifies knowledge according to the principle faculties of the mind. As they are set out in the *Encyclopedia,* all facts come under memory; all science under reason; all arts under imitation and the imagination; all the mechanical arts under the need for pleasure. If only historians, philosophers, orators, and poets were needed, there would be no problem in establishing the order of learning and knowledge. Since that is not the case, and the need for people in practical professions is great, it becomes evident that what works for speculation (based on the relationship among the sciences) does not always work in practice – utility based upon reason carries with it new demands.[13] This means that within each discipline an order must be established that corresponds both to the foundation of the discipline and to its use. ໖ Although Diderot agrees with Condillac that the association of ideas is the basic order of the mind, he maintains that such association can provide neither the order of the disciplines nor the order of learning. What may be good for the writer, for example, cannot be recommended for the student. Whereas the writer must be led by the natural threads that link thoughts together in the mind and guide the pen, instruction demands a structured system of knowledge. The real task of public education, therefore, is, first, to order and limit association, and, then, to apply reason to empirical phenomena in order to develop judgment.[14] ໖ What interests Diderot in the innovation of ideas is how *analogy and analogical thinking* create a 'new' philosophy between rational and experimental philosophy: specifically in *De l'interprétation de la nature* and *Le Rêve de d'Alembert.* This kind of thought must be reserved for the intellectually gifted, and is dangerous in the ordinary mind. Logic, the art of thinking correctly, or of making legitimate use of one's senses and reason, represents a safer model. One must begin by perfecting this instrument because it is the way in which the human being verifies received knowledge, learns methods of investigation in the search for truth, distinguishes errors of ignorance, and identifies the sophisms of the passions. ໖ Literature plays a crucial role in education, and its glory founds all others. By exploring the limits of rational thought, through association and analogy, literature becomes the vehicle for thinking in general. And because literature and language remain inseparable, the study of the maternal language is crucial to education: French for the French, Russian for the Russians, though French should be the model for clarity and distinctness. As for criticism, it is the art of appreciating the different, and even the contradictory, qualities of those authorities upon whose work knowledge is based. ✿ Overall, Diderot's project for the university shows restraint. Nowhere in this project does a critique of rationalism appear openly.[15] Rather, he states that the function of the university is to pass on knowledge to posterity, to 'the nephews' as he calls them. It is the same function he attributes to the *Encyclopedia*, the purpose of which was to present the sum of all knowledge based on an order of intelligibility. But beyond this, the larger purpose of the encyclopedic project was *to change the way in which men (and women) think*. The accomplishment of that goal would be the work of the French Revolution, as the laboratory of rationalism and a good deal more. ✿ The 'Discourse on National Education' (subtitled 'Public Instruction, or, On the Organization of the Teaching Corps') was a speech prepared by, and largely attributed to Mirabeau.[16] Mirabeau, who spearheaded much of the work at the National Assembly during the early days of the French Revolution, died before he was able to present it to the National Assembly. In this speech, Mirabeau describes the relationship of an educational system to the future society that the instigators of the Revolution hoped to create. The voice of an entire nation, he states, had conferred upon the members of the National Assembly the task of regenerating opinion, and the abuses that constituted the former 'servitude' of the people within society formed a system. All aspects of life in society were interdependent and could be identified at some level with public life so that – and this was a rallying cry for the Revolution – *it was necessary to demolish everything in order to reconstruct everything*.[17] ✿ As the body politic or organ of this new society, the National Assembly was to establish the basic principles of liberty. Although these principles had been enacted through a number of laws, much remained to be accomplished between the newly created constitution and the traditions and habits of the people to bring legislative and religious reforms in consonance with public opinion. Mirabeau announces a fundamental principle for freedom and equality: enlightened public opinion protects the people against political and moral abuse; a free people requires instruction in which, as Montesquieu wrote in *De l'esprit des lois*, 'The laws of education must be relative to the principles of government.'[18] ✿ Although the reinvention of the social order came about in the name of the people, it was the work of no single person or faction of the population, but the work of an entire nation.[19] The need for a system of education imposed itself at the time when the basis for a free constitution was being developed. The idea was not to force citizens into a mold, but rather to give them the chance to form themselves. Where social hierarchy had been dictated by birth, and the monarchy by divine right, revolutionary society was to be a voluntary association in which education would be available to all. The distinction between education and instruction is very important here. Public instruction required high schools, colleges and academies, and books and instruments for calculating. National education required circuses, public games, and national holidays. Education was for all; instruction for a few.[20] The means for installing a system of instruction were there, Mirabeau states; it was a question of applying principles. In order to bring about 'orderly and rational change,'[21] institutions of public instruction were needed. The function of these institutions would be to stabilize the new society, for without them, the threat of anarchy and despotism would remain. ❧ Mirabeau affirms that teaching liberty, equality, and fraternity would at once liberate the people from the past and lay the groundwork for the future. Such a view of innovation presumed a radical break from the past in which the new society, and the new education, were to be created *ex nihilo*. Through reason, the National Assembly was to become a legitimating power whose mandate was to restructure society, among other things, through education and instruction. ❧ Because the 'science of freedom' can neither be dissociated from other operations of the mind nor from morality in this view, political regeneration, founded upon virtue as an expression of reason, required a good public system of instruction. Mirabeau asserts that in a free regime the people must learn to make use of, and benefit from, the strengths of the system. In addition to strict rules that maintain such freedom, a great deal would be demanded of the ideal citizen to make the system work: reflection, caution, and practice. The whole of society was to be hewn by an incessant pedagogy, a school of morals intended to perfect a model for what was to come.[22] ❧ How would this be enacted? What would the role of the National Assembly be in giving birth to such a system? And how must it proceed? Charged with putting into action the basic operations of man's (and woman's) perfectibility, and charged with founding the political machinery for a complete transformation of

society, what was its mandate? Was it to create the applications or consequences of these principles in extensive detail? The National Assembly's
response was no. Questions of detail, whether of teaching methods, tuition demands or particular problems, would be dealt with through
progress in public development and the indirect influence of laws. The
duty of the National Assembly was *to create the means for social development, the putting into motion of institutions.* Its purpose was to ensure
that men and women develop their faculties and enjoy all the rights due
them in order to create the best possible situation for the citizen to develop. ❧ The question of invention and self-determination was one of
authority within the system: who, for example, would decide what constitutes error and how 'facts' were to be taught? Condorcet would subsequently argue that knowledge is in a constant state of change, so that in
order to avoid the imposition of dogma, public authority must refrain
from judgment on any body of knowledge or doctrine. 'Instruction in
the truths defined by scientific consensus should therefore be entrusted
to the independent direction and control of the republic of science.'
What this meant was that the 'goal of instruction' was to render men 'capable of evaluating and correcting' legislation in order to give the institution self-autonomy.[23] ❧ In other words, philosophy was to preside
over the teaching of politics in the instruction of young citizens. What
mattered was that natural law should determine the underlying notion
of truth.[24] ❧ Public education cannot achieve its end, however, unless
the model for social organization reinforces the model for education;
there must be a pact that fixes the limits and the nature of the institution
in accord with the definition of society. In a society based on the super-
imposition of natural and conventional rights, the individual develops
his or her 'natural' talents and desires. At the same time, the sum of
these individual existences must be an all-enveloping whole. As Rousseau had formulated it, the problem was to ensure that each person 'uni-
ting with all, nevertheless obeys only himself and remains as free as
before.' The solution he proposed was a social contract based on the
general will: 'Each of us puts his person and all his power in common
under the supreme direction of the general will; and in a body we receive
each member as an indivisible part of the whole.'[25] ❧ The question of
freedom was the most difficult of all, and the National Assembly had
been given a clear and adamant mandate to defend its cause. Because the
hope of the nation rests in its youth, and the spirit of the younger gener-

ation is indissoluble from the teaching of the elders, writers and teachers *must never oppose public morality.* Because it is the teachers of youth, the writers and the philosophers who make nations free, or precipitate them into slavery, it is necessary that these people *always act in the public interest.* Just how one could adhere to public morality in education without infringement on freedom remained unclear. What was very clear was the principle of a consonance of purpose in both. ❧ Mirabeau saw the primary duty of education as instruction in the skills of reading and writing, skills needed for future men (and women) of the nation. Without the light of reason, without literacy, there could be no public morality. Like Diderot and Condillac, Mirabeau believed the teaching of language to be primordial. It is essential that public education be taught in the *language of the nation: the French language.*[26] Why such emphasis on language as the center of education? What was it in these texts and others that followed that equated the importance of the maternal language, and its use in the literary context with a powerful national pedagogy? ❧ Mme de Staël answered by relating language to the foundation of a democratic state. In 'De la littérature,' she writes: 'The purity of language, the nobility of expressions, as images of the pride of the soul, are necessary especially in a state founded on democratic principles.' The perfectibility of thought through its expression in language, and the progress of literature, are unequivocally tied to the establishment and preservation of liberty. 'Among the diverse developments of the human spirit,' she continues, 'it is *philosophical literature,* it is eloquence and reasoning that I consider to be the veritable guaranty of liberty.'[27] And political equality was the inherent principle in a philosophical constitution. ❧ As for equality in the education of the sexes in such a democratic state, her views go further than either those of Mirabeau or Condorcet. Mirabeau states that men who are destined for public affairs are brought up in public, while women, destined for a domestic life, should only leave the paternal household on rare occasions. Education for women is lacking: college forms a greater number of worthy men than the best domestic education can provide for women; and convents ruin more women than they form. Invoking Rousseau, Mirabeau distinguishes between the roles that women and men play in nature and society. The constitution of man is robust; he is able to cultivate the earth, negotiate, travel, fight, and plead his rights. He concludes that when education is in tune with nature, it is to these ends that one is trained. On the other hand, the 'delicate constitution' of women makes them suited to childbearing and rearing; women were, it seems, given the irresistible power of weakness. To impose tiresome tasks on such 'frail organs,' to charge such 'feeble hands' with heavy loads, would outrage nature with the most cowardly kind of barbarity. Woman must reign inside the house, and there only. She is out of place everywhere else, unless she maintains the demeanor of a mother, or mother to be. 'Reason' ordains that domestic life be the true destination of women.[28] She is loved and respected within the family, though even there she has no power of decision. Mirabeau regrets only that she cannot be admitted to the family council. ❧ What this argument about the appropriate education for women leaves out is Rousseau's distinction between natural and conventional inequality. Although there is natural inequality among men, as there is among animals, the social contract must institute conventional equality. ❧ Mirabeau does not request suppression of all public education for women. He suggests maintaining the schools of reading, writing, and arithmetic that already existed for them, and creating more – based upon the same principle as the ones for young men. Women, like all citizens, should receive the basic skills that education teaches to enable a person to participate in society. ❧ Condorcet, in his text concerning the admissibility of women to the city, states that until the time of the Revolution, legal inequality between the sexes had existed, and it was one of the main causes of corruption. He goes further than Mirabeau in his advocacy of education for women, stating that the legal equality afforded all under the new constitution had found no worthy opposition, nor would the equality of the sexes.[29] ❧ Mme de Staël, however, raises the question of women and women's education to another level in 'De la littérature': she shows how women might assume power and take a role of leadership within society, and at a certain level she assesses what the consequences might be. In writing a work like 'De la littérature,' she declared that she came under more than local attack. The kind of criticism she received could repeat itself indefinitely because she was blamed for being a woman who writes and a woman who thinks.[30] In analyzing what women have contributed to literature, she acknowledges their greater sensibility and knowledge of the emotions. This, she points out, is evident in their contribution to contemporary literature; the novel is a product of the modern spirit, unknown to the thinkers of antiquity. Most important, *one could show on every page of these books ideas that had never before been possible, ideas that could only emerge with the attainment of equal civil status for women.*[31] Because of the influence of women, the general spirit had become philosophically more open: broadening or changing the sense of generosity, value and humanity within society. ᶾᵃ Although a woman with exceptional talent might be recognized, it was still difficult for her to lay claim nobly to a reputation as author, to maintain an elevated place within society without losing grace and dignity. All serious study for women was considered pedantic, and it was difficult to rise above the scorn and mockery to which a woman who wanted to write and study would be subjected. ᶾᵃ The hope was that some of these ills might be eliminated with the creation of the Republic. In all free countries, de Staël states, education of women had been directed according to the spirit of the constitution that was established: in Sparta, they trained women in warlike exercises while in Rome they required of women austere and patriotic virtues.[32] Thus she reasons that for revolutionary thought to come into harmony with the enlightenment of philosophy, it would be not only reasonable but necessary to encourage the cultivation of women's minds. ᶾᵃ Mme de Staël's criticism is sharp: the lesson of the Revolution had been that men thought it politically and morally useful to downgrade women, attempting to reduce them to absurd mediocrity. Although the Revolution changed many things, in effect it changed nothing in the status of women. To ensure the Republic, it is necessary to enlighten, instruct, and perfect women like men, and nations like individuals. The nation requires an enduring foundation, and this is the best way to achieve political and social goals for the future.[33] It is *useful* to society and to the happiness of all that women develop their minds and reason to the fullest. Mocking the general feeling of the time, she comments that the only bad effect of such training might be that certain women would become so distinguished that they might begin to covet glory for themselves. These women, she says, would suffer more from the torment of their superiority than would society from seeing them get ahead. And she remarks acidly that examination of the social order shows it to be totally 'armed against' any woman who might rise to the heights of men's reputations. The public tends to turn against any distinguished woman. The power of outstanding men may be in some measure enjoyed by those around him. All a woman can offer is *high sentiments and new ideas;* her celebrity can be no more than an irritating noise to the surrounding men. ᶾᵃ Despite her impatience, Mme de Staël recognizes that the period of the Revolution opened a new era for the intellectual as well as the political world. By examining such notions as perfectibility in literature and philosophy, the foundation of a free and just republic, she hopes that these ideas will be translated through institutions with more maturity. ❧ Mirabeau had been emphatic: *The French revolution was the work of letters and philosophy.*[34] Together they linked language to the notion of the homeland and showed the arts of the most apolitical nature to be inextricable from political considerations. Perhaps the same could be said today, with all the differences that nevertheless intervene. The humanities are not 'dispossessed humanities in their search for an imaginary empire,' as Allan Bloom would have it, nor do responsibility and truth necessarily lie elsewhere. Rather, literature and philosophy offer the possibility of reflecting about ways of thinking within and without the institutions of learning. ❧ Bloom writes his balance sheet for the revolutions in America and France: 'The misunderstanding between America and the Continent is that where Americans saw a solution, Continentals saw a problem. The American Revolution produced a clear and unified historical reality; the French Revolution, a series of questions and problems. Americans have tended to look at the French Revolution with indulgence. It represented the good things, akin to ours, but did not succeed in providing a stable institutional framework for them.'[35] In all of the texts from the eighteenth century to which I have alluded, the writers struggled to articulate the relationship between the individual and the institution, change and stability, truth and value. None presents the final version either for education or society. Were it possible, however, to combine the French spirit of problematizing with the American tradition of stable institutionalization, one might hope to achieve the following: orderly change dependent upon the Enlightenment principle that the 'spirit of criticism' relies upon, while at the same time questioning the place of language and reason, as well as the role of education, within society.

NOTES

1. E. D. Hirsch, *Cultural Literacy* (Boston: Houghton Mifflin, 1987); Allan Bloom, *The Closing of the American Mind* (New York: Simon and Schuster, 1987).

2. Bloom, *The Closing of the American Mind*, pp.378–79.

3. See Richard Rorty, *Philosophy and the Mirror of Nature* (Princeton: Princeton University Press, 1979), p.4.

4. Etienne Bonnot de Condillac, *Oeuvres philosophiques*, 3 vols., ed. Georges le Roy. (Paris: Presses universitaires de France, 1947), vol.1, p.398.

5. Ibid., p.399.

6. Ibid., pp.400–402.

7. Ibid., p.404.

8. Denis Diderot, 'Plan d'une université,' *Oeuvre complètes* (Paris: Club français du livre, 1971), pp.756, 750.

9. Ibid., pp.758–59.

10. Ibid., pp.750–51.

11. Ibid., p.763.

12. Ibid., p.756. 'Je reviens à la comparaison . . . d'un cours de la science universelle à une grande avenue a l'entrée de laquelle il se presente une foule de sujets qui crient tous à la fois: "Instruction, instruction! Nous ne savons rien; qu'on nous apprenne" ' (p.759).

13. Ibid., p.786.

14. I have argued this elsewhere: Christie McDonald, 'Resonances associatives: La pensée analogique selon Denis Diderot,' *Etudes françaises* 22, 1 (Spring 1987), 9–21; and 'Traduire la philosophie affectivement,' *Texte* 4 (1985), 53–65.

15. I have discussed Diderot's critique of rationalism in 'The Utopia of the Text,' *The Dialogue of Writing* (Waterloo, Ontario: Wilfrid Laurier Press, 1984), pp.73–89; and in 'The Sophistry of Heuristics,' MLN, 100, 4 pp.780–88.

16. This text can be found in *Discours et opinions de Mirabeau*, vols. (Paris: Chez Kleffer et Aug. Caunes, 1820), 3:502–36. All references here come from the following edition: *Une éducation pour la démocratie: Textes et projets de l'époque révolutionnaire*, ed. Bronislaw Baczko (Paris: Garnier, 1982), pp.68–105. A few months after the death of Mirabeau on 2 April 1791, D. J. G. Cabanis published *A Work on Public Education*, found among his papers. In it were four discourses that Mirabeau proposed to present to the National Assembly. Mirabeau had probably worked on them during 1790–91, and was to present them at the debate around the report to be presented by the constitutive committee assigned to work on public instruction. The particular speech that I deal with here has sometimes been attributed to Chamfort.

Maurice Pellesson argues, in *Chamfort* (Geneva: Slatkine Reprints, 1970), pp.232–57, that Chamfort's role in the speech writing of Mirabeau, Talleyrand, and Condorcet is not totally clear. His role in many of their speeches may have been considerable. Talleyrand presented his long report on public instruction on 10, 11, and 19 September 1791. That report was never discussed. Condorcet developed his policies between 1791 and 1792. He had already published *Memoires sur l'instruction publique*. Condorcet was designated as a member of the committee on public instruction instituted 14 October 1791.

17. 'Quand la voix d'une nation tout entière, ou les sages commençoient a régénerer l'opinion, vous a confié le soin d'effacer jusqu'aux moindres vestiges de son anciènne servitude, vous avez senti que les abus formaient un système dont toutes les ramifications s'entrelaçoient et s'identifioient avec l'existence publique, que pour tout reconstruire, il fallait tout démolir.' Mirabeau, Baczko, ed., *Une éducation,* p.71.

18. See Keith Michael Baker, *Condorcet: From Natural Philosophy to Social Mathematics* (Chicago: University of Chicago Press, 1975), p.286.

19. These were the words of Chamfort: 'La Révolution n'est l'ouvrage d'aucun homme, d'aucune classe d'hommes; elle est l'oeuvre de la nation entière.' Ed. Anguis, 2:361, cited in Pellesson, *Chamfort,* p.223.

20. See Baczko, ed., *Une éducation,* p.30.

21. Baker, *Condorcet,* p.299.

22. Baczko, ed., *Une éducation,* pp.17, 33.

23. Baker, *Condorcet,* p.301.

24. Michèle Crampe-Casnabet, *Condorcet lecteur des lumières* (Paris: Presses universitaires de France, 1985), p.121.

25. Jean-Jacques Rousseau, *On the Social Contract,* ed. Roger Masters, trans. Judith Masters (New York: St. Martin's Press), p.53.

26. Mirabeau, in Baczko, ed., *Une éducation,* pp.75–82.

27. Germaine de Staël, 'De la littérature,' *Oeuvres* ed. crit. Paul von Tieghem, 2 vols. (Geneva: Droz, 1959), 1:30–32.

28. Mirabeau, in Baczko, ed., *Une éducation,* p.89. 'La vie intérieure est la véritable destination des femmes.'

29. Crampe-Casnabet, *Condorcet lecteur des lumières,* pp.115–16.

30. De Staël, 'De la littérature,' p.199n.

31. 'En lisant les livres composés depuis la renaissance des lettres, l'on pourrait marquer à chaque page quelles sont les idées qu'on n'avaient pas avant qu'on eut accordé aux femmes une sorte d'égalité civile.' Ibid., p.243.

32. Ibid., p.302.

33. 'Éclairer, instruire, perfectionner les femmes comme les hommes, les nations comme les individus, c'est encore le meilleur secret pour tous les buts raisonnables, pour toutes les relations sociales et politiques auxquelles on veut assurer un fondement durable.' Ibid., p.303.

34. 'La révolution actuelle est l'ouvrage des lettres et de la philosophie.' Mirabeau, *Discourse*, p.79.

35. Bloom, *The Closing of the American Mind*, p.160.

# 3

The Injured University

*by Timothy Bahti*

In an earlier essay on Immanuel Kant's *Conflict of the Faculties* in its relations to Wilhelm von Humboldt's 1809–10 document on the university
to be founded in Berlin ('Uber die innere und äussere Organisation der
höheren wissenschaftlichen Anstalten in Berlin'), I attempted to examine how historical study was included or not included, inscribed or
ellided within the two men's respective models of the modern university.[1] In that essay, my interest in the status of history in these texts on
the university conjoined with a focus on an aspect of the history or historical fate of the modern university since then, that is, its preponderant
investment in historical studies from the early nineteenth century up to
the present. Jacques Derrida's writings on the modern university and the
state – on the potentially critical, but also potentially powerless position
of the university within a state apparatus of rationalization and technical
control – entered less explicitly into this essay; I confined my references to
several points in his 'Mochlos' essay where he alludes to a possible contradiction within the reasoning of Kant's university model.[2] ✸ As I continue an inquiry into Kant's *Conflict of the Faculties,* I also want to bring
this inquiry somewhat closer to Jacques Derrida's essay on the same text.
Kant asks about a philosophy faculty that is powerless with respect to
the state and the university's 'higher faculties' (theology, law, medicine),
except for its power to judge the truth – and from this small but leveraged vantage point, Kant hints or points toward a reversal of massive
proportions, whereby (as he puts it), 'The last shall be first,' the weak
strong. Indeed, the philosophy faculty shall not only judge, but it shall
control and guide, as philosophy leads the university and, along with
this, leads the state.[3] ✸ But this is already to overstate matters, for Kant
is no gushing proto-utopian, and his text, as is well known, is replete
with hedges and qualifications, ironic asides, and flirtations with despair
as to the prospects for a philosophically guided university and state. It is
here that Jacques Derrida's own meditation on the modern university

with respect to the state is so helpful. For what Derrida notices, toward the end of '*Mochlos,*' is that Kant's proposal for a critically guiding and controlling philosophy faculty in the university and within the state involves *leverage,* the leverage of one side or wing or part of a body against another, in order to be able to exert pressure and change direction. The example, from Derrida and from Kant, is roughly as follows. In his text, Derrida recalled to us, from Kant, that the 'higher' faculties of the university are aligned with the state (from whom they receive their orders) and, in the parliamentary model from which Kant draws, are thus lined up on the 'right,' on the side of those in power. The philosophy faculty, on the other hand, is 'lower' for the moment, and although guardian of the truth, it is also for that very reason in opposition – *for* the truth, *against* mere commands from might – and thus aligned on the 'left.'[4] Derrida then makes a stunning leap. Remarking that the hour is growing late, the light dim, the audience weary (he was speaking at the centennial celebrations of the founding of the Columbia Graduate School), he jumps to the issue of the impossibility of a juridical-legalistic settlement to the 'conflict of the faculties' when the university's rights and responsibilities are a consequence of its sheer founding. Its status, and the intrauniversitarian conflict that follows from this status as both institution of the state and organon of truth, are baseless except for the base provided by the sheer act of founding. Its foundation no more justifies its organization and the internecine conflicts that arise around its power sharing, than does one part of this organization – say, its law faculty – justify its foundation. As Derrida puts it, 'An event of foundation cannot simply be comprehended within the logic of that which it founds. . . . The foundation of a universitarian institution is not a universitarian event. . . . Although it is not simply illegal, such a foundation does not yet make recourse to the internal legality which it institutes.'[5] ❧ To settle or, more correctly, simply to respond to our responsibilities in the face of the conflict of the faculties which, in Kant's and Derrida's analyses, arises from the modern university's foundation, Derrida suggests a new foundation, particularly a new foundation of universitarian rights or of a 'legality' of the university ('en particulier d'un nouveau droit universitaire'). But such a new foundation, which he suggests is already occurring, will not simply break with or usurp the rights of the extant foundation of the modern university. Rather, it will negotiate a compromise with the extant rights and legal structures. How, Derrida then asks, does one orient oneself toward the foundation of a new right, a new legality?[6] ⤷ One does so by seeking leverage, by seeking to use the traditional institution – the extant university – as the point from and by means of which one could spring to a new foundation. It is clear from Derrida's language, and he underscores this by referring to Kant as well, that the image is that of the human being standing, walking, leaping. The university, Kant had said, has to stand and walk on its own two feet, the right one and the left, and each provides the support and leverage while the other rises and steps or leaps. But how, the question remains, does one *orient* oneself toward such leveraged movement from one established position to a new, still-unfounded or unsolid one? The difficulty, Derrida suggests by way of reference to another Kant text, is that left and right, in their opposition as well as in their coordination, 'arise from no conceptual and logical determination, but only from a sensible topology which one can only refer back to the subjective position of the human body.'[7] ⤷ Allow me to expand upon this dilemma a bit, in the terms of my own understanding. When we ask after direction, we customarily ask after *one*. That is, we have the sense and the presumption that direction can be given or taken in a singular and absolute manner. When Derrida asks, 'Comment *s'orienter* vers la fondation d'un nouveau droit?' ('How do we orient ourselves toward the foundation of a new principle of right, a new legality?'), his language is, as usual, precise and revealing. To ask after direction in terms of orientation is to appeal to absolute or cardinal direction, to appeal – in this case – to the east and to the movement of the sun rising in the east; as Kant puts it, 'Sich *orientieren* heisst in der eigentlichen Bedeutung des Worts: aus einer gegebenen Weltgegend, . . . die übrigen, namentlich den Aufgang zu finden.'[8] We may go one step further and suggest, with Kant, that our appeals to left and right also often – in many or perhaps most cases – tend toward appeals for and toward absolute direction, and are crucially in the assistance of establishing the latter. Even if, as Kant correctly argues, left and right are not a conceptual opposition but a subjectively corporeal one (thus a sensible and empirical one), he also argues that this merely '*subjective* ground of differentiation,' what he further specifies as 'the feeling of a difference in [one's] own *subject*,' is 'provided by nature' and is sufficient and necessary for geographical, mathematical and even logical orientation. 'To *orient* oneself at all in thinking, means,' Kant writes, 'to decide, in the insufficiency of objective principles of reason, upon taking something for true according to a subjective principle of reason.'[9] ❧ Be this as it may in the context of Kant's argument in his essay 'What does it mean to orient oneself in thinking?', in our context it only takes one step away from one's own body, with its subjective feeling of a primordial left-right differentiation, to twist or contort the very opposition between the conceptual and the corporeal. The single step is from the body to the body politic. In the parliamentary situation, the left – the 'opposition' – is located from the perspective of the president or the speaker, but the speaker's left is obviously the left's right. And yet within that political-discursive context, as well as outside of it, in all of our modern political discourse, this relative, corporeal or sensible orientation of left and right rapidly becomes the fixed opposition of left and right, the opposition of actual opposition and authority. The 'left,' in the parliament, allows its right to be named and called the left, and so we, too, generally speak of the political left and right as if they were fixed directions, without regard to their original corporeal motility. ❧ What each of us experiences daily before our mirrors, that our left is the Other's right, is disappropriated from our sensible or corporeal 'knowledge' and reappropriated as the claim of the speaker of the body politic: my left is your left. As my friend the ethnographer and cultural analyst James Siegel put it in a conversation, when we use corporeal directions we mean, 'Be like me.' The very nonabsolute or relative character of the corporeal directions of left and right turn, in their articulation, into absolute appeals, or the appeal of the absolute. The gesture of appropriation, of *Aneignung* – which is always the gesture of the Absolute – is the one that speaks of left and right and expects the interlocutor to see it that way: to reverse a possible or even likely opposition from opposition to identity. Absolute or cardinal directions, those of north and south and east and west, reappropriate their other, the corporeal directions of left and right, and this is why Derrida rightly asks how we *orient*, or 'eastern' or 'begin' ourselves vis-à-vis the left and right of the university, standing on its own two feet and conflicting within itself between opposition and allegiance to authority.

❧ ❧

This is what I thought I knew as I prepared a contribution on *The Conflict of the Faculties* in America. I was also at the time, for entirely unrelated reasons, beginning a more or less thorough rereading of Kafka's stories. It occurred to me, as I received Richard Rand's request and the provocation toward thinking which it brought with it, that I might find in Kafka something of assistance – something that might serve as leverage – for this task of thinking through the left and the right in Kant's text and our situation before the questions of the modern university. ❧ I no longer remember which came first, my reading in Kafka or the invitation from Richard Rand, but I found something in Kafka. What I found was in one of his earliest stories, 'Conversation with the Supplicant,' published in 1909.[10] In that story, the narrative 'I' goes daily to church, in order to be able to gaze upon the girl he loves. One day, when she does not come, he notices instead another person in prayer, the supplicant of the story's title. This man is prostrate upon the floor, sighing and occasionally clutching his head and beating it upon the ground. He periodically looks about to see if anyone is watching him. 'This I found unseemly,' the narrator says, 'and I made up my mind to accost him as he left the church and to ask him why he prayed in such a manner. Yes, I felt irritable because my girl had not come' (p.186; 9). ❧ The narrator makes preparations:

*I set myself in a direct line between the basin and the door, knowing that I was not going to let him pass without an explanation. I screwed up my mouth as I always do when I want to speak decisively, I advanced my right leg and rested all my weight upon it, balancing my left leg carelessly on the points of my toes; that too gives me a sense of firmness. (Pp.186; 9–10)*

One can perhaps imagine some of the pleasure I experienced in coming upon this passage, for it will be recalled that it corresponds quite symmetrically to the passage from Kant's *Conflict* with which Derrida's 'Mochlos' ends: the image of the Prussian infantryman, advancing the left leg forward, 'as if on a *hypomochlium*,' so as to be able to swing into attack with the right.[11] ❧ Kafka's narrator, however, misses his target, and in fact does not even get a chance to spring into attack: the supplicant in question dashes by before the narrator has a chance to move in response. 'He made a sudden unexpected dash out through the doorway. The glass door banged shut' (p.186; 10). But several days later, when the narrator's girl is once again absent from church, he again sees the young man lying on the floor. This time he hides for hours behind the church door and accosts the supplicant as he finally attempts to leave. What follows, and constitutes the remainder of the story, is an astonishing dialogue that cannot be analyzed in sufficient detail here. But the sa-

lient point for our purposes is the following: the narrator and the supplicant come to exchange positions, even to the point of identification,
whereas the story had first opposed them. When the narrator gleefully
begins to interrogate the supplicant about his strange habits in church,
the latter replies, 'My bad luck is like a seesaw teetering on a very fine
point, and it will fall on anyone's head who lays a questioning finger on
it' (p.187; 11). The remark proves to be prophetic. For as the narrator
questions the supplicant, he increasingly already knows the answers before he receives them – he understands him as if from within – while the
supplicant begins to question the narrator in turn. The narrator begins
to feel panicky in the face of the supplicant's turning upon him, and he
is made to utter: 'Haven't you a comic way of wriggling out of things,
projecting your own state of mind like that on other people?' (p.189; 13)
When the supplicant denies that he can do this – while we, the readers,
recall the narrator's projection from his absent girl to the present man –
the narrator responds with a further reversal and exchange: 'I never
wanted to come here, I said to myself, but the creature forced me to give
him a hearing' (p.189; 14). Where the narrator began, well poised and
balanced for decisive speech, with his forcing of the supplicant to submit
to his questions, he is here reversed into projecting upon the supplicant
that *he*, the supplicant, forced him, the narrator, to submit to the supplicant. ❧ The supplicant's bad luck, whatever it was, has indeed fallen
upon the narrator's head; the balanced legs, ready for leverage, gave way
to the teetering seesaw of the supplicant's fate. The story continues, or
continues to unravel, along this structure of reversal of opposition, of
exchange from opposition to identification: after hearing yet another
even more fantastic anecdote from the supplicant, the narrator can only
respond in the penultimate paragraph, 'The story you told me about
your mother and the woman in the garden seems to me not in the least
remarkable. Not only have I heard many like it and experienced them,
but I've even played a part in some of them. It was quite a natural inci-
dent' (p.191; 16). ❧ My interest and pleasure in this story had to do with
its posture of leveraged foot position, which gave way not to a decisive
attack – like Kant's Prussian infantryman – but to a teetering and falling
into reversals of opposition and projections of identification. Could this
have something to do, I wondered, with the tendency toward absolutism
(or absolutization) that was being postulated in corporeal directions? If
'left' or 'right,' in their opposition to the opponent's left and right, could

swing around to become fixed or cardinal directional points on a com-
pass of the body politic, could it also be the case – as it was in this Kafka
story – that the positioning of the left and right legs would ultimately establish absolute identifications rather than leveraged oppositions? ❧ At
least two things happened as I continued to pursue these questions, all
the while naively confident that I knew in what direction my preparations on this topic were heading. One was that in the course of my more
or less systematic rereading of Kafka's stories, as well as of his diaries,
such a coincidence of the indication of left and right directions with the
plot of reversals and identifications never again occurred. This frankly
astonished me, and for several reasons. Kafka's attention to the body is
well known, as is his admiration for gymnastics and other skilled move-
ments. His stories are furthermore quite replete with exact, precisely
noted detail of clothing, furnishings, and general surroundings – all
without, I noted with surprise, any particular mention of right and left.
Finally, and perhaps most astonishingly, there are many well-known stories about oppositions reversing into projections of identification: one
thinks, for example, of Georg Bendemann in 'The Judgment' opposing
his youth and accession to marital maturity with his father's old age and
widowed state, and then being reversed into a position of childlike pow-
erlessness and submission; of Gregor Samsa in 'The Metamorphosis' opposing his responsible role to his family's near helplessness, and then
awakening to find, in his insect's form, a helplessness and entrapment of
his own before the newly re-empowered family; of the officer in 'The
Penal Colony' who, about to execute the prisoner on the writing machine, exchanges places and becomes himself the executed one, prisoner
to the machine and its traditions; of the doorkeeper and the man from
the country symmetrically before the law in the parable of that title.
What was astonishing, I experienced, was to find that in each of these
stories of massively manifest reversals of opposed positions into projections of identification, there was no mention of left and right. For all of
the detail of Georg carrying his father to bed and then having him tower
above him, or of Gregor in his room and having his father pelt him with
apples when he tries to leave, or of the officer first explaining the machine to the explorer, then strapping himself in instead, or of the man
from the country noting every feature of the doorkeeper's clothing and
appearance, one looks in vain for the corporeal directions. ❧ What was
I to make of this; specifically, what was I to make of the singular charac-

ter of that very early story of the 'Conversation with the Supplicant' relative to all that followed? Could it be that Kafka, once – and at the very beginning of his oeuvre – having positioned one of his protagonists with a left-and-right detail vis-à-vis the 'opponent,' only to have this corporeal opposition reverse into psychic projection and identification, Kafka never had to do it again? Had Kafka understood decisively and at an early age (the 'Conversation' is thought to have been written before Kafka was twenty-four) the tendency of left and right toward absolutization: their tendency or 'will' toward an identification on the part of those who are otherwise their opposites? Be opposed to me, Kafka seems to say, or let me be opposite you, and we will exchange places before this story is out. And, we might add, why bother with left and right when the otherness they would signal will be absorbed and appropriated, reversed and identified, anyway? ❧ Where is leverage in such a situation? How might left use right – other than to wind up identifying with, or being usurped by, its other? To return to the context of our original deliberations, how might one side or wing – one 'faculty' or capacity – of the university use the other and its longstanding, well-positioned foundation and rights to swing into action and step toward a new foundation of a new set or order of rights and responsibilities? Or would such a position of leveraged opposition yield only an absorption into identification? 'Your left, opposed to my right, becomes my right: be like me, identify with me!' ❧ How can opposition itself be leveraged? This dilemma, which is the position at which Kant's example of the *hypomochlium* and Kafka's exemplary stories appear to leave us, is predicated upon the image of a *stance*, a well-positioned, upright body, whether it is Kant's university walking on its feet, or his Prussian infantryman poised for attack, or Kafka's narrator, ready to spring into discursive action. This apparently healthy body, assuming a stance prepared for decisive action, may only be preparing, however unwittingly or at least irresistibly, for a come-down or a take-down, a stumble or reversal. What if the university, like many of Kafka's characters, cannot stand but to fall, cannot swing around on a pivot foot or leveraged point but to collapse into the previous position that one had thought to oppose? Where would leverage, or opposition, then be? ❧ At this point, one more thing entered my discourse, and it is the 'other thing,' alluded to earlier but not yet introduced, that happened while this paper was initially being prepared. My essay came to change its direction, to reorient its thought, in a way that I shall try to explain and develop. Six weeks before the conference at which this paper was first delivered, I experienced in Paris, France, a collapsed lung. This condition, called a pneumothorax, was accompanied by hemorrhaging in the thoracic cavity – the pneumothorax became a hemopneumothorax – and so the initial procedure I underwent in an attempt to reinflate the lung was rapidly followed by surgery to stop the bleeding and complete the lung's reinflation. Now in France, lung surgery is immediately accompanied by efforts to restore lung capacity (I owe this information and much of what follows to my physician, Dr. Edouard Touaty, and my physical therapist, M. Claude Montfermé). In my case, this meant that the day I was moved from intensive care to an ordinary hospital ward was the day that I began respiratory exercises. It is the principle involved in this therapeutic practice that I would like to try to introduce into the present discussion. ❧ The healthy body has two lungs; it was my left lung that was injured. The balance between the two lungs in a healthy body is an exact and delicate one: they both work best when they each work at most nearly the identical capacity. The balance, in other words, is between equals. It is furthermore between equals to the point of indifference: there is no physiological difference or interest in difference between the left and right lungs in the instance of the healthy body. This, then, is a first point: while the difference between left and right may indeed be, as Kant says, a strictly subjectively topological – sensible or corporeal – one, one rooted irrevocably in the body (and rooted there by nature, he also argues), it is one that makes no difference to the healthy disposition of the body's regular and indispensable respiratory function. ❧ When one lung is injured, the situation changes by virtue of a dangerous imbalance that sets in. Even if the one lung has no serious or long-term diminishment of its capacity, its temporary impairment threatens to allow the other to usurp its functioning altogether and permanently. In my case, the fact that the left lung had to function within a chest wall and thoracic cavity that had undergone surgery put it at a disadvantage with respect to the balance obtaining between the two lungs. To use the image of my physician, it was as if a balance between two light-weight balloons had been disturbed by a football being added to one side, with this added weight of the football representing the stiffness and weakness against and within which the left lung had to function. Just as the balloon could not lightly drift upward on its own when the added weight was holding it down, so would my

left lung not have the lightness and motility of the right, while the right
one would appear and behave as if it were the *only* light and active one.
So this is a second point: a balance between left and right can be disturbed from the outside, or from the surrounding context, such that one
side usurps the functioning and ultimately the place of the other. It
seems important to note here that one is not initially speaking of an
organic process such as muscular atrophication, but rather of a simpler
physical or mechanical principle whereby one side replaces another,
such that atrophy might then eventually and permanently set in. ❧ Now
in such a situation the need for therapy is obvious and immediate. The
injured lung has to be reempowered, while the healthy, now-dominant
lung has to be inhibited. By this means, a balance might be immediately
reinstated, with a view toward a long-term balance being retained as the
surrounding injury heals. The therapy, in other words, artificially pressures the healthy lung, or uses it for leverage for the sake of the impaired
one. Thus the body's weight, for example, is placed upon the healthy
side – and pressure is artificially increased by means of several pillows or
'soft levers' placed beneath the healthy side – inhibiting the free and
strong use of the healthy lung, while forcing the injured side to do more
of the breathing while it is also released of its 'share' of the body's
weight. And in this same position, the respiration can then be manipu-
lated – extended, for example, into long and deep breaths, or speeded
up – further compensating for a diminished capacity which is now being
given leverage over the strong side that had threatened to replace and
usurp the former's function. And so a third point I would adduce is this:
leverage can occur between left and right horizontally as well as ver-
tically; lying down as well as standing up; in the injured as well as in
the healthy body – but always, as with all leverage, where the one side
or position of strength is 'weakened,' so that the weak one might be
strengthened. ❧ The usefulness of this example and its procedure, I
would now suggest, is that it takes off from an image of injury rather
than of health. How healthy is the modern university, the topic and occasion around which these essays are gathered? Surely any faculty member could report some occasional symptom of ill health from his or her
home institution – or, even worse, some cancer growing upon the *corpus
academicus,* some life-threatening disease from within or without. Or is
it rather just the annual epidemic of semiliterate undergraduates, or the
hundred varieties of that familiar ailment, not the common cold but the

Common Colleague? Closer to our present topic, let us recall that Kant significantly takes the university as he finds it, which is to say not as an ideally healthy institution, but as the empirical and sensible body that it is, with all the ailments and symptoms of more serious dis-ease which make it precisely a *conflicted* place. It is conflicted between serving a master and mastering its own self-empowerment, between being judged from outside and judging itself, between its own principles and all that would be laid down or decided as law within its walls. It is unhealthy as long as such conflicts impair what Kant sees as the ideal function of the university, which is to judge and, through judging, to advance the truth. With such internal judging and advancement, the advancement of the state will follow and, with it, the social or cosmopolitan community it heads. ❧ Let me suggest then, not dramatically but analytically, that the modern university is injured. If an image of injury is accompanied by a model of therapy, what might the view and outlook of the university appear to be? The injured university might be seen less as one poised for an advance from, and by virtue of leverage placed upon, a stance or foundation already achieved, than as a body reclining, virtually immobile, with one side or faculty variously weak, another side or faculty for that very reason strengthened and threatening to get even stronger. Indeed, to continue this image, the injury could, left unattended or without therapy, lead to the usurpation of one faculty or function altogether. ❧ What might this mean more concretely? I would like briefly to sketch out a few versions of the injured university and some possible corresponding therapies. To follow through one last step from the earlier discussion of left-and-right corporeal directions tending toward a reversal of opposition and an assertion of identity, I want to suggest that within the academic body, the diagnosis of an injury and the prescription of a therapy might go further toward establishing and distinguishing illness and health if it occurs *without* recourse to the corporeal directions. All that would be needed is a strictly contextual, strictly tactical sense of relative strengths and weaknesses, coupled with an awareness that damage is damage and strength is strength whether they are found on the right or the left; and the therapy will be similarly leveraged, only reversed. And so I would sketch two injuries to the contemporary university, the first involving the capacity or faculty called the 'philosophic' one with respect to other faculties around it, the other involving an internal division within the philosophy faculty or what it has come to mean today.

❧ In institutions of higher learning (at least in those where I have taught) one has heard in recent years a considerable amount from leading academic officers about this or that university's obligation to pursue high technology research or to enter into the risks and rewards, the costs and payoffs of advanced applied scientific discovery. I daresay that we shall hear yet more of this in the coming years. At the same time, from another direction – usually Washington, D.C., and various departments, foundations, and columnists seated there – but in a nonetheless persistent voice, we have heard about values in university education, and especially about values taught or, so the allegation more frequently goes, not taught in the humanities. Now the injury to the university that this situation describes is the following: an imbalance between wings or projects of the university, such that one faculty or capacity – that of 'science' (by which I distinctly do *not* mean *Wissenschaft*) – is being celebrated and enhanced from within the university, while another – the humanities – is being belittled and reprimanded from outside. (Let us note in passing that this injury or dis-ease was one that Wilhelm von Humboldt proleptically diagnosed and sought to avoid in his founding memorandum on the University of Berlin: the anticipatory response to the danger of 'applied' *Wissenschaft* is in fact his argument for 'invisible' *Wissenschaft*.)[12] What allows one to view this as a single, correlated injury – an imbalance with two corresponding sides, one strengthened, one weakened – is the common language and stake or *enjeu* of *value*. The university will itself profit, and will allow the surrounding, supporting society to profit from it in turn, if it enters into the valuation of high-tech, cutting-edge applications of science, while it is threatened with suffering loss, both within its own self-identity as well as in its outside image, its evaluation from the surrounding community, if it does not know and value the 'humanistic' values it ought to maintain. This is an injury of values or of evaluation: one part of the academic body becomes the *locus* of a promise of greatly increased values, while another part suffers an attack against its ostensible undervaluing or devaluing of values. ❧ A therapy for this injury suggests itself, which would take the academic body as a whole, embodying imbalance, and seek to vitalize the very issue of evaluation, of the production and ascertainment of values. By this I mean that the faculty or capacity – the 'humanities' – which stands accused of ignoring or abandoning values, would take on this very stake and reroute its address toward the university, which

would appear to be momentarily strengthened and more highly empowered by the appeal toward science. In the image of physical therapy
invoked earlier, the academic body would have its 'strong side,' with the
very strength of enhanced values, used for leverage so as to allow the
provisionally weakened side to take up and exercise the function of evaluation for which it stands challenged. For the 'humanities' to defend not
purportedly timeless and substantial values – which do not exist except
as *functions* – but rather the function of evaluation, of asking anything
claiming value or having value claimed for it to justify such evaluation:
this is the leveraged response to an unequal distribution or an imbalance
within university values. As the humanities ask about the values of scientific knowledge in the university and – by extension – in the society,
they will accept the very conditions of injury and imbalance within the
university, and use them to apply leverage toward their critical examination. 'Where are the values?' is the question put to the humanities at the
same moment that values are everywhere claimed for university sciences – this is the injury. The same question, 'Where are the values?' put
forcefully and insistently back to the university by the humanities, is the
leveraged therapy. ❧ This use of the term 'humanities' (as in the National Endowment for the Humanities) introduces the second university
injury and therapy I would like to sketch. We are a long way today from
Kant's usage in his *Conflict of the Faculties,* when he could oppose the
philosophy faculty to the other three, 'higher' ones, and then propose
dividing the philosophy faculty itself into what he called two 'departments': a department of 'historical knowledge' and one of 'pure rational
knowledges.'[13] We are a long way from this, in the sense that today the
divisions within what Kant would have designated as the 'philosophy
faculty' are such that we do not so much recognize two departments
within the same thing as we recognize three distinct units within one
strictly administrative conglomeration or confederation. Thus what is
often called the College of Arts and Sciences (or what my institution
quaintly calls the College of Literature, Science, and the Arts) does not
have philosophy arching over its parts, but rather most commonly has
the natural (or physical and life) sciences in one corner, the 'social sciences' in a second, and the 'humanities' in a third. It is within today's
'humanities' that the intrafaculty issues of Kant's 'philosophy faculty' are,
for better or for worse, played out. ❧ I recall this shift in university topography, however familiar it surely is, to remark that the issue now for

the 'humanities,' as then for Kant's 'philosophy faculty,' is one of the balance of roles and functions between philosophy – its reasoning and judgments – and 'historical knowledge,' by which I mean, much more narrowly than Kant, the production and accumulation and transmission of positive historical knowledge in the 'humanities.' One last historical remark: we have never, to my knowledge, been in danger in the modern Western university of a nonhistorical, 'purely theoretical' doctrine of knowledge in the 'humanities'; perhaps the only doctrine resembling such a bogeyman was Fichte's 'Deduced Plan' for the university to be founded at Berlin, written in 1807, and it never stood any chance of adoption anyway. Contrast with this, on the other hand, the preponderance of historical material and infrastructure that the modern university has unfolded from the 1820s and 1830s in Germany throughout that century, and then again in this country throughout the twentieth century. Few of us could deny, I believe, that the curricula we offer our undergraduate and graduate students, and the scholarship we expect and accept from our graduate students and colleagues, is preponderantly the history of literature, the history of art, the history of culture and society. ᐤ The injury, then, is one in which one part of the 'philosophy faculty,' or – let us now accept the translation – the 'humanities,' has become so empowered that the other part, once called philosophy and now perhaps awkwardly designated as method, theory, and metacritical, nonpositive analysis, is threatened with usurpation and atrophy.[14] What one might mean by 'philosophy' here is not some ghettoized department of logic and analysis, but rather something closer to what Kant meant by 'philosophizing,' and which would have informed the whole 'philosophy faculty': inquiring rationally, judging freely, and doing both all the way down to the principles of inquiry, reason, judgment, and freedom. By contrast, the injured university today often breathes a superhistorical oxygen with one specialized, 'historicist' lung, while another means for potential functioning has scarcely a place for ventilation and entry into circulation. ᐤ A therapy would once again begin with the distribution of strengths, and would leverage the present strength toward the weakness. For all the activity devoted to historical knowledge – by which I mean the courses, the examinations, the papers and dissertations and submitted manuscripts – there would be the repeated occasion, on each such occasion, for these small and simple questions: How? Why? So what? That is, the present distribution which, for

some century and a half, has favored historical knowledge over its philosophic judgment, need not be revamped or done away with (which is
hardly realistic anyway), so much as used as the fulcrum for the corresponding questions of how and why one knows such knowledge, questions weakened almost to muteness but thereby given voice by virtue of
their very other. My sense of injury within the 'humanities' leads me
to insist, quietly but firmly, that all historical knowledge without an
accompanying rationale for its constitution and existence is counter-
intellectual, and ultimately counterrational. My sense of a possible
therapy suggests that each bit of historical knowledge, each occasion for
its articulation and transmission, should become the occasion for inquiry into its methodology and teleology. Even to acknowledge, and to
insist upon the acknowledgment, that history has a history, and that the
history 'known' is not a substantial object but a subjectively constructed
cognition, can be critical in this context. Put more polemically: no history of literature, no history of art, no history of society, without a philosophy of history, a method of historiography, an internal and external
accounting. Only when the two sides lever, each against the other, will
the humanistic *corpus academicus* begin to creak and wheeze with a
newfound health, perhaps even approaching a joyful science. ❧ Allow
me to conclude with two sets of remarks. I should first like to ward off a
possible misunderstanding that might arise with the employment of the
analogy of injury as imbalance. The misunderstanding might accordingly assume that a certain symmetry verging on stasis, or perhaps a certain version of a golden mean, is perhaps being held out as either an
original health to be restored, or an ideal state to be attained, or both. If
the only set of instances upon which I drew were those of two lungs –
or two feet, for that matter, for the case of a temporary limp is not that
different from that of the damaged lung – a suspicion of incipient
symmetry-and-balance-as-health would be well warranted. But I would
wish to recall that considerations of balance, endangered or restored, between two sides of the body only followed upon Kafka's 'lesson' of the
*indifference* between directional designations of the two sides. And if I
have a real lesson, that is, a real *reading* of the examples from Kant,
Kafka, my own injury, and those of the university, it is this. Left posed
against right, or right against left, it is not a matter of righting an
imbalance – or even so much of healing an injury – as it is of recognizing imbalance as the condition within which leverage can and does take

place. Injury – specifically, an imbalance between two functions or functional parts of a body – ought to be recognized, without any pathos, as the condition that confronts us in the university, before any supposed balance, be it supposedly preexistent or about to be reestablished. This means the need and the occasion for leverage, which at any one moment and from any one perspective will appear as left against right, and then at or from the next moment or perspective, will be right against left. ❧ To suggest a condition of injury in the absence of any definitive sense of direction is perhaps to pose injury before health, and leverage in advance of direction. This may be less Manichean than it is Kantian, for whom, as Jean-Luc Nancy has suggested, we have the need for the desire for the good, for practical reason, precisely because there *is* evil;[15] so, too, perhaps we have the desire for health, and for leverage, because there is injury, and imbalance. *In-jur-,jus,* the unjust, the non-right, the damaging or violation of the law: perhaps we have injury because the right is always wronged, the law broken. It would then be less the case that the right is always stronger, or that the left is always weaker, as Kant appears to have mistakenly thought, apparently misled by his own subjective, corporeal topology,[16] than it would be the case that *there is always weakness,* and thus always the condition for leverage of one side against another. When Walter Benjamin, levering *against* Kant and against his own given, proper name, as it were, said that 'all the decisive blows will be struck left-handed,' he indicates not a corporeal direction tending toward a cardinal one, but rather (as his preceding sentence makes clear: 'In der Improvisation liegt die Stärke') the decisive strength issuing from the untrained, off-balance member: the awkward one that is not dexterous.[17] As if to say that in *this* German, the right hand could also be *linkshändig.* ❧ A second and last, concluding remark. If injury is the condition of leverage, of leverage within the university, and the condition of injury is imbalance, then balance would seem to preclude a therapy based upon leverage. We might take small comfort in the fact that our universities have injuries and imbalances of strength, however misguided, and injuries and imbalances of favor, however blindly bestowed; we might take comfort in this in the face of the weaknesses and disfavor of our reasoned judgments and our attempted theories. Kafka, you will recall, suffered from tuberculosis of both lungs, which eventually became tuberculosis of the larynx and of the epiglottis. A symmetrical injury, one that allowed for no reversals or leverage. Symmetrical injuries are the fatal kind.

NOTES

1. Timothy Bahti, 'Histories of the University: Kant and Humboldt,' MLN 103, 2 (April 1987), 437–60.

2. See Jacques Derrida, *'Mochlos; ou, le conflit des facultés,'* Philosophie 2 (1984), 28 and 311, and my 'Histories of the University,' pp.455, 456.

3. Immanuel Kant, *Der Streit der Fakultäten* (1798), in *Werke in 12 Bänden,* ed. Wilhelm Weischedel (Frankfurt: Suhrkamp, 1968), 11:280–300 (my translation).

4. Kant, *Der Streit,* p.299; Derrida, 'Mochlos,' pp.48, 49.

5. Derrida, 'Mochlos,' p.50.

6. Ibid., pp.50–51.

7. Ibid., pp.51, 52.

8. Kant, *Was heisst: Sich im Denken orientieren?* (1786), in *Immanuel Kants Werke,* ed. Ernst Cassirer (Berlin: B. Cassirer, 1922), pp.352, 353.

9. Ibid., pp.353, 354.

10. Franz Kafka, 'Gespräch mit dem Beter,' in *Sämtliche Erzählungen,* ed. Paul Raabe (Frankfurt: Fischer Taschenbuch Verlag, 1970), pp.186–91; 'Conversation with the Supplicant,' *The Penal Colony: Stories and Short Pieces,* trans. Willa and Edwin Muir (New York: Schocken Books, 1961), pp.9–17. Subsequent references are given in the text, with the first number referring to pages in the German edition, the second to the English.

11. Kant, *Der Streit,* p.382.

12. See my 'Histories of the University,' esp. pp.445–52.

13. Kant, *Der Streit,* p.291; see also my 'Histories of the University,' pp.453–56.

14. What J. Hillis Miller, 'But Are Things as We Think They Are?' *Times Literary Supplement,* 9–15 October 1987, p.1104, has called 'the universal triumph of theory' is only, I think, to be understood ironically. So, too, what has recently been trumpeted and discussed as 'the new historicism' in literary and cultural studies should be understood more soberly as familiar, nontheoretical historical studies.

15. Jean-Luc Nancy, 'Le Katègorein de l'excès,' in *L'Impératif catégorique* (Paris: Flammarion, 1983), pp.12, 13, and passim; see also his 'Dies irae' in Jacques Derrida et al., *La Faculté de juger* (Paris: Les Éditions de Minuit, 1985), pp.9–54.

16. See Kant, *Der Streit,* p.382, and, for a 'pre-critical' version of the same argument, his 'Von dem ersten Grunde des Unterschiedes der Gegenden im Raume' (1768), in *Werke in 12 Bänden,* 2:997.

17. Walter Benjamin, *Einbahnstrasse* (1928), in *Gesammelte Schriften,* vol.4/1, *werkausgabe Band 10,* ed. Rolf Tiedemann and Hermann Schweppenhäuser (Frankfurt: Suhrkamp, 1980), p.89. Benjamin, whose name means 'son of the right hand,' reflected upon the fantasy of having other names in his 'Agesilaus Santander,' *Gesammelte Schriften,* 6:520–23.

# 4

The University Founders:

A Complete Revolution

*by Peggy Kamuf*

In examining our academic contract, how should one proceed? What, in other words, are we doing here? Perhaps such a question must look for a response in the place where it is asked: in this very particular place of a colloquium, which is also always in some way the negation of the particularity of place and its limits. A colloquium takes place but it has no proper place. It actualizes for a brief time what may be called a space of interrogation which, at any other time, is a phrase whose figurality seems to go without saying. What we are doing here, then, is making a space for that question: what are we doing here, in the university? ❧ As prelude to or as already part of a negotiation with our academic contract, that question would describe a fundamental space and the acts of our colloquium would be foundational. The university is founded and because it is founded, writes Jacques Derrida in 'Mochlos,' 'There can be no pure concept of the university, there cannot be within the university a pure and purely rational concept of the university.'[1] The ground of our interrogation cannot be delimited by a rational concept, which is precisely why it permits and requires a fundamental questioning. And a responsibility for our acts. 'We are here,' continues 'Mochlos,' 'in that place where the founding responsibility passes by way of acts or performances,' acts and performances whose law is not simply that of reason. But there is nothing at all simple about this 'not simply.' It gives space to our interrogation, to that which 'il s'agit ici d'interroger,' it is a matter of interrogating here. Such an interrogation

*would be inseparable from new acts of foundation. We live in a world in which the foundation of new rights – in particular of new academic rights – is necessary. To say that it is necessary is to say in this case both that one must take responsibility for it, a responsibility of a new type, and that this foundation is already under way. . . . Such a foundation cannot simply break with the tradition of inherited rights nor submit itself to the legality it authorizes, including within the conflicts and violent episodes that al-*

*ways make way for the installation of a new law, a new age of rights.*
(pp.50–51)

Of necessity, we are in that place – a space of interrogation – which requires from us new acts of foundation. A double constraint, a neither/nor stands at the gate of this foundation: neither a radical break with the law it inherits but would disavow nor a submission to a law it institutes but cannot cite. Between the two uprights of this gate, which support not a stable structure but an arena of conflict, a necessity makes its way beneath the arch connecting the two sides, pulling their opposed positions together. No revolution tears down the palace gates; a deconstruction of their opposition allows for a passage at the limit of what passed for a closed structure. ᴥ Besides, what would a revolution in the university today look like? Or a revolution in the educational apparatus in general? Who today speaks of revolution as the future of our educational institutions? No doubt many do, but they might be surprised to have to count among their number the former secretary of education, William J. Bennett. And yet, for a speech delivered to the Heritage Foundation in July 1986, the secretary chose the title 'Completing the Reagan Revolution: A Resumption of Responsibilities.'[2] This ingenious title works on two levels in Bennett's address, which I want to consider very briefly before taking a step back – about two hundred years – to a predecessor discourse on educational revolution. ᴥ First of all, 'the Reagan Revolution' is said to refer to 'fundamental shifts in national policy' in two areas: economics ('historic tax reform') and foreign policy ('the rebuilding of our nation's defenses'). In this connection, the phrase 'completing the revolution' has an additive sense: A fundamental shift in educational policy must supplement the Reagan Revolution in order to complete it and to cement it in place. And because at stake is the nation's future, our realization of 'our potential as a people,' this additive or complementary sense sketches a linear course. Bennett says, 'National wealth and military strength are necessary means to national greatness; but they are not, of course, sufficient. . . . National greatness, in the end, depends on – is embodied in – the character of our people' (p.611). This 'character' depends in turn on the well-being of institutions created to express the beliefs of a people, 'and on the values according to which we shape the next generation of Americans.' Here, 'in the somewhat amorphous realm of beliefs and attitudes and values,' Bennett proposes to 'mount an effort of national recovery . . . if we are to realize our potential as a people' (p.611). 🐾 But Bennett is also aware that his title is working not only in this progressive, linear sense but in another sense as well.

*It is worth pausing for a moment to ponder what a peculiar revolution the Reagan Revolution has been. True, we seem to have broken with the past, or at least the immediate past. And true, we look forward with fresh expectation to a future of our own shaping. [It might be recalled here that Bennett is speaking to the Heritage Foundation whose role in 'shaping' Reagan's foreign and economic policy he has cited as 'indispensable' and 'vital.'] But this has been a revolution presided over and executed by conservatives – which means that it has been accomplished not by abandoning but, to the contrary, by recovering and conserving fundamental institutions, fundamental principles, and fundamental truths.* (p.611)

In this other, 'peculiar' sense, 'completing the revolution' describes not a linear progress but a circular return, the completion of a cycle of revolution. These two senses, however, are continually playing off against each other in this rhetorical performance, the one covering for the other in a game of blindman's bluff. Consequently, it would be equally possible to read the 'progressive' sense as an alibi for the 'conservative' sense and vice-versa. That is, the vague appeal to the future's promise of 'greatness' could be seen as a rhetorical mask laid over an unyielding rejection of the changes already in motion toward some future or, conversely, the equally vague appeal to 'fundamental institutions, fundamental principles, and fundamental truths' could be heard as reassuring sounds that drown out the demolition of such institutions, principles, and truths. Bennett's discourse would not want to choose between these alternatives, because the two are dependent on each other for their effects. This is not to say that this rhetorical construct somehow enjoys a status beyond the traditional political division of 'conservative' from 'progressive'; it is, rather, to remark that some of the standard rhetorical indicators have become – and no doubt for a long time have been – uselessly imprecise tools with which to delineate political effects. Here I would recall a remark Derrida has often made, for example in 'Mochlos.' The charge that deconstruction is politically 'demobilizing' often comes, suggests Derrida, from 'those who recognize the political only with the help of prewar road signs.' However, the questioning of politico-institutional structures undertaken by deconstruction 'should no longer necessarily rely on inherited codes of politics or ethics' (p.42). 🐾 Although there would be much still to say about Bennett's speech, 'Completing the Reagan Revolution,' we will leave it aside for the moment and be content to draw some questions from this preliminary sketch. The questions are the following: Is there perhaps a connection to be sought between discourse on education – reforming, revolutionary or conservative – and the tendency of these political codes (or their rhetorical indicators) to cover for each other? When 'education' is taken as the object of a political program or a state policy, is discourse about that object thereby made vulnerable to a dissociation from its codes or a disruption of their pertinence? And finally, do such disruptions and dissociations have their source in a fictional topology according to which the thing called 'education' can be comprehended as an 'object' or objective *within* a state's purview? ✺ In a rather simple sense, Bennett's speech, for example, could be taken as a singular demonstration of this fiction since its advocacy of any educational policy must remain within the strictly decentralized tradition of the American structure of compulsory education. Thus he must recognize that 'the work to reinvigorate and renew and restore our common culture . . . is *not primarily the work of government.* But it is work that those of us in government must be attentive to and supportive of, work to which we can contribute in careful and limited ways' (p.612; emphasis added). As to what these 'careful and limited ways' might be, I will let you fill in from memory some of the more recent interventions of our federal Department of Education in the affairs of school desegregation, affirmative action, tuition waivers for sectarian schools, prayer in school, and so on.[3] But it would be, at least for the imaginable future, out of the question for a U.S. secretary of education to propose a centralized, national system of public education. Perhaps you recall the resistance Jimmy Carter encountered when he created the Department of Education and added its secretary to his cabinet. And if I am not mistaken, Ronald Reagan promised his conservative constituency, during his first campaign, that he would eliminate the Department of Education at the first opportunity.[4] Instead, we have the somewhat anomalous situation of a federal government department and its resources being used to *intervene in favor of nonintervention* of the federal government in those areas (segregation, affirmative action) which had been the only valid areas of intervention recognized up until then. ✺ Yet the idea of state-controlled, national public education has currency everywhere else in the West and what I have called the fictional topology of this idea has been with us for at least two hundred years. Kant, in the second essay of the *Conflict of the Faculties,* is concerned with this idea and would even seem to have been making allusions to proposals for a national system of public instruction which were at the time – in 1795 – preoccupying the legislators of the new French Republic. As you recall, before inserting this essay into the *Conflict of the Faculties,* Kant gave it the title 'An Old Question Raised Again: Is the Human Race Constantly Progressing?' The answer to this question is given in the affirmative by means of a complex and cautious reference to 'the revolution of a gifted (*geistreichen*) people which we have seen unfolding in our day.' It is not, however, the French Revolution as event or series of acts that 'demonstrates the moral tendency of the human race' but rather the 'disinterested sympathy' that the spectator of these events experiences for the revolutionaries over against their *ancien régime* adversaries: 'It is simply the mode of thinking of the spectators which reveals itself publicly in this game of great revolutions, and manifests such a universal yet disinterested sympathy for the players on one side against those on the other, even at the risk that this partiality could become very disadvantageous for them if discovered,' says Kant. This sympathy is also called 'a wishful participation that borders on enthusiasm.'[5] Jean-François Lyotard has given fine analyses on two occasions of this complex 'historical sign' as well as the potentially dangerous enthusiasm it almost inspires in its distant spectators.[6] ❧ In a later passage in the essay Kant makes the first of only two allusions to educational institutions. Section 8 is titled 'Concerning the Difficulty of the Maxims Applying to World Progress with Regard to Their Publicity.' It is under this heading of publicity or publication that Kant takes up the subject of public instruction in order, it seems, to denounce a disguise or concealment (*Verheimlichung*)[7] within the relations of a state to its people and to the instructors of the people, the philosophers, those whom the state deems dangerous and calls *Aufklärer.*

*Enlightenment of the masses is the public instruction of the people in its duties and rights vis-à-vis the state to which they belong. Since only natural rights and rights arising out of the common human understanding are concerned here, then the natural heralds and expositors of these among the people are not officially appointed by the state but are free professors of law, that is philosophers who, precisely because this freedom is allowed to them, are objectionable to the state, which always desires to rule alone; and they are decried, under the name of enlighteners, as persons dangerous to the state.* (p.161)

A first disguise is indicated here, the one that calls those responsible for 'public instruction of the people in its duties and rights' appointees of the state rather than free professors of law, 'das ist die Philosophen.' The point would seem to be not that professors of law should necessarily remain free of any official tie rather than being appointed and supported by the state (this was, by the way, one of the questions that was most hotly debated by the French legislators at the time), but rather that such appointment cannot preempt the freedom that must be allowed to them. Philosophers are appointed to teach *as* free professors of law; this freedom is 'allowed to them' and indeed it is the condition of their appointment. The deception is to refer to these instructors as 'officially appointed by the state' and then to pretend that this appointment must entail a subservience to the will of the state, rather than a freedom from any will other than that expressing 'natural rights and rights arising out of the common human understanding.' ❧ A second deception or concealment concerns the 'danger' posed by such freedom, which puts at risk only the desire of the state to be the sole ruler of the people. What is concealed in the charge against the enlighteners is the far greater risk that would be posed were this voice of 'natural right' to be silenced in obedience to the state's desire to rule absolutely. Kant spells this out as the passage continues:

*They are decried, under the name of enlighteners, as persons dangerous to the state,* although their voice is not addressed confidentially [vertraulich] to the people (as the people take scarcely any or no notice at all of it and of their writings) but is addressed respectfully to the state; *and they implore the state to take to heart that need which is felt to be legitimate. This can happen by no other means than that of publicity in the event that an entire people cares to bring forward its grievances* [gravamen]. *Thus the prohibition of publicity impedes the progress of a people toward improvement, even in that which applies to the least of its claims, namely its simple, natural right.* (p.161, emphasis added)

The censorship or 'prohibition of publicity' of the philosopher's voice conceals one danger beneath another, the danger to simple, natural right beneath the danger to the state's absolute rule over a population ignorant of its rights. But Kant's particular formulation of the relation between the state and its educators needs to be heeded. The 'free professors' ' voice, he writes, 'is not addressed confidentially [*vertraulich*, on a

level of familiarity] to the people (as the people take scarcely any or no
notice at all of it and of their writings) but is addressed respectfully to
the state.' There is, then, yet another form of deception or disguise that
holds that these official appointees of the state are appointed to address
the people familiarly, in their own language, as one says, and to instruct
them in how to be good citizens of the state according to the state's
wishes. Instead, writes Kant, it is, in effect, a fiction that public instruction exists in an address to the people who pay little or no heed to the
philosophers' voice and writings. In fact, public instructors respectfully
address their teachings to the state. In speaking to the people of their
'duties and rights vis-à-vis the state,' these free instructors are really always addressing the state, instructing it in its duties and rights vis-à-vis
the people. Far from serving the wishes and at the pleasure of the state,
the free professors are appointed to instruct the state in the limits of its
wishes. ✿ We could say that the fiction Kant exposes as such is that of a
privately hired tutor instructing sons in the service of the father. This
cannot be a model for *public* instruction, a lesson that Kant would have
learned, perhaps, from Rousseau's *Emile,* of all places. Rousseau's fiction
of a tutor and his pupil is a model for *public* instruction only in the
sense of its *making public* a teaching of rights and duties through, precisely, publication and publicity. The fact that *Emile* was officially censored by many of the states of Europe situates it within Kant's problematic of the philosopher's freedom to address the state as the state's
teacher. And in this regard, we must ask how to read the novel's own
confidential and familiar address to the mother: 'C'est à toi que je m'ad-
dresse, tendre et prévoyante mère' (I address myself to you, affectionate
and provident mother).[8] One could argue that this familiar address, in-
citing the people to subversion of state authority, constituted Rousseau's
greatest offense. But was it also necessarily the work's greatest fiction?
That is, in addressing itself to the mother, was *Emile* disguising its address to the state which had to go to great lengths to avoid heeding that
address? Beyond that, we could ask: Is public instruction a mother
which the father state must keep in check? ✿ Kant, however, does not
name Rousseau. The passage from the second essay of *The Conflict of the
Faculties* we are reading never departs from the form of the general
proposition, to wit: public instruction concerns the state and yet is not
an object within its power. The state has the duty to maintain publicity
'of the rights arising out of common human understanding' and to that

end it supports 'free professors of law, that is philosophers.' The state, in other words, appoints its own teachers, the teachers of the *res publica,* overcoming what is objectionable to it in this limitation on its desire to rule without heeding any other voice. To better resist the lesson addressed to it, however, the state has several fictions at its disposal, for example, that teachers are the servants of the state, that their instruction is addressed in familiar terms to the people, that censorship of instruction preserves the people in their respect for the state. ❧ These fictions remain, in fact, formidable resources and not only for absolutist states, as the history of the debate over public instruction during the first French Republic can demonstrate. This situation – that of a newly constituted democratic state which proposes to institute a national system of public instruction in order, in Bennett's phrase, to complete the revolution – has no obvious precedent. The observations of Kant's sympathetic spectator on this scene will have, nonetheless, prepared us to see how certain of the conflicts were, if not wholly predictable, then at least liable to be explained by the force of the fictions Kant identifies. ❧ The debate began in 1791 with the creation of the first Committee on Public Instruction of the Legislative Assembly, which was charged with presenting a proposal to fulfill the article of the Constitution promising a system of free public instruction common to all citizens at the elementary level. It continued over at least the next four years, during which time numerous proposals were presented, rejected, neglected or accepted only to be thrown out in abrupt reversals of direction. In 1795 – *An IV* of the republic – the law of 3 *brumaire* decreeing the organization of public instruction was adopted but remained in place for only three years before debate was opened again by the Directoire which sponsored many reform proposals. The law of 3 *brumaire,* however, was not officially replaced until 1802.[9] ❧ Of necessity, we can evoke only in passing some of the organizing questions in this debate, questions that persistently returned. Of the many proposals and projects, let us take the most well known as a guide to these questions, that of the *philosophe* Condorcet, who was an eminent mathematician and disciple of d'Alembert, as well as an elected representative to both the Legislative Assembly and the National Convention. His 'Report on the General Organization of Public Instruction,' presented to the Assembly in April 1792, was the first project to come out of the Committee on Public Instruction. Although it received little debate before being summarily tabled, it remained a princi-

pal point of reference for all succeeding proposals. After the fall of the
monarchy, Condorcet himself diverted his attention from education to
the drafting of a new constitution. When this constitution was presented
and rejected by the Robespierrists, Condorcet was one of the few who
defended it publicly and denounced the makeshift proposal adopted in
its place. His defiance of the Committee of Public Safety precipitated his
arrest decree; he went into hiding but was eventually imprisoned and
died there in 1794.[10] It was, then, not as a spectator nor with Kant's
'wishful participation' that Condorcet beheld the Revolution, but with
the dangerous proximity of one of the principal actors in the spectacle.
It was also, however and as we shall see, precisely such a distinction between men of action and scholars or intellectuals that fueled the debate
over public instruction.[11] ⅍ As the work of an exemplary *Aufklärer,*
Condorcet's proposal relied on a boundless faith in the emancipatory
power of science. Not only was elementary knowledge the means of
guaranteeing the freedom of citizens from a dangerous dependence on
more advantaged neighbors, but advanced knowledge – the perfection
of the arts and sciences – promised a general benefit and prosperity even
to those members of a society who did not, or could not cultivate such
knowledge themselves. Condorcet identifies this as the double point of
view that any general system of instruction must embrace: on the one
hand, in the name of justice and so as to 'realize the political equality
recognized by the law,' that system must be universal and equally available to all; on the other hand, in the name of truth, that system must be
'as complete as circumstances can permit.'[12] The double exigencies of
universality and completeness are, insists Condorcet, complementary
rather than contradictory or mutually exclusive. He reasoned that all citizens had the right to as much instruction as they were willing or able to
pursue. Any other reasoning would have to be ready to designate a limit
to the knowledge necessary for citizens of a republic, and Condorcet understood that such a gesture could only be equivalent to tracing limits
on knowledge in general, which is to say submitting reason to an arbi-
trary tribunal.[13] It was thus the obligation of the people's government to
maintain and support the development of every science to the highest
degree possible. This support, however, could only be conceived as one
with no strings attached. The principle of the autonomy and self-
regulation of instructional institutions must be respected, he argued, *as
far as possible.* 'The first principle of any instruction being to teach only

truths, the institutions which the government consecrates to this end must be as independent as possible from all political authority' (Baczko, p. 182). Or in somewhat stronger terms: 'Finally, no public agency ought to have either the authority or even the means to prevent the development of new truths or the teaching of theories that go counter to its particular political program or its interests of the moment' (Baczko, p.183). ⪧ After this preamble, the Condorcet plan sets in place the five levels of a public education system (*primaire, secondaire, instituts, lycées* – corresponding to what we would today call universities – and the Société Nationale des Sciences et des Arts) as well as the four 'classes,' which group, in the last three levels, the different disciplines (mathematical and physical sciences, moral and political sciences, applied sciences, and literature and beaux-arts). It was a meticulous plan and would serve as the groundwork for the legislation eventually adopted. ⪧ And yet, Condorcet and his proposal became a touchstone for many things the revolutionary republicans sought to eradicate or at least to contain. The principal fault found with the proposal was its virtual exclusion of 'national education' in favor of 'public instruction.' The distinction of *éducation* from *instruction* became a commonplace in the debate.[14] That distinction was formalized by a number of the proposals, for example that of Rabaut Saint-Etienne in his 'Project for a National Education' presented some months after Condorcet's and in reaction to it:

*One must distinguish public instruction from national education; national education should instruct the heart, the former must impart enlightenment while the latter imparts virtue; the former will be the light of society, the latter will be its character and its force . . . national education is everyone's necessary sustenance; public instruction is the lot of the few. They are sisters, but national education is the eldest. What am I saying! It is the mother common to all citizens, who gives them all the same milk, who raises them and treats them as brothers and who, through the commonality of her maternal care, imparts to them that family resemblance that distinguishes a people raised in this manner from all the other peoples of the earth.* (Baczko, pp.297–98)

This impassioned rhetoric, with its figure of tutorship in the Republic as *alma mater,* suggests the seriousness of Condorcet's crime: he had proposed, in effect, a *lèse-maternité* and a severing of the Republic from its source. (We also hear, by the way, just one of the echoes from Rousseau's address to the mother. The debate might even be summed up as a struggle for the mother: is the mother *éducation* or *instruction?*) But the passage also suggests that the hierarchical distinction between instruction and education was still being thought in complementary terms rather than oppositional ones. Later projects, however, would go so far as to propose that the public space of the Republic – its festivals, meetings, and tribunals – was the only reliable educational institution, a kind of school without walls. The Montagnard Bouquier, for example, would write:

*What need have we to seek far and wide for what is right before our eyes? Citizens! the finest schools, the most useful, the simplest, there where our youth can find a truly republican education, are, without a doubt, the public meetings of departments, districts, municipalities, tribunals and especially popular societies . . . the Revolution has, by itself so to speak, organized public education and distributed everywhere limitless sources of instruction.* 🙰 *Let us not then substitute for this organization that is as simple and sublime as the people who created it a factitious organization which imitates the academic hierarchies that should no longer infect a regenerated nation. Let us carefully preserve what the people and the Revolution have done; let us be content to add to it the little that is lacking in order to complete public instruction. This complement should be as simple as the work created by the genius of the Revolution.* (Baczko, pp.419–20)

In other proposals, public ceremonies and celebrations almost entirely displaced formal instruction. In the course of this considerable shift, Condorcet's proposal was increasingly seen as a masked elitism and an aristocratic throwback that would replace inherited titles with graduated academic degrees.[15] To Condorcet's vision of a future stretching out to perfection through the unhampered cultivation of all the sciences, of an education completing the revolution of an enlightened people, Bouquier and others evoked a revolution virtually complete in itself, needing only a minimal supplement, and indeed they saw a positive threat to this integrity coming from what Bouquier described as 'a cast of speculative scholars [whose] speculative sciences detach [them] from society and become, in the long run, a poison that undermines, weakens and destroys republics' (Baczko, p.418). 🙰 Yet, despite their fierce opposition, these two sides of the ongoing debate can be seen as reverse mirror-images of each other if they are viewed through the role each foresaw for the state in the system of public instruction. Condorcet envisioned a complete educational system totally financed by the state from primary school up to a national society of eminent scholars in all disciplines. This system would be self-regulated and self-appointed, with no intervention by the state. Except for some fundamental training in non-religious moral thinking and some public ceremonies, Condorcet's proposal made no provisions for civic education, which was thereby to be left to the family and religious institutions. The role of the state was thus severely circumscribed in every regard. By contrast and on each point, the other side reversed the state's role. Most plans provided for only primary schooling, state-financed in some cases and in others funded by parents directly. The principal concern would be civic education, and the state would have the major role in determining curricula and teaching staff. The Republic was thus both the model of the educator and the object of the education. This more active role aimed at forming men of action. As Bouquier put it, 'The people who have conquered liberty need only vigorous, robust, hardworking men of action (*des hommes agissants*)' (Baczko, p.418). As for formal instruction beyond the most basic level, it was to be left to private institutions and was not the concern of the state. ❧ The point is not to argue that, despite such reversals, the two sides come down to 'the same thing.' Rather, it would be to remark the reversibility inscribed *at a certain beginning* in modern thought about education as an object bounded by the *polis* and falling, therefore, within its purview. Whatever their views on the intervention of the state, neither Condorcet nor his opponents would have questioned this topology, or, to put it less subjectively, this topology supplies the metaphoric ground for one and the other construction of a national education, the education of citizens for the nation. ❧ This reversibility has had time to act itself out through at least one full revolution, and no doubt more than that. If, for example, we circle back now to William Bennett's speech, how does it sound against the background of these other discourses seeking to complete that other revolution? I will cite just one paragraph whose sympathetic resonances with Montagnard preoccupations are most striking. Bennett is addressing 'the failure of our institutions' to teach our children 'about our nation – about our history, our heroes, our heritage, our national memories.' He asks 'What is to be done?' and replies:

*Government has a role here – especially the localities and states that govern our public schools; and the national government has an important educational part to play as well – through speeches, reports, recommendations, recognitions and ceremonies, through the dissemination of ideas and the setting of a national agenda, as well as funding for various enterprises. Individuals have an even more central role – at home, and in voluntary associations. But above all, we as a society, as a common culture, have to respond to the call of our national history, and to the responsibility it imposes upon us of instilling in our children an informed appreciation of American principles and American practices. The variety of ways in which this can be done will become clearer once we rise above all the pseudo-sophisticated claims and counter-claims, all the educational cacophony and cultural confusion, and decide: yes, we need to know our national experience, so as to know our national purpose.*[16]

When a U.S. secretary of education talks in 1986 about public ceremonies as a means for the state to intervene in the 'education' of its citizenry, to inspire admiration and youthful enthusiasm by means of state spectacle, he is, of course, not saying 'the same thing' that Robespierre said in 1793.[17] Even though it is not perhaps tragedy being repeated as farce, a revolutionary rhetoric has clearly been emptied out so that it continues to turn on itself and on its own. At the very least, the repetition and the difference suggest that the options for this kind of discourse have remained more or less fixed even as the historical, cultural, and economic conditions for it are considerably changed. If we think the options seem less limited on the 'left' than on the 'right,' then it may be largely because we are reluctant to relinquish our faith in coded political 'road signs' to point the way to a changed social future. In this regard, one could cite the new old *doxa* that charges any attempt to dismantle this code as a disguised return to some unacceptable doctrine labeled reactionary, liberal, conservative, and so on. One might consider the effects of this *doxa* on the discourse of feminism, for example, when the latter relies on such coded markers to set off its own political relevance from another, putatively 'apolitical' territory in which these familiar signs have become to some extent unrecognizable. Sexual difference, as we have already suggested, may have had a more central role in the revolutionary debate about education than at first appears. On the surface, the revolutionaries on both sides of this debate gave but little thought to the education or instruction of their daughters. The exception was once again Condorcet who, unlike almost all of his successors on the Committee for Public Instruction, unlike his predecessors or mentors Diderot and Rousseau, unlike Kant even, could think of no reason to differentiate between the proposed education of girls and boys, young women and young men; he even went so far as to argue for complete coeducation, rather than any 'separate but equal' principle.[18] In so doing, he counted on the 'reunion of the two sexes' to foster a new principle for the advancement of science, a principle he named quite simply – or naively – 'the desire to be loved.' As he wrote in his 'Première Mémoire sur l'Instruction publique,'

*The reunion of the two sexes in the same schools favors emulation, and brings forth a kind of emulation that has as its principle feelings of good will rather than personal sentiments . . . an emulation that will be inspired by the desire to earn the esteem of the beloved or to obtain that of one's family. . . . An emulation that would have as its principle the desire to be loved or to be considered for one's absolute qualities rather than for one's superiority over others could also become very powerful.*[19]

It should be quickly acknowledged that no first principle is being uncovered here: even if one did not have to distinguish between a 'good' and a 'bad' emulation, there would still be the fact that emulation remains essentially a dual or specular structure and thus fundamentally related to the public spectacle that constituted, for Condorcet's opponents, the keystone and the touchstone of the best civic education, the education that Condorcet's proposal had neglected. As such, 'good' emulation is a version of model formation and imitation.[20] And yet just as clearly, by situating this emulation in a proximity to the 'reunion of the two sexes,' it is not simply a matter here of the desire *to be like*. Rather, only a different desire or a desire for the different could introduce something 'powerful' within the institutional model. ❧ Does this 'powerful' something also propose another foundation for our academic contract, one that neither the state of reason nor reasons of state can, in themselves, supply? By 'other foundation' one should hear an appeal to a foundation which, finally, *is not one* because it takes place only with or in the other, that is, from the place of an *address* whose singular demand has no model and gives no model to the response. It will have been perhaps this question of address – as Kant discerned in part by attending to Rousseau – that discourse about education or the university has mistaken for the question of the purpose and perfectibility of these institutions and that has kept it turning around in circles. Although this discourse has been recently revived with much publicity, its appeal remains the very familiar one to the choice between a unifying model of national identity and what Bennett calls 'cultural confusion.' Some of our 'free professors of law, that is the philosophers' have agreed that we have this choice and have made themselves into spokesmen urging it on the people just as if they had been 'officially appointed by the state' to do so. They too would prefer to believe that *there is* still the choice between identity and confusion, the institution of the one and the address of the other. ❧ With no regard for this choice, the question of the other address asks one to take responsibility for it. The grounds on which to found this new reponsibility lie at the limits between the university's erected knowledge and its exclusions of what should not be known or make itself known, all that which has the potential of rearranging the space of our interrogation. While such grounds have only begun to be surveyed, we have long been receiving warnings that the university *founders* where it is *founded*. A warning, or perhaps rather just a question addressed from beyond the university's walls, interrogating its topology? Listen, for example and in conclusion, to the interrogation passed along by the poet of Amherst – by which, of course, is not meant the college of that name, one of whose founders was Edward Dickinson, the poet's father, a man with severe ideas about the uselessness of educating one's daughters.

*I went to School*
*But was not wiser*
*Globe did not teach it*
*Nor Logarithm Show*

*'How to forget'!*
*Say – some – Philosopher!*
*Ah, to be erudite*
*Enough to know!*

*Is it in a Book?*
*So, I could buy it –*
*Is it like a Planet?*
*Telescopes would know –*

*If it be invention*
*It must have a Patent.*
*Rabbi of the Wise Book*
*Dont you know?*[21]


NOTES

1. 'Mochlos; ou, le conflit des facultés,' *Philosophie* 2 (April 1984), p.50, my translation; further references to be given in the text.

2. In *Vital Speeches of the Day*, 52, 20, pp.610–13. Further references are given in the text.

3. On some of these points, see Bennett's speech to the National Press Club of March 1985: 'Educators in America,' in *Vital Speeches of the Day* 51, 9 (1985), 128–32.

4. As to why this did not happen, the conservative *National Review* offers two opinions. Lawrence Uzzell blames the entrenched liberal ideology of education 'science' which, once it had hold of a major federal bureaucracy, was not about to let go ('Education's Mad Science,' *National Review*, 11 April 1986, pp.39–41). Chester E. Finn, Jr., assistant secretary of education for research and improvement, defends the department's right to exist and even argues for the 'virtues of centralization.' He also notes that, although the liberal establishment created the department, since William Bennett took it over, some representatives of that same establishment have called for its abolition ('Two Cheers for Education's G-Men,' *National Review*, 15 August 1986, pp.35–37).

5. Immanuel Kant, *The Conflict of the Faculties/Der Streit der Fakultäten*, trans. and intro. Mary J. Gregor (New York: Abaris Books, 1979), p.153. Further references are given in the text.

6. See Jean-François Lyotard, *L'Enthousiasme: La Critique kantienne de l'histoire* (Paris: Galilée, 1986), pp.45–77; and *Le Différend* (Paris: Minuit, 1983), pp.232–46.

7. This term occurs in the first sentence of the paragraph immediately following the paragraph next quoted, and in a manner that suggests that, in the foregoing, Kant has been penetrating disguises. 'Another disguise, which is easily penetrated indeed, but is one to which a nation, nevertheless, is legally committed, is that pertaining to the true nature of its constitution.' Kant, *The Conflict of the Faculties*, p.165. The note to the passage on the British monarchy makes it clear that by disguise or concealment, Kant means the

lack of publicity, maintained by censorship, concerning a certain state of affairs.

8. Jean-Jacques Rousseau, *Oeuvres complètes*, 4 vols. (Paris: Pléïade, 1969), 4:246.

9. See the 'Repères chronologiques' (pp.59–62) in Bronislaw Baczko's excellent anthology *Une Éducation pour la démocratie: Textes et projets de l'époque révolutionnaire* (Paris: Garnier, 1982): subsequent references are given in the text. I have also relied on the richly documented study by Robert J. Vignery, *The French Revolution and the Schools: Educational Policies of the Mountain, 1792–1794* (Madison: State Historical Society of Wisconsin, 1966) which includes the best available bibliography of the subject. For translations of some earlier eighteenth-century texts as well as of Condorcet's 'Report,' see F. de La Fontainerie's *French Liberalism and Education in the Eighteenth Century* (New York: Burt Franklin Reprint, 1971; orig. publ. 1932).

10. See Catherine Kintzler's fine study, *Condorcet: L'instruction publique et la naissance du citoyen* (Paris: Minerve, 1984).

11. By pointing to this distinction, I am not at all suggesting, as Jean-Claude Milner does in his introduction to Kintzler's book (ibid., p.12), that one can simply oppose Condorcet's 'activist' knowledge to Kant's spectatorship or to the division of the First from the Second Critique.

12. Baczko, ed., *Une éducation*, pp.181–82, my translations. Further references are given in the text.

13. On this point, see Kintzler, *Condorcet*, pp.239 ff.

14. On this distinction, see Baczko's 'Introduction,' *Une éducation*, pp.30 ff.

15. Vignery, *The French Revolution*, p.43, is probably correct to attribute this shift in part to the deposing of the constitutional monarchy.

16. 'Completing the Reagan Revolution,' *Vital Speeches of the Day*, p.612. Lynne V. Cheney, who replaced William Bennett as head of the National Endowment for the Humanities (neh), echoed these positions in almost every particular; see, for example, her interview with *The Los Angeles Times*, 8 June 1987, as well as the neh's study (1987) of the failures of public education to teach the basics of Western culture and American history. The neh, of course, has a certain power (albeit not a legitimate one) to limit what it considers nefarious influences within the study of the humanities, through its Research Grants Program and through a decision not to fund proposals which are favorable to 'theory.'

17. Although Robespierre did not himself draft any of the proposals of the Committee on Public Instruction, he endorsed the proposal of L.-M. Lepeletier and presented it to the Convention after the death of the latter. This proposal, which went further than any other in the direction of state control, would have assumed complete responsibility for children between the ages of five and twelve.

18. In fact, Condorcet's 'Rapport,' in contrast to the 'Mémoires,' accepts the idea of separate education, at least in primary schools: 'In the villages where there will be only one primary school, children of both sexes will be admitted to it, and will receive the same instruction from the same teacher. If a village or a town has two primary schools, one of them will be in the charge of a mistress, and the children of the two sexes will be separated. This is the only arrangement concerning the education of women that we have made in our preliminary work. Their education will be the subject of a special report.' Baczko, p.212. This special report was never written.

19. Jean-Antoine-Nicolas Caritat, marquis de Condorcet, *Oeuvres complètes* (Paris: 1804), 9:80.

20. In his 'Rapport' as well, Condorcet warns against fostering a 'spirit of emulation which would make professors desire to increase the number of their students' and which 'does not proceed from sentiments so exalted that we may permit ourselves to deplore its loss' (Baczko, p.202) while on the other hand he proposes measures to encourage a worthy emulation that would make scholars aspire to the highest achievement of science (pp.205, 206, 209).

21. From poem 433 in *The Poems of Emily Dickinson*, 3 vols., ed. Thomas H. Johnson (Cambridge: Harvard University Press, 1979), vol.1.

# 5

The Idea of a Chrestomathic University

*by Robert Young*

Should education have any use? The question seems hardly worth asking, let alone answering. Yet this apparently absurd topic constitutes the major issue that has dominated debates about higher education in Britain for the past two hundred years. What is perhaps most remarkable is that such a controversy should have managed to sustain itself into such extreme old age; that indeed even now, as I write, it reasserts itself. ❧ It is true that not even Oscar Wilde dared to assert publicly, at least, that universities should be like art – that is, perfectly useless. But to suggest that universities should be useful, that they should teach practical forms of knowledge, has been for many to go too far. And that has not been because like Foucault, they have suspiciously regarded the university as an 'institutional apparatus through which society ensures its uneventful reproduction, at least cost to itself.'[1] On the contrary, they have considered that society is best served and sustained by the universities teaching knowledge that is useless. The knowledge of the university, in this account, should not have a use value: it should be outside the circuit of exchange; its very exteriority assures it its special value as a signifier, no doubt transcendental, that guarantees the stability of society itself. ❧ This by no means implies, however, that the university's special function is to embody the principle of reason.[2] No English university – English because the systems elsewhere in Britain are separate and would require altogether different analyses – is founded on reason. If we pose the question of the basis, principles, and function of the university, we find that, suitably enough for a country with an unwritten constitution, there is no founding document or even prospective philosophical account: only a charter by which the university is granted certain privileges by the state. In this sense, no English university can claim that it even thinks that it knows what it is doing. Even the institution of the Ph.D. had no more glorious rationale than the fact that in the 1920s, discovering that their Master of Arts degree could not compete with the Ph.D. of foreign universities in attracting overseas graduate students, the British universities pragmatically introduced a doctorate of philosophy.[3] ❧ Nor do we find in the eighteenth or nineteenth centuries any conflict of faculties such as Kant describes, if for no other reason than because by then the higher faculties had largely disappeared, leaving the faculty of arts in uncontested domination of the university.[4] But if there was no conflict within the universities, the state itself constantly challenged the validity of the knowledge that was taught within them. The history of the universities in the nineteenth century is about the contestation of academic freedom in that sense: Do the universities have the right to teach what they like? Does the state have the right to call into question the knowledge that the universities teach – and given that the universities are themselves by definition the highest authorities on the subject of knowledge and its validity, what are the grounds on which the state opposes them? ❧ To contest the authority of the universities is no easy matter. Oxford and Cambridge – which have always most seriously defended their right to teach useless knowledge – are, as ecclesiastical corporations, founded on nothing other than the *Logos* itself.[5] No lesser word than the Word has constituted the authority of the university – exclusively from the beginnings of the University of Oxford in the twelfth century to the founding of the secular University of London in 1826. For six centuries, Oxford and Cambridge held a monopoly over university education in England. The charters on which they were established, which guaranteed them certain forms of freedom from the state, the monopoly they exercised over the degrees necessary for candidates for ordination in the Church of England, and the successive endowments they accrued over the centuries meant that they became immensely wealthy – and, in the opinion of many, virtually useless. ❧ It is generally agreed even by the official historians of the universities themselves that by the eighteenth century they had fallen into almost irretrievable decay: testimony after testimony can be found of their appalling state at that time – one of the best known is Wordsworth's description of Cambridge in *The Prelude,* published after his death in 1850 at a very timely moment, just when the university was under investigation by a Royal Commission. Edward Gibbon recalls of his tutor at Magdalen College, Oxford:

*Dr Winchester well remembered that he had a salary to receive, and only forgot that he had a duty to perform. Instead of guiding the studies and*

*watching over the behaviour of his disciple, I was never summoned to at-*
*tend even the ceremony of a lecture; and except one voluntary visit to his*
*rooms, during the eight months of his titular office, the tutor and pupil*
*lived in the same college as strangers to each other.*[6]

The state of the universities at this time is most economically summed
up in Adam Smith's remark, which seems to have gone uncontested, that
'in the university of Oxford, the greater part of the public professors
have, for these many years, given up altogether even the pretence of
teaching.'[7] No doubt this was the period when the idea was advanced
that the real education of Oxford comes not from any pedagogic instruction, but from its social environment – in the eighteenth century in
some sense this was literally true inasmuch as the B.A. was conferred as a
result of the fulfillment of residency requirements rather than by any
formal examination. College fellowships were regarded as a reward for
achievements attained rather than for any teaching to be done. Other
factors were also important – in Newman's day, Oriel College was the
only college in Oxford that elected its fellows on the sole grounds of academic merit.[8] ✇ Demands for reform began in the eighteenth century
but achieved little; the universities' close affiliations to the Church and
the Tory party kept them unharmed until the state itself changed. Although the universities claimed that, as ecclesiastical institutions, no
contract between them and the state existed beyond that between church
and state, in 1854 despite strong opposition, particularly from Oxford,
the state reasserted its ultimate legal powers and rewrote the statutes.
The subsequent history of Oxford and Cambridge during the nineteenth
centuries is a story of reforms directly or indirectly imposed upon them.
This history is not a reassuring one for any advocate of an absolute academic freedom. ✇ The assault on Oxford and Cambridge from outside
the universities focused on two related issues: the exclusion of anyone
who was not a member of the Church of England, and the curriculum
that was, nominally, taught, both of which were ultimately justified by a
notion of truth. In 1809, declaring that he had been long waiting for an
opportunity of saying something on the subject, Sidney Smith attacked
the whole rationale of classical education which at Oxford formed almost the entire extent of the syllabus (Cambridge by contrast demanded
a little classics, but mostly pure mathematics). In the place of truth he
substituted use. 'The only proper criterion of every branch of education,' Smith argued, is 'its utility in future life.' According to this criterion,

*There never was a more complete instance in any country of such extrava-*
*gant and overacted attachment to any branch of knowledge, as that which*
*obtains in this country with regard to classical knowledge. A young English-*
*man goes to school at six or seven years old; and he remains in a course of*
*education till twenty-three or twenty-four years of age. In all that time, his*
*sole and exclusive occupation is learning Latin and Greek: he has scarcely a*
*notion that there is any other kind of excellence; and the great system of*
*facts with which he is the most perfectly acquainted, are the intrigues of the*
*Heathen Gods: with whom Pan slept? – with whom Jupiter? – whom*
*Apollo ravished? These facts the English youth get by heart the moment*
*they quit the nursery; and are most sedulously and industriously instructed*
*in them till the best and most active part of life is passed away. Now, this*
*long career of classical learning, we may, if we please, denominate a foun-*
*dation; but it is a foundation so far above ground, that there is absolutely*
*no room to put any thing upon it.*

Smith concluded that 'nothing would so much tend to bring classical literature within proper bounds, as a steady and invariable appeal to utility
in our appretiation [*sic*] of human knowledge.'[9] In this way he set up the
terms of a debate that was to last to the present day. ❧ His attack stirred
Oxford even to the extent of provoking a reply. In 1810 a don named Edward Copleston published *A Reply to the Calumnies of the Edinburgh Review against Oxford,* and, then, *A Second Reply to the Calumnies* and
even *A Third Reply to the Calumnies.* It was hard to defend the Oxford
curriculum in terms of the idea of a liberal education, since, with its
exclusive emphasis on Latin and Greek, it could hardly be described as
liberal; nor could Copleston invoke the other meaning of liberal as 'freedom,' given the severe financial, sexual, and religious restrictions on at-
tendance at the university. So instead he fought his ground on the long-
established claim, to be often repeated subsequently, that if a literary
education did not prepare the student for any specific kind of employment or profession, its very lack of specificity meant that it prepared
him (as women were not admitted I say 'him' advisedly) for everything:

*Without directly qualifying a man for any of the employments of life, it en-*
*riches and ennobles all. Without teaching him the peculiar business of any*
*one office or calling, it enables him to act his part in each of them with bet-*
*ter grace and more elevated carriage. . . . ❧ There must surely be a cultiva-*
*tion of the mind which is itself a good: a good of the highest order; without*

*any immediate reference to bodily appetites, or wants of any kind. . . . And if Classical Education be regarded in this light there is none in which it will be found more faultless. A high sense of honour, a love of enterprise, and a love of glory, are among the first sentiments, which those studies communicate to the mind.*[10]

A sublime elevation versus a rational ground, useless Truth versus vulgar utility, quality of mind versus particular or practical use: such were the terms of the debate which, in spite of local variations, has remained the basis of discussions of university education from that day to this. ❧ Copleston's argument assumes that the recipient of such a form of education is in a position to disregard such trivialities as 'wants of any kind'; in other words, that he does not need education in order to provide the wealth to support him afterward. In fact one could argue that a classical 'literary' education survived precisely because anyone who could afford at that time to go to Oxford or Cambridge by definition was not in need of a profession, and therefore was not in need of anything but a gentlemanly education. This is clear from the failure of attempts to transplant the Oxford model to the new University of Durham in 1832. That university was founded because in the year of the Reform Bill, the Church of England was afraid that the government might appropriate some of its obvious surplus wealth; thirty years later, however, Durham still had no more than forty-six students.[11] A similar fate befell the new Catholic University of Dublin, founded in 1852, whose rector, John Henry Newman, ironically provided in his rectorial addresses the most eloquent defense of this ideology of university education. The 'cultivated intellect' that is its object produces the true gentleman, whose magnanimous and fastidious qualities are described by Newman with some fervor for several pages.[12] However, the reality of such high ideals, at a university designed solely for Irish Catholics who had been oppressed and prevented from holding office or power for several centuries, was rather different: as Newman himself admitted, 'The great difficulty is that there seems to be no class to afford members of a University.'[13] In fact, only the useful part of the university, the medical school, survived. ❧ If the idea of a literary education appealed to upper class interests, also at stake was the authority and power of the Anglican Church, which in Britain, of course, is constitutionally part of the state. For this reason, as Newman's lectures make abundantly clear, the argument about useful as against useless knowledge is also an argument about secular, or free

thinking, versus religious education – and about the place of religion
in knowledge generally, which was, in the sphere of natural philosophy,
being increasingly contested. This is apparent from the controversy that
surrounded the founding of the University of London in 1826 – the first
English university designed to teach useful knowledge. What shocked
the more conservative members of the public, including Coleridge who
immediately announced that he would give three lectures on the subject
of the university, which he never gave, was that the University of London
was, as it was termed, a 'godless university.' The Church of England's
monopoly over university education had at long last been broken: not
only were the teachers not clergymen, as they were still required to be at
Oxford and Cambridge, not only did students not have to take a religious test by swearing allegiance to the doctrines of the Church of England in order to matriculate, but religion was not even taught. The
University of London was founded if not on reason as such, then at least
upon the reasoned argument of the utilitarians that a university should
teach useful knowledge. Modeled not on Oxford and Cambridge but on
the universities of Edinburgh and Virginia, and the new reformed universities of Germany, from which it took the professorial and lecture system, its intellectual inspiration was derived from the ideas of the radical
utilitarian, Jeremy Bentham, whose mummified body is still preserved in
University College London, and which – perhaps rather less reason-
ably – on the instruction of his will is still carried out to take its place at
certain college functions each year, allegedly on the grounds that his silence will amount to more sense than the rest of what is said. Bentham,
though too old to take an active part in the planning of the new institution, had established an important precedent in his *Chrestomathia, Being a Collection of Papers explanatory of the Design of an Institution, proposed to be set on foot under the name of the Chrestomathic Day School, or
Chrestomathia School, for the Extension of the New System of Instruction
to the higher Branches of Learning. For the Use of the middling and higher
Ranks in Life* of 1816.[14] This remarkable work proposed a new system
of instruction for more efficient teaching, based on the latest theories of
associationist psychology, together with the abolition of flogging, the
admission of girls on an equal basis with boys (a principle that University of London, however, did not endorse until 1878), right down to such
details as the employment of what Bentham with his love of abstruse
terminology called the 'Psammographic principle,' that is, the use of

sand-writing instead of slates. The school itself was to be built as a panopticon, so as to allow the most efficient use of the teacher's capacities, with additional instruction by pupil-monitors on the 'Madras system' (so called because such a method had first been tested in Madras in India). Efficient methods of teaching, together with a detailed scheme of progressive structures through which knowledge could be taught, meant that instead of just a 'scraping together,' as Milton had put it, of 'so much miserable Greek and Latin,' pupils could be taught an impressively wide range of knowledge. Here we may recall that J. S. Mill, who was himself taught by his father on strictly Benthamite principles, reckoned that by the age of eighteen he was, in intellectual terms, twenty-five years ahead of his peers. ❧ An influential review of the *Chrestomathia* in the *Westminster Review* of 1824 suggested pointedly that its method could be adapted to higher forms of learning, declaring: 'Here then is a machine of immense power capable of producing the most extraordinary effects.'[15] Accordingly, the University of London adopted Bentham's 'Chrestomathic' principle, chrestomathic, as Bentham himself explained, meaning 'conducive to useful learning' (he might have added that the word was not, as a word, an example of itself). This spanned the whole range of contemporary knowledge at both a theoretical and technical level. The 1825 *Prospectus* of the University of London announced that 'the object of the Institution is to bring the means of a complete scientific and literary education home to the inhabitants of the metropolis.'[16] The university therefore offered comprehensive instruction in all forms of knowledge – in medicine, engineering, mathematics, the sciences, political economy, law, classical and modern languages, Hindustani and Sanskrit (suggesting the extent to which the university, many of whose original shareholders were British administrators and businessmen in India, was designed to service the needs of the East India Company, a colonial connection made more explicit with the subsequent founding of Imperial College) as well as, for the first time in an English university, 'British literature.'[17] The kind of professors appointed, who were mostly Scottish or German, with a few from Cambridge, ensured that the university taught the most advanced subjects and forms of knowledge of its day (except, that is, in British literature, where a candidate, whom Bentham supported, specializing in the new German science of philology, was passed over in favor of a traditional moralist, as a sop to the nonconformists who had given the university such strong support).[18]

New forms of knowledge, as always, involved important political stakes.[19] The University of London embodied, for the first time in competitive institutional form, the counterideology of the antithetical social class to that of Oxford and Cambridge. British higher education since that time has been the product of these two different systems whose politics and effects can still be found at work today. Schematically but only provisionally we could characterize them as conservative and radical, corresponding, as the opponents themselves often specified, to the politics and religion of the upper and middle classes. The first, identifiable with Oxford and Cambridge, the Tory party and the Church of England (itself, as Disraeli observed, 'the Tory party at prayer'), regarded the universities as sustaining the state by embodying its religious and cultural heritage through an elite form of education for a privileged few, namely the ruling class. Here the university's function was to be an organ for the transmission of truth, with knowledge regarded either as an end in itself or at most as a form of morality. Its preferred activity, consequently, was pedagogy, and, if not altogether anti-intellectual, such an ethic was certainly hostile to 'research' and to the idea of the 'advancement' of knowledge; its preferred subject area was rather the past, particularly the Greco-Roman tradition and the literature of the classics. By contrast, the competing radical educational tradition rejected such truth as both political and partial. Its strategy, however, was not so much to challenge it on the grounds of its class interests as to characterize it as useless, a strategy later modified with great success into 'science' versus 'arts.' The Liberal utilitarians and nonconformists, who were science- and therefore research-oriented, argued that knowledge should be up to date, useful, practical, changed according to theoretical and scientific investigation, and taught in a democratized secular form. Representing the interest of the dissenting middle classes, they saw education as a political force – specifically as a potential means of liberation for disadvantaged groups, such as religious nonconformists, women, the poor, colonized peoples, in fact anyone suffering political oppression.[20] If they placed much greater emphasis on a belief in the possibilities of education than on a change in the capitalist system to which they were fully committed, in some respects these radical utilitarians were less different from Marx than is often suggested: in their different ways, after all, both Marx and Adam Smith were economic determinists. And it was Bentham who declared of the German idealist philosophers long before Marx's more famous statement in the theses on Feuerbach: 'The Germans can only inquire about things as they are. They are interdicted from inquiring into things as they ought to be.'[21] ᐟ One effect of utilitarian radicalism's belief in education as a force for change, however, is the striking absence of a politics of higher education that can be identified with the working class. In the first place, this is because in the nineteenth century the political aspirations of the working class were fixed on a national system of primary – let alone university – education. But in addition, as we shall see, from the time of Chartism onward the universities were mobilized as a significant form of resistance to working-class demands and their alternative institutions of education, such as the mechanic's institutes which were eventually safely absorbed into the state education system. This lacuna accounts for the extent to which the issues of 'truth' versus 'use,' arts versus sciences, continue to dominate the politics of education.[22]

## USEFUL USELESSNESS

It is not without significance that the most famous analysis of the university by an English writer should take the form of a defense of the university as Truth itself. Newman's work could be said to define not so much the idea of a university as such, as the English idea of a university, since all contemporary alternatives are based on foreign models, be they Scottish or German. No doubt it is also significant that at the very moment when Newman was proposing such an ethos, the university that inspired it was already in the process of being reformed by the Liberals. Nevertheless the idea of the university that Newman advanced remains the basis of a whole educational and political ethic. ᐟ Newman's lectures, gathered together at various times under different titles but best known by the last, *The Idea of a University* (1852–73), demonstrate an ambivalence between an endeavor to reassert the religious basis of education against the advance of secular knowledge and an attempt to treat religion as separate from the general idea of a 'liberal education' whose function would be to produce quality of mind, social cohesion, and, ultimately, once again religious truth. While Newman tries on the one hand, in the best Oxford fashion, to justify the idea of a university education as one of knowledge for its own sake, on the other he attempts to establish the place of theology as the faculty that functions as the architectonic, or Idea, of all the diverse knowledges in the university. ᐟ New-

man bases his idea of a university – ominously enough – on what ety-
mologists consider to be a false derivation, claiming that a university 'by
its very name professes to teach universal knowledge.'[23] This allows him,
according to what Freud would characterize as the logic of the broken
kettle, to offer three defenses of the role of theology in the university.
First, if a university is a place of universal knowledge, then it must include theological knowledge. Second, although all such knowledges
must be understood in their connections together in an institution that
claims to teach universal knowledge, only religious knowledge can complete and correct the other sciences and give each particular field an appreciation of its place from the perspective of the whole; and, third, if
theology is not taught, then its place will be usurped by other sciences
which will teach other, irreligious, doctrines in the place where theology
should have been. Theology is thus, like philosophy for Kant, both a
part of the system of the sciences of the university and also that part
which operates over and above the rest. It does not, however, as in Kant,
have the function of judging the truth of other forms of knowledge but
of fusing such knowledge of partial truths into a higher truth, truth itself, correcting the 'false peculiar colouring of each' (Newman, p.151)
into the Platonic whiteness of the Idea. Theology is both a science in itself and the product of all other forms of knowledge, a higher knowledge
that transcends all others; the perspective of the whole that theology
provides comprises the function of a university education, with the result that it finally becomes identified with the institution of the university itself. As Newman puts it, the student 'apprehends the great outlines
of knowledge, the principles on which it rests, the scale of its parts, its
lights and its shades, its great points and its little, as he otherwise cannot
apprehend them. Hence it is that his education is called liberal. A habit
of mind is formed which lasts through life . . . what . . . I have ventured
to call a philosophical habit. . . . This is the main purpose of a university
in its treatment of its students' (p.82). What, however, Newman is
obliged to ask, is the *use* of such an education? The answer is: none.
None, that is, if use is thought of only in terms of 'ulterior objects,' such
as training for the professions or for commerce. Knowledge, he coun-
ters, does not have to have a use, for it 'is capable of being its own end.
Such is the constitution of the human mind that any kind of knowledge,
if it be really such, is its own reward' (p.83). ❧ This reward, if it has no
use value, nevertheless brings a surplus value in its wake: that well-

established institutional product characterized by Newman as the 'state or condition of mind' of 'the gentleman' (p.93): 'Liberal education makes not the Christian, not the Catholic, but the gentleman. It is well to be a gentleman, it is well to have a cultivated intellect, a delicate taste, a candid, equitable bearing in the conduct of life – these are the connatural qualities of a large knowledge; they are the objects of a university' (p.99). Although Newman claims to separate the benefits of a liberal literary education from those of religious education, he does so only to unite them again in the same terms, so that the second is the product of the first. For if the object of the university is a gentlemanly condition of mind, then this condition is indistinguishable from the form of religious truth: 'Religious truth is not a portion, but a condition of general knowledge. To blot it out is nothing short, if I may so speak, of unravelling the web of university education' (p.54). Newman mixes his metaphors, literary and religious, blots and webs, in order to appropriate that comprehensive knowledge which, as John Barrell has argued, was contested in the eighteenth century between the 'man of letters' and the 'gentleman,' producing a synthesis in which the two contending parties are uplifted into the higher universal term of the university.[24] 🍂 Newman does this by invoking the aid of a powerful literary-political tradition, but in doing so he demonstrates that the defense of useless knowledge is made because such knowledge serves an important and indeed highly useful function. As will have become obvious to any student of Romanticism by this point, Newman's literary education, 'the philosophic habit,' is remarkably reminiscent of what Wordsworth and Coleridge termed 'the philosophic mind'; similarly Newman's description of the place of theology in relation to the university, and of the university in relation to knowledge, repeats a version of Coleridge's theory of organic form, where the 'esemplastic' imagination holds all knowledge together as a whole and gives it its life and spiritual center. What is less obvious to students of Romanticism is the no less political than spiritual function of this impressive unification. Newman suggests that

*the process of imparting knowledge to the intellect in this philosophical way is its true culture; that such culture is a good in itself; that the knowledge which is both its instrument and result is called liberal knowledge; that such culture, together with the knowledge which effects it, may be fitly sought for its own sake; that it is, however, in addition, of great secular utility, as constituting the best and highest formation of the intellect for social and political life.* (My emphasis, pp.185–86)

Even useless knowledge, it seems, can sometimes turn out to be useful. It is not hard to chart the relation of the secular utility of Newman's Idea back to Coleridge's *On The Constitution of Church and State According to the Idea of Each* (1829) or forward to Matthew Arnold's *Culture and Anarchy* (1869). In what he terms his 'concluding address to the parliamentary leaders of the Liberalists and Utilitarians,' Coleridge makes the connections quite explicit between his attack on secular knowledge, on useful knowledge, and the necessity for the conservation of religion and the state:

*A permanent, nationalized, learned order, a national clerisy or church, is an essential element of a rightly constituted nation, without which it wants the best security alike for its permanence and its progression; and for which neither tract societies nor conventicles, nor Lancasterian schools, nor mechanics' institutions, nor lecture-bazaars under the absurd name of universities [that is, the University of London], nor all these collectively, can be a substitute. For they are all marked with the same asterisk of spuriousness, shew the same distemper-spot on the front, that they are empirical specifics for morbid symptoms that help to feed and continue the disease. But you wish for general illumination: you would spur-arm the toes of society, you would enlighten the higher ranks per ascensum ab imis [by ascent from the lowest levels]. You begin, therefore, with the attempt to* popularize *science: but you will only effect its* plebification. *It is folly to think of making all, or the many, philosophers, or even men of science and systematic knowledge. But it is duty and wisdom to aim at making as many as possible soberly and steadily religious; – inasmuch as the morality which the state requires in its citizens for its own well-being and ideal immortality, and without reference to their spiritual interest as individuals, can only exist for the people in the form of religion. But the existence of a true philosophy, or the power and habit of contemplating particulars in the unity and fontal mirror of the idea – this in the rulers and teachers of a nation is indispensable to a sound state of religion in all classes. In fine, Religion, true or false, is and ever has been the centre of gravity in a realm, to which all other things must and will accommodate themselves.*[25]

Coleridge could hardly have made the alliance between truth and power, between politics and knowledge clearer: the very extent of his claims indicates the scope of an argument which I have not space to analyse further here: I would only point to the deep complicity between a literary and a political ideology in a founding text of a literary theory that in the twentieth century has been supposed to be defined by the separation of the two. ⟨ Arnold's purposes, though secular, work toward the same end. In *Culture and Anarchy* he retransposes Newman's Idea back to the university from which it was derived, although in its own way it still remains just as much an ideal:

*Oxford, the Oxford of the past, has many faults; and she has heavily paid for them in defeat, in isolation, in want of hold upon the modern world. Yet we in Oxford, brought up amidst the beauty and sweetness of that beautiful place, have not failed to seize one truth: – the truth that beauty and sweetness are essential characters of a complete human perfection. When I insist on this, I am all in the faith and tradition of Oxford.*

In evidence of this Oxford spirit, Arnold cites Newman himself and his attempt to uphold the power of the Anglican Church over the university. Arnold, like many lapsed Christians of the nineteenth century, wished to preserve the religious perspective by presenting it in as ecumenical a form as possible. In the face of the potentially dangerous, growing calls for democracy and socialism, culture could act as a force of 'civilization' upon the people at large. The repository of culture, the ideal toward which the whole country should strive, Arnold posits as nothing less than the university: it acts as a bastion against anarchy – specifically class division – preserving and producing a metaphysical aspiration that can counter political unrest. Arnold maintains that culture 'does not try to teach down to the level of inferior classes; it does not try to win them for this or that sect of its own, with ready made judgements and watchwords. It seeks to do away with classes; to make the best that has been thought and known in the world current everywhere; to make all men live in an atmosphere of sweetness and light.' Although Arnold can no longer appeal to religion for this ideal, its secular substitute, literature, will function just as effectively. If for Marx, the class struggle between the bourgeoisie and the proletariat constitutes, as he puts it, 'the great lever' – *mochlos* – 'of the modern social revolution,' for Arnold literature is the power that can dissolve the division on which that lever pivots.[26] ⟨ After Arnold, literature became the privileged repository of culture assigned the role of truth itself both within the university and in society at large. Whereas for Kant the lower faculty of philosophy judged the rest by the truth of reason, in England this function, abandoned by philosophy, was appropriated by literature which gave judgment according not to rational but poetic truth.[27] We might speculate that if religious truth was followed by poetic truth as the architectonic of knowledge, the contemporary assertion of political truth as the most comprehensive metalanguage, specifically and noticeably in the realm of literary theory, is an attempt to win back that higher function extending over society at large – Newman's 'imperial intellect' – which poetic truth has now lost. ❧ The influential 1921 report for the British government by Sir Henry Newbolt, *The Teaching of English in England*, gave institutional endorsement to Arnold's position, and set up the terms of the form and function of the teaching of literature in secondary and tertiary education that have been maintained ever since.[28] Significantly enough, Newbolt cites Wordsworth's discussions of education in *The Prelude*, Newman's *Idea of a University*, and misquotes Arnold as claiming that 'culture unites classes,' before concluding that an education based upon the English language and literature would dissolve the effects of class differences through an appeal to a civilizing common national 'English' culture. ❧ The discomfort felt at the discovery of the explicit nationalistic and political origins of English as an educational subject, recently demonstrated even further by analyses of its role in the service of colonial subjugation in India, has resulted in a call to transform literary studies into cultural or communication studies, that is to shift it from an elite to a mass culture.[29] Literature and the literary as such has certainly been under attack of late, and in many quarters they now have very strongly marked negative connotations. But what suggestions about changing the object of literary studies have perhaps neglected is the place of literature in the theory and institutional practice of the university whose origin, as we have seen, goes back to Newman and beyond, and which cannot be changed quite so simply. In other words, to convert the disciplinary object from English into Cultural Studies merely inverts the site of its truth. The attempt by Raymond Williams and others on the left to reappropriate the Arnoldian cultural tradition into an oppositional mode preserves absolutely unharmed its political and ideological function in the university and in society at large. This has led to some acute political difficulties in recent years. ❧ Since 1979 the attacks on higher education by the Conservative government have been conducted strictly according to the terms of the debate that I have been charting. The disorienting part, however, is that they have, as it were,

come from the wrong political side, invoking all the utilitarian arguments against the humanities and advocating instead science and a strict
criterion of utility. ᵺ For more traditional literary critics, this has presented no problem, for the whole literature of the nineteenth century
was already to hand: F. R. Leavis even refers to the anarchy, barbarian-
ism, or, as he likes to put it, 'Americanism,' that he is fighting against as
the 'technologico-Benthamite' age. Perhaps nothing illustrates so clearly
Leavis's place in a tradition of argument about the function of education
than this anachronistic and no doubt deliberately inelegant phrase.
Dickens's *Hard Times,* to which Leavis attached special significance, is
the most famous literary attack on what was represented as the utilitarian view of education, but it is easy to find many other writers of the
'great tradition' who opposed such a philosophy just as passionately. As a
literary critic, therefore, one is already positioned in the debate: both in
terms of the arguments of the literary and critical texts themselves, and
in terms of the very existence of one's own discipline within the institutions of higher education. Even current Conservative education policy is
derived from the *Black Papers* on education of a literary journal, the
*Critical Quarterly.*[30] ᵺ The difficulty for literary theorists, when faced
with a new 'technologico-Thatcherite' assault on the humanities, was
that the terms by which their subject was established historically, and the
only effective terms with which it could still be defended, were those of
the cultural conservatism and humanist belief in literature and philosophy that 'literary theory' has, broadly speaking, been attacking since the
1970s. When theorists found themselves wanting to defend their discipline against successive government cuts they discovered that the only
view with which they could vindicate themselves was the very one
which, in intellectual terms, they wanted to attack. One might say that
the problem was that the oppositional literary or theoretical mode was
not the oppositional institutional one – a situation that in itself illustrates the limitations of oppositional politics. In short, for theorists the
problem has been that in attacking humanism they have found themselves actually in consort with government policy. This has meant, effectively, that it has often been left to those on the right to defend the study
of the humanities as such: symbolized, perhaps, when the University of
Oxford, traditionally, as we have seen, the main object of utilitarian hos-
tility, refused to award Margaret Thatcher the customary honorary degree given to British prime ministers. ᵺ What this suggests is that a

curious historical mutation has occurred by which the Conservatives, as they claim, have indeed become the radical party, if not of today, then of yesterday, by returning to a middle-class radicalism which regards not Edmund Burke as its founder, but Adam Smith. This means that the Conservatives, in turn, are also already positioned in terms of their attitude toward education and the universities.

### USELESS USEFULNESS

In the mid-1980s, Margaret Thatcher began telling interviewers that what the press called 'Thatcherism' was really nothing other than the ideas of Adam Smith. In the context of today's renewed demand that knowledge be useful, therefore, university teachers of the humanities in Britain, who have been feeling the brunt and uncertainties of successive educational cuts since the Conservatives came to power in 1979, might also find it worth their while to turn to *The Wealth of Nations* to find out what theory of the university Thatcherism involved. ❧ Smith discusses education in Book 5 of *The Wealth of Nations*, where he broaches the question of what we now call public expenditure, and addresses such topics as defense and the administration of justice. Education appears in a section entitled 'Commercial Institutions,' which discusses the public institutions designed to facilitate commerce and to instruct the people. In certain cases these pose the problem that however beneficial they may be for society as a whole they cannot be left to the efforts of individuals because the profit obtainable from them does not repay the expense that individuals would need to incur in order to maintain them. Education falls under the category of a noneconomic institution whose ultimate benefit however makes it 'in the highest degree advantageous to a great society.' Smith then immediately focuses on the difference between what might be called the immediate and deferred profits of education: education is an institution whose use-value cannot be measured by the immediate exchange value of its product, or, to put it another way, whose cost is greater than the direct exchange-value of the product that it produces, that is, the newly graduated student.[31] ❧ Smith solves this difficulty by elaborating a version of an educational theory that later became popular in the 1960s and has recently given rise to precise quantification exercises at the Department of Education and Science: that is, the theory of human capital, developed by T. W. Schultz and Gary Becker.[32] Smith formulates this theory very succinctly when accounting for wage differentials: one of the factors he points to is that 'the wages of labor vary with the easiness and cheapness, or the difficulty and expence of learning the business.'

> When any expensive machine is erected, the extraordinary work to be per-
> formed by it before it is worn out, it must be expected, will replace the capi-
> tal laid out upon it, with at least the ordinary profits. A man educated at
> the expense of much labor and time to any of those employments which re-
> quire extraordinary dexterity and skill, may be compared to one of these
> expensive machines. The work which he learns to perform, it must be ex-
> pected, over and above the usual wages of common labor, will replace to
> him the whole expense of his education, with at least the ordinary profits of
> an equally valuable capital. It must do this too in a reasonable time, regard
> being had to the very uncertain duration of human life, in the same man-
> ner as to the more certain duration of the machine. (1:103)

Smith illustrates his argument in relation to apprenticeships, adding that 'education in the ingenious and in the liberal professions, is still more te-dious and expensive. The pecuniary recompense, therefore, of painters and sculptors, of lawyers and physicians, ought to be much more liberal: and so it is accordingly' (1:104). For Smith, this line of reasoning suffices to excuse the state from any necessity for providing such forms of edu-cation. ❧ On the basis of this argument Smith is fiercely critical of any subsidy for higher education, which he considers would only lead to an academic freedom that would be abused. The human capital theory of education allows him to consider the remuneration of teachers, as well as the contents of courses of instruction, from the perspective entirely of market forces. Smith contends that the best system occurs where teachers are directly rewarded according to the estimation of their students – a system under which Smith himself worked in part at the University of Glasgow, and which was originally proposed for the Uni-versity of London. Any form of endowment, salary, or organization as a corporation will, he argues, set a teacher's duty in opposition to the teacher's interest; as proof of this argument, Smith instances the state of the University of Oxford. Similarly, all forms of university discipline over students Smith merely considers to be 'contrived, not for the bene-fit of the students, but for the interest, or more properly speaking, for the ease of the masters' (2:253). In other words, they are an attempt to assert authority through force where it cannot be derived from intellectual respect. ❧ The argument against the insulation of universities from market forces becomes a powerful weapon with which Smith attacks academic freedom, by which he means the intellectual decadence of contemporary English universities. Such protection means that any estimate of the value of knowledge itself becomes irrelevant. Accordingly, Smith blames the public institutions of education for the teaching of knowledge 'universally believed to be a mere useless and pedantic heap of sophistry and nonsense. Such systems, such sciences, can subsist no where, but in those incorporated societies for education whose prosperity and revenue are in a great measure independent of their education, and altogether independent of their industry' (2:266). He goes on, 'Few improvements in philosophy have been made by universities, and fewest by the richest universities'; instead they have acted as the shelter of 'exploded and obsolete systems'; the poorer universities, by contrast, by which he means the Scottish universities, in which teachers depend upon their individual reputations, have been more forward-looking and receptive to 'the current opinions of the world' (2:260). At Oxford and Cambridge, by contrast, 'The diligence of public teachers is more or less corrupted by the circumstances, which render them more or less independent of their success and reputation in their particular professions' (2:265). ❧ The argument seems almost convincing until, in the next paragraph, Smith compares the academic system, where a gentleman finishes his education ignorant of everything that is of interest or use in the outside world, with the education of women: they, by contrast, are taught 'what their parents or guardians judge it necessary or useful for them to learn,' that is, 'either to improve the natural attractions of their persons, or to form their mind to reserve, to modesty, to chastity, and to oeconomy; to render them both likely to become mistresses of a family, and to behave properly when they have become such' (2:266). Unlike the Benthamites and utilitarians, Smith was no advocate of feminism or of equal opportunities of education for women: suddenly usefulness has become a criterion that ensures the ideological control of certain groups. ❧ The logic of this aspect of the argument is brought out when Smith reverses his position according to which university education ought to operate solely on the basis of market demand and suggests that the state ought to provide for the education of the working class – who might well neither demand it nor be able to pay for it. Smith argues that whereas people of rank and fortune will look after the education of their sons, who will then take up chiefly intellectual occupations providing variety and stimulation, the division of labor that has been accentuated under capitalism means that work for the poor has often been reduced to a few mindless activities. This situation has the effect of reducing the populace to a condition of virtual imbecility; the state ought therefore to provide education 'in order to prevent the almost entire corruption and degeneracy of the great body of the people' (2:267). Smith suggests that some basic education in reading, writing, arithmetic, geometry, and mechanics could be provided by subsidized schools, financed, on the Scottish model, by local parishes. The reason for this apparent benevolence on the part of the state is then given very clearly:

*The more they are instructed, the less liable they are to the delusions of enthusiasm and superstition, which, among ignorant nations, frequently occasion the most dreadful disorders. . . . They are most disposed to examine, and more capable of seeing through, the interested complaints of faction and sedition, and they are, upon that account, less apt to be misled into any wanton or unnecessary opposition to the measures of government.* (2:272–73)

This theory of what Samuel calls 'nondeliberate social control' is entirely predicated upon an Enlightenment belief in the power of reason that never countenances the idea that the interests of the poor may be at variance with those of the ruling class.[33] Smith's suggestion should, however, also be seen in the context of the contemporary Tory opposition to any education for the poor whatsoever on the grounds that it might lead them to question their poverty and work less efficiently. Marx, who was scornful of Smith's prescription for education to alleviate alienation 'in prudently homeopathic doses' as he puts it in *Capital*, notes how Garnier, Smith's more conservative French translator, protests at this point.[34] But *The Wealth of Nations* is a theory of contracts rather than conflict, in which institutions are utilized as a means of resolving the different interests of individuals into the general interest of society as a whole – on the face of it, at least, a benevolent theory of institutions. The strategy becomes clear when Smith goes on to suggest that the state should also encourage regular carnivals (2:281; it is hard to understand why it is that those on the left who make great claims for carnival as radically subversive of the social order always seem to forget to mention that Adam Smith shared their enthusiasm). If Smith proposed education and carnival as a way of easing the ills of alienation, the opportunities a state system of education afforded for the behavioral training of the industrial classes were soon recognized, as William Godwin, the great critic of state institutions, had predicted.[35] ❧ This points to a significant paradox in the logic of Smith's account of the free market, where an attack on public educational institutions for the wealthy is accompanied by a prescription for public instruction for the poor. The ambivalence of the place of education merits attention, for its function points to nothing less than a problem in the theory of *The Wealth of Nations* as a whole. If Smith was the first to produce an economic interpretation of history, the progress and increase of the wealth of nations leads paradoxically, in his account, to a moral and material decline.[36] The material decline is based on a proto-Malthusian principle of economic growth that leads to a population explosion, which, in turn, produces eventual economic stagnation; Smith attributes the ensuing moral decline as a condition of reduced well-being produced by the effects of industrialization:

*In the progress of the division of labor, the employment of the far greater part of those who live by labor, that is, of the great body of the people, comes to be confined to a few very simple operations; frequently to one or two. But the understandings of the greater part of men are necessarily formed by their ordinary employments. The man whose whole life is spent in performing a few simple operations, of which the effects too are, perhaps, always the same, or very nearly the same, has no occasion to exert his understanding, or to exercise his invention in finding out expedients for removing difficulties which never occur. He naturally loses, therefore, the habit of such exertion, and generally becomes as stupid and as ignorant as it is possible for a human creature to become. The torpor of his mind renders him, not only incapable of relishing or bearing a part in any rational conversation, but of conceiving any generous, noble, or tender sentiment, and consequently of forming any just judgement concerning many even of the ordinary duties of life. . . . His dexterity at his own particular trade seems, in this manner, to be acquired at the expense of his intellectual, social, and martial virtues. But in every improved and civilized society this is the state into which the labouring poor, that is, the great body of the people, must necessarily fall, unless government takes some pains to prevent it. (2:267–68)*

Smith contrasts this state of alienation with the conditions of what he calls 'barbarous societies,' that is, societies without manufacturing and foreign commerce, where necessity spurs the population into a quickness of intelligence and its accompanying virtues. In such societies, 'The varied occupations of every man oblige every man to exert his capacity, and to invent expedients for removing difficulties which are continually occurring. Invention is kept alive, and the mind is not suffered to fall into that drowsy stupidity, which, in a civilized society, seems to benumb the understanding of almost all the inferior ranks of people' (2: 268). According to the first theorist of capitalism, then, the division of labor necessary for the economic progress of commercial societies leads to an intellectual and moral decay – an alienation that sounds very similar to the argument of a later theorist of capitalism. The paradox in Smith's whole account has been neatly summarized by Robert Heilbroner: 'The deterioration of the human condition cannot be rationalized in terms of the very purpose for which the system of perfect liberty is espoused – namely, the material betterment of mankind that is supposed to flow from its workings.'[37] Smith's analysis of the effects of the division of labor, therefore, eventually does lead to a class division in which the different interests of society conflict. This is the point where the contract founded on the mutual interest of a general desire for 'self-betterment' breaks down and antagonism begins: the point at which Marx's analysis could be said to start. ❧ Yet, as we have seen, Smith does offer one major palliative with which he attempts to sustain that contract, that is, the general education of the populace. This, he suggests, would be primarily an education in the principles of useful sciences, particularly geometry and mechanics, which would be of practical help in the trades to be followed later in life; but of course this by itself would be contradictory, insofar as education, which is supposed to be an anodyne for the effects of capitalism, would merely constitute a training for the trade that will go on to produce capitalism's enervating effects. Smith therefore proposes that such education would involve what he terms 'the necessary introduction to the most sublime as well as to the most useful sciences' (2:270). But what would be the use of a knowledge that is 'sublime' in a scheme according to which everything must be justified by its usefulness? A curious passage a couple of pages earlier in the description of the virtues of a barbarous society before the division of labor gives a hint:

*Though in a rude society there is a good deal of variety in the occupations of every individual, there is not a great deal in those of the whole so-*

*ciety. . . . In a civilized state, on the contrary, though there is little variety in the occupations of the greater part of individuals, there is an almost infinite variety in those of the whole society. These varied occupations present an almost infinite variety of objects to the contemplation of those few, who, being attached to no particular occupation themselves, have leisure and inclination to examine the occupations of other people. The contemplation of so great a variety of objects necessarily exercises their minds in endless comparisons and combinations, and renders their understandings, in an extraordinary degree, both acute and comprehensive. Unless those few, however, happen to be placed in some very particular situations, their great abilities, though honourable to themselves, may contribute very little to the good government or happiness of their society.* (2:268–69)

Capitalism, therefore, though it reduces diversity for each individual, increases the total variety at play in society as a whole. Those who can contemplate this reach a state of comprehensive understanding unavailable to anyone in a precapitalist society. Unless, however, they 'happen to be placed in some very particular situations,' such philosophers can contribute little to society's happiness. 'Notwithstanding the great abilities of those few, all the nobler parts of the human character may be, in a great measure, obliterated and extinguished in the great body of the people' (2:269). ❧ Whatever place or institution Smith may have had in mind in his comment about 'some very particular situations,' it is obvious that this special function for society's philosophers, who have access to a form of sublime knowledge that could link to the general education system as a palliative for capitalism, cannot be justified insofar as it contradicts the very grounds for the basis of public institutions of higher education that Smith has been at pains to elaborate.[38] According to the logic of *The Wealth of Nations*, those institutions should be restricted to the utility of the knowledge that they can sell and which the student can accumulate as a form of capital for increased remuneration. To impart knowledge on the grounds of its sublimity for the alleviation of the population as a whole could form the basis of no such academic contract. ❧ Even according to the rigorous analysis of Adam Smith's economics, then, in which education is constituted solely according to market forces, knowledge outside the orbit of a strict criterion of utility has to be invoked in order to provide something beyond the system that can save it from its own consequences. That philosophical knowledge can only not be assigned to the university because, having in the first instance been rigorously excluded, its introduction would contradict the rest of Smith's argument so absolutely as to call his entire premises into doubt. Smith therefore leaves his suggestion hanging, on the borderline of the aesthetic and the political, outside the logic of his text, in the sublime aerial situation of the philosophers he describes – perhaps the place of the Idea of the university itself. The conclusion we, as readers, may draw is that in *The Wealth of Nations* the university, though in the first instance made directly useful, is then called upon to fulfill a role strikingly similar to that which it would be required to play in the theories of Newman, Arnold, or Leavis – who present themselves specifically in opposition to the utilitarian ethics of the function of education in the free-market economy. ❧ As it stands in *The Wealth of Nations,* with little apparent prospect of those who possess such higher knowledge being placed in the very particular situations from which they can contribute to the happiness of society, Smith's account means that the paradox for the universities is that the more useful to the state that they are, the quicker the system to which they contribute will succeed and therefore go into decline. In other words, the most beneficial thing the state could do to ensure its own survival would be to encourage the universities to be useless. Or to put it the other way around, the most politically subversive thing you could do would be to help the universities to be useful. ❧ But first it would be wise to recall that if you cannot stop uselessness from becoming useful, neither can you stop usefulness from becoming useless. ❧ Useful or useless for whom, though? What becomes clear is that both ideas of the university, which seem to be set directly in opposition to each other as radical to conservative, are equally necessary to the state, as is the conflict between them. To enter into that conflict by resisting one with the other is to remain blind to the extent to which they are interimplicated and therefore not in any sense alternatives. Such a strategy can only ensure that you lose any point of leverage whatsoever. A more successful point of leverage might begin with the recognition that Thatcherism did indeed operate not just by the ethos of *The Wealth of Nations* in general, but according to its own precise contradictory logic, whereby the creation and maintenance of a 'free' market for the economy can only be sustained by an ever-increasing authoritarian and centralized control by the state apparatus of everything 'outside' that market that services its needs – such as education. The question today's philosophers therefore need to ask is this: In what ways and with what effects can the university, both inside and outside the market economy, useful and useless, function as a surplus that that economy cannot comprehend?

NOTES

1. Michel Foucault, *Language, Counter-Memory, Practice: Selected Essays and Interviews,* ed. Donald F. Bouchard, trans. Donald F. Bouchard and Sherry Simon (Ithaca, N.Y.: Cornell University Press, 1977), p.224.

2. The texts of the German idealists on the subject of the university are collected and translated in L. Ferry, J.-P. Pesron, and A. Renault, eds., *Philosophies de l'université: L'idéalisme allemand et la question de l'Université; textes de Schelling, Fichte, Schleiermacher, Humboldt, Hegel* (Paris: Payot, 1979). See also Jacques Derrida, 'The Principle of Reason: The University in the Eyes of Its Pupils,' *Diacritics* 13,3 (1983), 3–20.

3. See Renate Simpson, *How the Ph.D. came to Britain: A Century of Struggle for Postgraduate Education* (Guildford: Society for Research into Higher Education, 1983).

4. Immanuel Kant, *The Conflict of the Faculties/Der Streit der Fakultäten,* trans. Mary J. Gregor (New York: Abaris Books, 1979); Jacques Derrida, 'Mochlos; ou, le conflit des facultés,' *Philosophie* 2 (April 1984), 21–53.

5. Historically, both universities were founded as a result of academic diaspora: the standard method of resisting papal control was for the university simply to disperse: thus Oxford began as a result of the dispersal of the University of Paris, Cambridge as a result of the University of Oxford. See Hastings Rasdall, *The Universities of Europe in the Middle Ages* (Oxford: Clarendon Press, 1895).

6. Edward Gibbon, *Memoirs of My Life* (1795), ed. Betty Radice (Harmondsworth: Penguin, 1984), p.83. William Wordsworth, *The Prelude, or the Growth of a Poet's Mind; An Autobiographical Poem* (London: 1850).

7. Adam Smith, *An Inquiry into the Nature and Causes of the Wealth of Nations,* 2 vols. (1776), ed. Edwin Cannan (London: Methuen, 1904), 2:251.

8. John William Adamson, *English Education 1789–1902* (Cambridge: Cambridge University Press, 1930), p.177.

9. Sydney Smith [Review of R. L. Edgeworth's *Professional Education* (1809)], *Edinburgh Review* 15 (1809), 42, 45–46.

10. Edward Copleston, *A Reply to the Calumnies of the Edinburgh Review against Oxford, Containing an Account of Studies Pursued at the University* (Oxford, 1810), *A Second Reply to the Calumnies* (Oxford, 1810), *A Third Reply to the Calumnies* (Oxford, 1810). See Michael Sanderson, ed., *The Universities in the Nineteenth Century* (London: Routledge and Kegan Paul, 1975), pp.37–38.

11. V. H. Green, *British Institutions: The Universities* (Harmondsworth: Penguin, 1969), p.108.

12. John Henry Newman, *On the Scope and Nature of University Education* (1859) (London: Dent, 1915), pp.181–83. For detailed analysis of Newman's essays, see A. Dwight Culler, *The Imperial Intellect: A Study of Newman's Educational Ideal* (New Haven, Conn.: Yale University Press, 1955).

13. Cited in John Henry Newman, *Select Discourses from the Idea of a University* (1873), ed. May Yardley (Cambridge: Cambridge University Press, 1931), p.xi.

14. Jeremy Bentham, *Chrestomathia, Being a Collection of Papers explanatory of the Design of an Institution proposed to be set on foot under the name of the Chrestomathic Day School, or Chrestomathia School, for the Extension of the New System of Instruction to the higher Branches of Learning. For the Use of the middling and higher Ranks in Life* (1816), in *The Works of Jeremy Bentham*, 11 vols., ed. John Bowring (Edinburgh: William Tate, 1843), vol.8.

15. 'Literary Education,' *Westminster Review* 1 (1824), 68.

16. *Prospectus of the London University* (London, 1825), p.1. For a history of University College, see H. Hale Bellot, *University College London, 1826–1926* (London: University College, 1929); for the history of the University of London, see Negley Harte, *The University of London 1836–1986: An Illustrated History* (London: Athlone, 1986).

17. Brian Simon, *Studies in the History of Education, 1780–1870* (London: Lawrence and Wishart, 1960), p.122.

18. For a full account of the first professorship, see D. J. Palmer, *The Rise of English Studies* (Oxford: Clarendon Press, 1965). Eventually even Oxford began to feel the effects of the arguments that it was not abreast of modern knowledge. At that time, for instance, as Simon notes (*Studies in the History of Education*, p.87), at Oxford, which considered itself the center of theological and classical studies, 'There was almost complete ignorance of the great advances in historical criticism and philology.' If Oxford did finally become receptive to historical criticism in the nineteenth century, it is perhaps characteristic of its slow pace in the advancement of knowledge that it has kept to the method of historical criticism ever since.

19. In 1824, for instance, Baden Powell, Professor of Geometry at Oxford, wrote: 'Scientific knowledge is rapidly spreading among all classes EXCEPT THE HIGHER, and the consequence must be, that that class will not long remain THE HIGHER. If its members would continue to retain their superiority, they must preserve a real preeminence in knowledge, and must make advances at least in proportion to the classes who have hitherto been below them. And is it not a question, whether the same consideration does not in some measure apply to the ascendancy and stability of the University itself?' *Quarterly Journal of Education* 4, 8 (October 1832), 197–98, cited by Simon, *Studies in the History of Education,* p.92.

20. 'Knowledge brings with it the want and necessity of political amelioration, a necessity which must be satisfied,' declared the opening issue of the *Westminster Review* 1 (1824), 81.

21. Cited by Elie Halevy, *The Growth of Philosophical Radicalism,* 2d ed., trans. Mary Morris (London: Faber and Faber, 1934), p.436.

22. For an account of socialist politics of education in the nineteenth century see Simon, *Studies in the History of Education;* and Michalina Vaughan and Margaret S. Archer, *Social Conflict and Educational Change in England and France 1789–1848* (Cambridge: Cambridge University Press, 1971).

23. Newman, *On the Scope and Nature of University Education,* p.9. Further references are given in the text.

24. John Barrell, *English Literature in History 1730–80. An Equal, Wide Survey* (London: Hutchinson, 1983), p.207.

25. Samuel Taylor Coleridge, *On the Constitution of Church State According to the Idea of Each,* ed. John Colmer (London: Routledge and Kegan Paul, 1976), pp.69–70. Matthew Arnold, *Culture and Anarchy,* ed. J. Dover Wilson (Cambridge: Cambridge University Press, 1932).

26. Arnold, *Culture and Anarchy,* pp.61–62, 70. Karl Marx, *Selected Writings,* ed. David McLellan (Oxford: Oxford University Press, 1977), p.575.

27. The authoritative text, widely deployed in this context, for literature's claim to the highest form of Platonic truth is of course Shelley's *Defense of Poetry* (1821), first published in *Essays, Letters from Abroad, Translations and Fragments,* ed. Mary Shelley (London: 1840).

28. Sir Henry Newbolt, *The Teaching of English in England* (London: HMSO, 1921).

29. This is the argument, for instance, of Terry Eagleton's *Literary Theory: An Introduction* (Oxford: Blackwell, 1983). The standard account of the political

strategies of the institution of English literature as a university discipline is Chris Baldick's *The Social Mission of English Criticism, 1848–1932* (Oxford: Clarendon Press, 1983); for its mission in India, see Gauri Viswanathan, 'The Beginnings of English Literary Study in British India,' *Oxford Literary Review* 9 (1987), 2–26.

30. C. B. Cox and A. E. Dyson, eds., *Fight for Education: A Black Paper* (London: Critical Quarterly Society, 1969), and *Black Paper 2: The Crisis in Education* (London: Critical Quarterly Society, 1970). For F. R. Leavis's writings on the function of the university (for him, more or less synonymous with that of English literature) see *Education and the University: A Sketch for 'English School'* (London: Chatto and Windus, 1943), and *English Literature in Our Time and the University* (London: Chatto and Windus, 1969).

31. Smith, *The Wealth of Nations*, 2:214. Further references are in the text.

32. T. W. Schultz, 'Investment in Human Capital,' *American Economic Review* 51 (1961), 1–17; Gary Becker, *Human Capital: A Theoretical and Empirical Analysis, with Special Reference to Education* (New York: Bureau of Economic Research, 1964). For the relation of the 'Human Capital' theory to Adam Smith see Andrew S. Skinner and Thomas Wilson, eds., *Essays on Adam Smith* (Oxford: Clarendon Press, 1975), pp.340–41, 573–74.

33. Mark Blaug, 'The Economics of Education in English Classical Political Economy: A Re-Examination,' in Skinner and Wilson, eds., *Essays on Adam Smith*, p.591.

34. Karl Marx, *Capital*, vol.1, trans. Ben Fowkes (London: Penguin, 1976), p.484.

35. William Godwin, *Enquiry Concerning Political Justice* (1793, 3rd ed. 1798), ed. Isaac Kramnick (Harmondsworth: Penguin, 1976), pp.616–17.

36. E. G. West, 'Adam Smith and Alienation: Wealth Increases, Men Decay?' in Skinner and Wilson, eds., *Essays on Adam Smith*, p.528.

37. Robert Heilbroner, 'The Paradox of Progress: Decline and Decay in *The Wealth of Nations*,' in ibid., p.532.

38. Moreover, in the early part of *The Wealth of Nations* Smith does not excuse philosophers themselves from the general process of the division of labor: 'Philosophers, or men of speculation, whose trade is not to do anything, but to observe everything . . . upon that account, are often capable of combining together the powers of the most distant and dissimilar objects. In the progress of society, philosophy or speculation becomes, like every other employment, the principal or sole trade and occupation of a particular class

of citizens. Like every other employment too, it is subdivided into a great number of different branches, each of which affords occupation to a peculiar tribe or class of philosophers; and this subdivision of employment in philosophy, as well as in every other business, improves dexterity, and saves time. Each individual becomes more expert in his own peculiar branch, more work is done upon the whole, and the quantity of science is considerably increased by it' (1:12). For further discussion see Barrell, *English Literature in History,* chap.1, and, for the essence of the university as the sublime, see Derrida, 'The Principle of Reason,' p.6.

**6**

Ancillae (The Concord of the Faculties)

*by John Llewelyn*

*Who today would presume to claim that he is at home with the nature of poetry as well as with the nature of thinking and, in addition, strong enough to bring the nature of the two into the most extreme discord and so to establish their concord?* – Martin Heidegger, 'What Are Poets For?'

ONE

In August of 1987, on my way back to Edinburgh from Perugia, where Jacques Derrida had been speaking about *Glas,* I broke my journey at the village of Classe, the Civitas Classis where Caesar Augustus based his Adriatic navy and where, as my train pulled in, there came into view, writ large on the station name-board, a replica of the title of that quasi book in which one reads a citation from a dictionary telling us that among the many meanings of the word *classis* may be listed 'endlich, zu Augustus zeit, auch "gruppe von knaben, die gemeinsam unterrichtet werden." '1 🍃 My topic here will be the classes, departments, and faculties that, on a classical analysis, might be judged to be the foundation of the classes, departments, and faculties of the university. Although what I say has implications for the ancient question of where in the academy, if anywhere, poetry stands in relation to philosophy, I shall be so busy with the question of foundations that I shall be hard put to get to the superstructural question in the form it takes in the two texts that participants in this symposium have contracted to treat: in the words of our convener, 'our academic contract, the conflict of faculties in America.' In the sense that I guess was intended in this allusion to a conflict, I shall not be talking, except by implication and aided by a pun, about the conflict of academic faculties in Scotland. However, I can appeal to a Scottish university institution for a precedent for my remiss behavior, namely to the practice of those many distinguished professors who, having accepted the invitation to deliver the Gifford Lectures in Natural Theology, have deemed it sufficient to fulfill their contractual obligation

to treat of God if they just mentioned Him once in their opening remarks. Well, in my opening remarks I have mentioned the university.
And now, in the hope of covering all eventualities, I have also mentioned
God. Indeed, making some reparation for the parsimony of those
Gifford lecturers, I shall be speaking quite a lot, in one way or another,
about the Upper Case and lower case creators and their Upper Case and
lower case work. ॐ Midday was striking as I walked toward the basilica
of Saint Apollinaris in Classe carrying in my rucksack a copy of that
work (is it a work?) where one can read: '*classum* lärm,' then, among the
succeeding entries, 'glas "sonnerie de toutes les cloches d'une église" . . .
"gazouillement des oiseaux" . . . "son de trompette pour convoquer" '
and, eventually, '*glas d'emprunt* "glas pour une personne décédée hors
de la paroisse." '[2] These entries convoke Literature before Philosophy, the
topic of Derrida's lectures at Perugia, and the questions I raise again
here. Where does what gets classed by Heidegger as *Dichten*, great poetry
or art, stand in relation to what he means by *Denken*, philosophical or
prephilosophical or postphilosophical thinking of being? How does
what Heidegger says about *Dichten*, poiesis as distinct from poesy, that is
to say, from poetry in the narrower sense, stand up to what Emmanuel
Levinas says about art and how art stands in relation to what he means
by ethics?[3] *Dichten* and *Denken*, which, if either, is the handmaiden of
the other? If neither, what mistress or master, if any, do they serve? Is
there hope that the conflict, the *Auseinandersetzung* between Heidegger
and Levinas might be resolved, despite the fact that according to Heidegger philosophy as the thinking of being is prior to the division of philosophy into natural philosophy, theory of knowledge, logic, and ethics,
whereas according to Levinas ethics is prior to philosophy and indeed
ethics is metaphysics, and further, if by *physis* is meant being or what
since the Roman rethinking of Greek thinking we have come to know as
essence or nature, ethics is beyond the thinking of being, *meta ta phys-
ika?* Is there a sign of hope in the Hellenic, Roman, and Judeo-Christian
elements of the masterpiece of sixth-century mosaic art representing the
Transfiguration in the apse of the basilica at Classe? ॐ Among the rocks
and stones and trees of 'the high mountain apart' of Matthew 17.1, birds
sing and, each side of Saint Apollinaris, who is erect center stage, his
hands raised upward, sheep stroll, three for Peter, James, and John,
twelve for the Apostles or, on another interpretation, the twelve stems of
Israel. The face of the God-man appears in the middle of a cross sus-

pended between the green earth and a golden sky in which Moses is visible to the left and Elijah to the right, while all that is visible of the Cre-
ator is a hand reaching down through the clouds from the zenith of the
proscenium arch. At either side of the arch, just above the level of the
Corinthian capitals of the columns of the nave, the archangels Michael
and Gabriel hold standards on which are inscribed the words 'Hagios,
Hagios, Hagios,' which I propose we rewrite 'Qadosh, Hagios, Sanctus'
in memory of Heidegger's statement that the default of God and the di-
vinities is absence, but absence which is 'precisely the presence, which
must first be appropriated, of the hidden fullness and wealth of what has
been and what, thus gathered, is presencing, of the divine in the world
of the Greeks, in prophetic Judaism, in the preaching of Jesus.'[4] Holy,
*heilig, saint*. A basic word for Heidegger and Levinas. But if we asked
them what of what is represented in the representation at Classe is holy,
and whether the representation itself is, we should receive what Levinas
at least would seem to regard as irreconcilably different answers. He
has remarked that it is the holy with which he has been preoccupied
throughout his writing life, the ethical being the holy by another name.
He would agree that the writings of Heidegger too are concerned with
the holy, but he would insist that for Heidegger, as for Hölderlin, holiness is the holiness of the pagan gods, those gods who dwell, as Levinas
is fond of saying, like the gods of Epicurus, within the interstices of
being. How could there be a rapprochement between polytheistic ontology on the one hand and monotheistic ethics on the other? If, as Levinas
observes, the idea of the holy is the idea of that which is set apart, his
idea of the holy seems so set apart from Heidegger's that it would appear
pointless to try to bring them together. Let us nevertheless try, for even if
we fail, there is much to be learned from the attempt. ❧ As a lever let us
use the 'classical protocol,' referred to in Derrida's 'Mochlos,' of asking
after the conditions of the possibility of a conflict of faculties in the university.[5] By rights, we should go back as far as Plato's account of the concord of faculties of the person, of the classes in the state, and of the
classes of the academy where the philosopher-kings and their auxiliaries
would be educated. However, because 'Mochlos' was occasioned by an
anniversary and by Kant, and because in 1981, the anniversary of the first
edition of Kant's first *Critique*, I presumed to predict that most of the
reasons for celebrating that anniversary would remain reasons for celebrating the anniversary of the second edition in 1987, let us restrict our-

selves to Kant's theory of the concord of the faculties, to Kant's account of justice in the soul, but reading it with the help of Heidegger's interpretation of Kant.[6] One advantage of this procedure for our purposes is that Kant is one of the philosophers on whom Levinas too most frequently draws. Although it is Plato's allusion in the *Republic* to the *epekeina tēs ousias* and Descartes's *Meditations* that Levinas most often invokes when he argues that the idea of infinity that overflows its idea is the common root of theory and practice, he several times suggests that the Idea in a Kantian sense, of which Husserl made so much use, could be employed to similar effect. On Heidegger's reading of Kant's first *Critique*, the common root of theory and practice, of constation and performance, is the productive imagination. Kant describes this, it will be recalled, as 'an art (*Kunst*) concealed in the depths of the human soul, whose real modes of activity nature is hardly likely ever to allow us to discover.'[7] That is no more than what we can expect of nature, one can hear Levinas say. Have we not known for a long while that nature loves to conceal itself? And as for imagination being an art, indeed, art is artful. *Kunst* is cunning. So let us not put so much reliance on imagination, nature, and art. Let us look more to the infinitely overflowing eyes of the Other in which I am commanded 'Thou shalt not kill,' and where the Other's mortality takes precedence over my being toward my own death. ❧ When Heidegger delivered his inaugural lecture at Freiburg, Levinas would remind us, he was in a dilemma. In a lecture one makes assertions. But assertions are made about beings, events, and states of affairs, whereas what the freshly inducted professor of philosophy wanted to get across somehow to the students and teachers of various faculties sitting before him was that beings, events, and states of affairs presuppose being and the advent of being out of nothingness. Heidegger knew that he was hindering his audience from attending to what he felt they should care for above all. Levinas is aware that he himself is in a similar predicament when he begs to differ from Heidegger, contending that beyond being and nothingness is the ethical, beyond ontology and meontology is the metaphysical, metaphysiognomic visage which is invisible trace, the proximity of God in the face of my neighbor.[8] The blinding light that makes visibility possible cannot itself be the subject of a photograph, no matter how dark a filter may be used. It cannot be caught in an image. If an image is a representation, there can no more be an *imago Dei* than there can be an appearance of the appearing, a phenomenon of the *pha-*

*inesthai,* a said that says its saying. Only man, of whom Heidegger says that no one can substitute for him in his being toward death, can be an *imago Dei,* man, of whom Levinas says that he substitutes for the other mortal man by being responsible for the other's responsibilities, and, moreover, more responsible than anyone else, with a responsibility that increases without end as these responsibilities are met. Once this is understood, there can be no occasion for a crisis like that experienced by the young John Stuart Mill, brought on by the thought that he must answer No to the question 'Suppose that all your objects in life were realized; that all the changes in institutions and opinions which you are looking forward to, could be completely effected at this very instant: would this be a great joy and happiness to you?' Nor could there be any excuse for supposing that a cure for such a crisis could be found by taking down from the shelf the nature poetry of William Wordsworth. *Paysage,* paganism, poet and peasant can only ease the symptoms. The cause of the malaise is not removed until one grasps what Mill at best only glimpsed when he wrote in his autobiography that the source of his anxiety 'may, perhaps, be thought to resemble that of the philosophers of Laputa, who feared lest the sun should be burnt out.'[9] What Mill failed to face up to was the truth that the sun can never be burned out, not if it represents the unrepresentable Good beyond Being that is envisaged by metaphysical, ethical Desire, the Good which is also the Holy for Emmanuel Levinas. And for Immanuel Kant.

T W O

'Critique' as Kant uses the word distinguishes the faculties of mind and shows how these elements – sensibility, imagination, understanding, will, reason – should, but can fail, to cooperate. Man is fully person, he tells us in *Religion within the Limits of Reason Alone,* when he is fully rational, and that means fully responsible. In section 13 of *The Basic Problems of Phenomenology* (1927), Heidegger's rethinking of Kant (already under way in *Being and Time,* in lectures to be published in 1929 as *Kant and the Problem of Metaphysics,* and continued meanwhile in a course on Kant's first *Critique*) distinguishes moral personality, psychological personality, and transcendental personality. Transcendental personality is man's self-consciousness, his capacity to prefix 'I think' to any of his thoughts in the broad sense of thought that Descartes ascribes to *cogitatio* in one of his uses of that word. Hence among those thoughts of which man is conscious that he thinks them will be any thought he may have of his empirical nature, any thought whose object is or is in his inner sense, the temporal flow of his stream of consciousness. The transcendental personality manifests itself too with those *cogitationes* that Descartes includes under the heading of will, thus in any action that, in the Kantian sense of the term, is performed out of respect for the moral law. That is to say, the transcendental personality manifests itself in any action of the moral personality, in any act of practical reason. It would therefore seem in order to take this activity of combining my *cogitationes* to be what Kant means by the action he identifies with intelligence. And that may be what Kant would have said at the time of the composition of the *Critique of Pure Reason*. The combining Kant is primarily interested in there is the combining of *cogitationes* treated as representations. But, Heidegger says in his study of Schelling's *Essay on the Essence of Human Freedom*, between writing the first *Critique* and the second, Kant comes to see that the real nature of the I is not the representative 'I think' of the Cartesian ego or the Leibnizian monad, but the 'I act,' *ich handle*.[10] Or, as Heidegger also says in the same place, Kant comes to see the 'I represent' as 'I act.' The idea *(Vorstellung)* is understood in terms of the freedom in which I give myself the law from the ground of my being and in which the I is truly together with itself. Indeed, although he does not fully realize it, Kant is some distance along this path when in the first *Critique* he maintains that I am conscious of the spontaneity of my intelligence even though this consciousness does not amount to knowledge. It does not amount to knowledge because for there to be knowledge the categories must be applied to data presented under the form of inner sense, time. As the Transcendental Aesthetic of the first *Critique* maintains, time is the form only, and only the form, of what is capable of being given in empirical or pure intuition, so I can have knowledge only of my psychological self which, Kant says (in Heidegger's opinion too hastily), is the self only as object. Kant does not grasp that although the categories temporalized by schematism do not apply to the self as subject, that is, as the agent which applies the categories, a more original temporality might enable us to supplement the categories through which we understand the given object with existentials through which we understand the giving, the *es gibt*, the being of spontaneous subjectivity. ❧ Heidegger argues that although Kant fails to work out a way of describing the unity of the theoretical and practical ego, this deficiency can be met by following guidelines laid down by Kant, in particular in his interpretation of the phenomenon of respect. Heidegger's claim to be able to arrive in this way at an ontology of the self presupposed by the distinction between theory and practice is not without paradox. It is doubly paradoxical, because a superficial reading of the first and the second critiques might lead one to conclude that Kant limits respect to practical reason, and because what he says about it is usually classed as moral psychology and could be expected to have little to offer to a thinker who, heeding Plato's warning that, instead of taking faculty psychology too seriously, we must take the long philosophical way around, had already written at length decrying psychologism. Yet Heidegger says that 'Kant's interpretation of the phenomenon of respect is probably the most brilliant phenomenological analysis of the phenomenon of morality that we have from him.'[11] If it is initially surprising that Heidegger seizes upon Kant's analysis of respect as a clue, we should bear in mind that his application of that analysis is a reapplication of some of the thoughts suggested to him by the doctrine of transcendental schematism sketched out by Kant in the first *Critique*. Those thoughts were later to be published in Heidegger's 1929 book on Kant. That book contains too some reflections on respect, and these in turn should be kept in mind as we read what is said on that topic in *The Basic Problems of Phenomenology*.[12] ❧ Respect is, in Heidegger's phrase, 'subjugative self-elevation,' *unterwerfende Sicherhaben*. As Kant himself says, the feeling of respect for the moral law is at one and the same time something like inclination and something like fear. We feel diminished and threatened when we compare our all-too-human humanity with the demand made by the moral law. We are upraised at the thought that submission to the moral law is a giving of oneself to what one is *par excellence*, a giving of oneself to 'the hero in one's soul.'[13] Respect, Kant says, strikes down self-love and self-conceit. However, there is a danger that in this striking down one form of self-love and self-conceit will be usurped by another kind unless we keep in view that although 'Respect always goes to persons only, not to things,' 'Respect for a person is properly only respect for the law (of honesty, etc.) of which he gives an example.'[14] This danger is only brushed under the carpet by Kant's insistence that I can never be sure that I myself and anyone else have acted from a moral motive and that therefore what we respect is the law which is *capable of* being adopted as the principle determining a person's will, a good will being, in Heideggerian terms, a possible modification of *Dasein,* the being that is the there, 'as we are *able* to be own to ourselves.'[15] Ignorance of whether I have ever been determined in my action by the moral law does not clear away the danger that self-love arising from turning a blind eye to the law may be succeeded by pride at the thought that I am capable of following it. On the other hand, if this latter danger is reduced by consciousness that respect for a person, hence self-respect, is properly only respect for the moral law, another danger looms for an interpretation of Kant that would see in his account of respect the promise of an ontology of the self. The risk now is that the law will be *too other* than self to be capable of grounding an ontology of the self. This risk is a threat to the possibility of an existential ontology based on Kant's doctrine of respect, not, like the other two, a threat to the possibility of moral behavior or what Heidegger holds to be its pre-moral condition, authenticity. Fortunately for Heidegger's project, these risks can be circumvented. We see that this is so as soon as we realize that Heidegger's ontology draws neither simply on the moral law nor simply on human sentiment, but on that special ambiguous sentiment, 'analogous to other sentiments,' of which Kant says no person can be destitute without ceasing to be a person.[16] ❧ The moral law is the object of a complex feeling, aspects of which are analogous to inclination and fear. If, with Heidegger, we understand inclination and fear as dispositions to seek and avoid, we have already taken a step away from the view that feelings are occurrent, extant or present at hand psychological states, a view Kant takes when he regards the psychological personality as a continuum of empirical states and processes. Feelings and moods – how we find ourselves *(wie wir uns befinden, comment on se trouve)* – are understandable only in terms of ways of comporting ourselves in the world. This is a break with one variety or aspect of psychologism. But this break is not one that has to do specifically with respect as compared with other feelings or emotions. Further, when Kant maintains that inclination or attraction and fear are only analogues of the conflicting dispositions combined in respect, he is concerned to underline that the motivation to and from distinctive of respect is intellectual. Heidegger interprets this intellectuality of respect by means of the existential notion of *Verstehen* described in *Being and Time,* just as he interprets the feeling of respect along the lines of the existential notion of *Befindlichkeit* described there. So that 'in respect I myself *am* – am *acting,*' 'ich selbst bin.' Here we do well to recall that in *Being and Time* and the *History of the Concept of Time* Heidegger speaks of an etymological connection between *bin* and *bei* and *innan,* words connoting dwelling and the home. In the 'Letter on Humanism' he associates the word *ethos* with these ideas.[17] This is important for our understanding of the debate between Heidegger and Levinas. It reveals that although Heidegger emphasizes that his thinking treats of what precedes the distinction of philosophy into logic, ethics, etc., he is treating of what can provisionally be called the ontology of ethics. His project is obviously not to develop a system of ethics as such. But the same can be said of Levinas. However strongly Levinas would resist the suggestion that he is developing an ontology of ethics, the ethical metaphysics that is his avowed concern has in common with Heidegger's reflections on *ethos* and *oikos* a radicality that means that they are for the most part dealing with the same question. When Levinas maintains that the ethical, in his sense of that word, is prior to ontology and the thinking of being, the impact of his argument cannot be accurately gauged unless we remember that Heidegger's topic is in a broad sense ethical, just as he is working toward a deeper understanding of humanism. Although the senses that Heidegger and Levinas give to their key words may differ, and although they differ violently over the scope of the words 'being' and 'ontology,' the question at issue between them cannot be seen in its proper perspective unless we notice the degree to which they share the same vocabulary. Recognition of this sharpens the point of their dispute. And the terms of that dispute are often terms they have carried over from their reading of Kant. 'Respect,' though not a term that Levinas employs frequently, is one that is associated in Kant and in Heidegger's reflections on Kant with terms that Levinas does employ frequently: 'responsibility,' 'holy,' and 'conscience.' We shall now consider each of these with a view to making clearer the extent of agreement and disagreement between Heidegger and Levinas as made manifest in the light of their reflections on Kant. It will become clear later how the tie these three notions have with the Kantian notion of moral respect helps to articulate a Heideggerian notion of ontological respect and how this relates to Levinas's notion of responsibility. ❧ Heidegger appeals to Kant's account of respect to support the claim made in *Being and Time* for the *Jemeinigkeit* of *Dasein.* The moral feeling, like other feelings, is a feeling-of or feeling-for which is at the same time a self-feeling. I feel myself feeling. As Descartes says, *cogito me sentire.* But, against Descartes, Heidegger maintains that this self-feeling is a direct self-having,[18] not an intuitive knowledge, and not reflective in the sense that implies a bending back. In the case of the direct self-feeling of moral feeling, respect, I know myself as responsible. 'Respect reveals the dignity before which and for which the self knows itself to be responsible. Only in responsibility does the ego reveal itself – the self not in a general sense as knowledge of an ego in general but as in each case mine *(als je meines)*, the ego as in each case the individual factical ego.'[19] Here Heidegger has recourse to the Kantian teaching on responsibility to help him spell out his reasons for rejecting the neo-Kantian, particularly Rickertian, gloss according to which Kant's logical ego is a nameless abstraction. The strength of this rejection depends, however, on the demonstration that the logical ego, that is, the transcendental unity of self-consciousness that Heidegger calls transcendental personality, is one with what he calls the moral personality. As long as that demonstration is accepted, Heidegger's argument for the concreteness of the Kantian ego can be supported by drawing our and Rickert's attention to the order of proceeding in Kant's *Groundwork* where the analysis has as its point of departure the concrete experience of the difference between prudential and moral necessity. Heidegger would add that it is important not to forget that the freedom and responsibility to which Kant believes we are committed by this *Faktum* of pure practical reason is not confined to virtuous action, but is the ontological freedom and responsibility that is the definition and vocation of personality as such, and is revealed in the respect for the moral law felt by the most vicious among us. In respect we know ourselves because respect, unlike other feelings, is self-wrought, *selbstgewirkt*. (Kant subscribes to a version of the Viconian *verum-factum* principle: we can know only what we make.) Hence 'mineness' is the ground no less of inauthentic than of authentic self-understanding.[20] This existential-ontological distinction between inauthenticity and authenticity corresponds to Kant's ontic-ethical distinction between heteronomy and autonomy. However, it is not especially on account of the mineness of *Dasein* that Heidegger makes a connection between his ontology and Kant's metaphysics of morals. Rather is it on account of the structure of *Dasein*'s mineness as *Dasein*'s being for the sake of its own self, *umwillen seiner selbst*. ❦ *Dasein*'s mineness is the existential-ontological ground of formal or logical self-identity and of ontological identity in the traditional sense of ontology that classifies according to

categories and according to the opposition of substance or essence
and predicate or property; this is what Heidegger means by 'formal-
ontological' here. Mineness is the phenomenological-ontological belonging of each *Dasein* to itself, its existed having of itself. ✿ *Dasein*'s
being for the sake of its own self, Heidegger writes, 'is the structural moment that motivated Kant to define the person ontologically as an end,
without inquiring into the specific structure of purposiveness and the
question of ontological possibility.'[21] Otherwise stated, Kant's doctrine
that the person is an end in itself begins, but only begins, to acknowledge that *Dasein* is a possibility-of-being, a *Seinkönnen,* whose unifying
principle is *Sorge,* care. I say 'end in *it*self' to mark the earlier-mentioned
fact that respect for persons is respect for the moral law. Personality on
Kant's account of it is distinguished by its impersonality. This being so, it
is difficult to see how this can be reconciled with the for-the-sake-of-
itselfness of *Dasein* that Heidegger's reading of Kant discovers in the
Critical doctrine, unless this is located on the animal side of the rational
animal, the side of which the principle is not the moral law, but the interest in the attainment of happiness. This is a difficulty Levinas sees in
Kant, one he tries to overcome by working out an analysis of concrete,
personal me-ness that is not based on the quest for happiness, but on rationality understood through the face-to-face encounter in which my
subjectivity is my ethical subjection to the Other's accusative regard. ✿
This difficulty for the interpretation of Kant that Heidegger advances in
his Marburg years against the Marburg and South-West German Neo-
Kantians looms too in Heidegger's statement in *The Metaphysical Foundations of Logic* that 'selfhood is free responsibility for and toward itself.'
It is followed half a page later by a statement that enables us to see in relief another deep difference between Heidegger and Levinas. Heidegger
writes: 'The surpassing of the factic beings that is peculiar to the world
as such, and thereby to transcendence and freedom corresponds to the
*epekeina.* In other words, the world itself is surpassive *(übertrifftig):*
beings of *Dasein*'s character are distinguished by overleaping *(Über-
schwung).*'[22] Here again is the Platonic *epekeina tēs ousias,* but with a difference, a difference not only from Plato, but a difference from Levinas.
The difference from Levinas is made all the more poignant by the presence in Heidegger's text at this point not only of this Platonic phrase
that Levinas too likes to quote, but also of the phrase 'primary in-
satiability,' where the noun is the one Levinas uses to describe the fact

that ethical Desire never achieves even momentary satisfaction, since the more I heed my responsibilities to the other man the more responsibility comes my way. The excession that Heidegger is describing, on the other hand, is not, like that to which Levinas refers, an excession beyond being. It is an excession beyond beings, but not beyond being. That for the sake of which personality acts, according to Kant, is the good will, and ultimately the highest good, which calls for the perfect accordance of the mind with the moral law. On Kant's interpretation of 'the moral destination of our nature,' there can be only an endless progress toward the *summum bonum* thanks to our acting out of respect for the moral law. And, he says, the moral law is holy. That is what he writes in the second *Critique*. In the *Opus Postumum* he writes: 'The highest ideal as person (of which there can be only one) is God.'[23] The words, at least, are the ones Levinas might well use, provided the asymmetry between the Other and myself be preserved, and ethical heteronomy, that is, my being the Other's servant without his being mine, is given priority over the autonomy that immediately implies universal impersonalism in the ethical teaching of Kant. Clearly, even though on Kant's teaching God would be a citizen of the Kingdom of Ends, he is also a Sovereign according to Kant's theory. So the Idea of God can be borrowed from Kant's theory by Levinas to help him explain what he means by saying that infinity is invested in the other man. This appeal to God is not theological in Kant or in Levinas. It is ethical, and religious only to the extent that religion and obligation have in common the idea of a bond. In Heidegger's thinking, certainly that of the 1920s and early 1930s, the very idea of a God, ethical or theological, would be the idea of a being or of beingness, and therefore beside the point of fundamental ontology. Similarly with the notion of Goodness. In Kant this notion, along with the idea of the *ought*, is sharply distinguished from the notion of what is, even though theoretical reason turns out to presuppose practical Ideas, for example, the Idea of freedom which Kant analyzes in terms of the *ought*. That gives priority to the ethical, rather as Levinas does. It would be quite mistaken to say that Heidegger gives priority to the theoretical, since he is concerned to expose to view, as far as that is possible, the common root of theory and practice. What Heidegger gives priority to is being. Allowance made for this rethinking of the tradition, he belongs, and Levinas does not want to belong, to the tradition that says, in Meister Eckhart's words, not only of goodness, but of holiness and the divine,

'Goodness depends on being, for if there were no being there could be no goodness, and thus being is purer than goodness.'[24] ❧ On Heidegger's rethinking of this tradition, however, goodness and in general value are not subordinated to being hierarchically. What follows from it is that value and obligation are no longer regarded as tertiary properties superimposed upon the primary and secondary qualities of things or upon the 'good-making' characteristics of human dispositions or actions, but are seen to be formative of the very structure of being in the world. That is another way of saying that ontological ethos is prior to the distinction between theory and practice, and it explains why Heidegger says that an authentic way of being in the world is a responsible, careful, resolved and open *(ent-schlossen)* way of responding to the call of being. ❧ There is a paradoxical alienness in this call which has analogues in the thinking of Levinas and Kant. In *Religion within the Limits of Reason Alone,* Kant distinguishes three classes or elements in the calling *(Bestimmung)* of man or, more precisely, 'of the original disposition for good in human nature': the disposition to animality of man as a *living* being, the disposition of *humanity* in man taken as living and at the same time as *rational,* and the disposition to *personality* as a rational and at the same time responsible and accountable being. This classification is made according to the functions or ends of man. So the first does not refer to life in general, life such as is manifest in creatures with a vegetable soul, plants. Nor, apparently, can the animality or animateness intended be that which man shares with nonhuman animals. For although Kant says that *Tierheit* is physical and mechanical self-love that manifests itself in the instinct for self-preservation, propagation of the species, and the social impulse, which we might call gregariousness, he associates with these various vices, for example the coarseness of drunkenness, sensuality, and lawlessness in regard to other human beings. True, he describes these as 'beastly' or 'brutish' vices, but we all do that without implying that they can be imputed to nonhuman animals and that to them can be attributed the corresponding virtues. Thus the animality of Kant's first class encroaches upon the humanity of the second.[25] ❧ As for this second class, it raises the question how humanity can be an *element* in the constitution, condition, definition, destiny, or calling of man. Is not humanness rather the whole, all there is to humanness? Is not humanity tautologically the whole duty of man, the wholeness, *Heiligkeit,* of his calling? Kant must be using the word *Mensch* in a wider and narrower sense, the wider sense being that of which each division mentions an aspect, the narrower sense being that specified in the second class, man's all-too-human humanness. Like the predisposition to animality, this predisposition to humanness or humanity is natural self-love, but whereas the predisposition to animality is mechanical *(mechanisch)*, the predisposition to humanity is comparative *(vergleichend)*. It is concerned with whether we are more or less happy than others. This concern gives rise first to an interest in acquiring at least equal esteem, and then, when we become aware that others seek to be esteemed above us, to an interest in being esteemed above them. The vices correlated with humanity are vices of culture, and in their extreme forms of envy, ingratitude and malice, they are described as devilish, that is, their evil is thought of as going beyond humanity, as being manifestations of man's inhumanity to man. Like the so-called beastly vices, they are abuses of humanity in the generic sense of the word. Unlike them, they and their correlated nondeviant uses are abuses and uses of reason, specifically reason employed as an instrument toward the satisfaction of physical desire, as ancilla of the passions. As in Kant's philosophy of theory the imagination's schematism participates in both the particularity of sensibility and the universality of intellectuality and is the medium through which the one is applied to the other in what the *Critique of Judgment* calls determinant, as opposed to reflective judgment, so humanity participates in man's animality and in the predisposition in which man manifests reason *par excellence*, the predisposition to personality. ❧ Unlike his predispositions to humanity and animality, man's predisposition to personality is not one upon which vices can be grafted. Hence, when this predisposition becomes a motive for man's elective will, that will is, as Kant says in the *Groundwork*, the only thing that is good without qualification. In the *Groundwork* Kant also says, in a passage reproduced by Heidegger, that 'man *and every rational being* exists as an end in himself; and not merely as a means to be used arbitrarily by this or that will.' That is, Kant wishes not to limit rationality to human beings. But if the rationality of superhuman beings is what commands human respect, how, we must ask, can it be true, as Heidegger says in interpreting Kant, that 'what constitutes the nature of the person, its essentia, . . . is an object of respect,' that 'Conversely, that which is objective in respect, what is revealed in it, makes manifest the personality of the person,' and that 'This interpretation of the personalitas moralis first makes clear what man is and defines his quidditas, man's essential nature, the rigorous concept of *Menschheit*, humanity'?[26] How can what is essentially superhuman according to the classification of humanity in *Religion within the Limits of Reason Alone* nevertheless be the essence of humanity? It is not just, as Suarez expresses it, that the human intellect is a mean between the angelic intellect and sense, or, as Kant himself says in the *Critique of Practical Reason*, 'The person as belonging to the sensible world is subject to his own personality as belonging to the intelligible' so that man is elevated (*erhoben*) above himself 'as part of the world of sense.' He is elevated above himself, it would seem, as human, that is, 'as living and at the same time *rational*.'[27] One is reminded of Aristotle's statement in *De Generatione Animalium*, which describes the active intellect as though it comes from without, almost as though it were identified with God, *leipetai de ton noun monon thurathen epeisienai kai theion enai monon* (2.3.736b28; cf. *De Anima* 3.5.430a10). This is not irrelevant to the question, asked by Kant in *The Conflict of the Faculties*, whether the philosophical faculty is ancillary to the faculty of theology or whether the latter is auxiliary to the former, a question in the answering of which it would not be irrelevant to recall Hegel's assertion in the Logic of the *Encyclopaedia*, with reference to logic, that 'the superexcellent is also the most useful, because it is the all-sustaining principle which, having a subsistence of its own, may therefore serve as the vehicle of special ends which it furthers and secures. And thus, special ends, though they have no right to be set first, are still fostered by the presence of the highest good.'[28] Mention of Hegel is relevant here for another reason also. Is not the anticipatory imbrication of the classification drawn up by Kant in *Religion within the Limits of Reason Alone* an anticipation of the dynamics of Hegelian dialectic? If religion is within the limits of reason, reason too seems to be within the limits of religion. In *Le Malheur de la conscience dans la philosophie de Hegel*, in connection with what Hegel says in the section on the spirit of Judaism in *The Spirit of Christianity*, Jean Wahl writes: 'If it is true that there is a need in man to surpass himself – and it is that which explains why it is possible for there to be a phenomenology of religious consciousness – it is none the less true that there have always been certain spirits for whom this being that is higher than man is absolutely separate from him.' Kant's *epekeina* is not that separate. It is both contrasted with humanity and identified with it, a predicament that is encapsulated in the statement that 'man . . . must regard *humanity in his own person* as *holy,*' as though the study of man's rationality, hence of his philosophical faculty, would be the study of God, and as though the philosophical faculty and the faculty of theology were inside and outside each other.[29] ❧ If the holy is the separate, as Levinas maintains, Kant's statement that man must regard humanity in his own person as holy anticipates Heidegger's reference to the way in which *Dasein* is foreign to itself, *fremd* and *übertrifftig* in its very own home, as expressed in his statement that the voice of conscience is both my voice and yet comes from above and beyond.[30]

### THREE

*Der Ruf kommt aus mir und doch über mich.* According to Kant the call of, from, and to conscience is the call of reason, whereas according to the Heidegger of *Being and Time* the call is of being and to the care of being. According to Levinas conscience is the voice of the Other, not of being. But it has the same angle of incidence. It tells me that the Other is nearer God than I am.[31] The Other is not *da,* indeterminately here or there, but *illic.* He is over and up there. I am his humble servant, even if, paradoxically, it is his humility that gives him the majesty and height from which his eyes teach me that I am with respect to him perpetually *in statu pupillari.* According to Kant the call is from and to rationality, and because for him rationality is freedom of the will, the call would appear to be a recall to that from which conscience, as understood by Levinas, would call us away: the 'I can' of the ego persisting in its will to life and power. This appearance is false. For, as we have seen, the Kantian account of personality is given in terms of reason and a moral law which, far from inflating the ego, deflates it to the point of impersonality. Levinas aims to show that such impersonality is inconsistent with the ethical. This is one reason why Heidegger's interpretation of Kant is so significant. It offsets the threat of anonymity by underlining *Dasein*'s *Jemeinigkeit* and being toward death. There is no denying that neither in Kant nor in Heidegger is the mortality of the other human being given priority over my own as it is by Levinas. Still, in Kant's metaphysics of morals respect for the moral law does bring with it the idea of a kingdom of ends, and if Heidegger takes this seriously then what both he and Kant refer to as the proper or authentic self (Kant uses the phrase 'das eigentliche Selbst' in the *Groundwork,* for example) will be a being that is ontologically being-with, whatever the ontic circumstances.[32] Although being toward death may set *Dasein* apart from the inauthentic self of *das Man,* this does not mean – as translating *'das Man'* by 'the they-self' could lead the unwary reader to think – that *Dasein* is isolated from others in authentic being toward death. Heidegger writes: '*Dasein* in itself is essentially Being-with.' He also writes: 'The expression "Dasein," however, shows plainly that "in the first instance" this entity is unrelated to Others, and that of course it can still be "with" Others afterwards.'[33] What follows from these statements taken together is that although ontically *Dasein* may be on its own, ontologically *Dasein* is with Others. Later on in *Being and Time* he says: 'As the non-relational possibility, death individualizes – but only in such a manner that, as the possibility which is not to be outstripped, it makes *Dasein,* as Being-with, have some understanding of the potentiality-for-Being of Others.' The qualifying clause is important. Evidently, the nonrelationality of my being toward my death no more cuts me off from others than it cuts me off from myself. What it cuts me off from is the purely general possibility of the 'one,' *das Man,* the merely constated fact that one dies, like Caius, Socrates, and so on. Heidegger emphasizes that '*Dasein* is authentically itself only to the extent that, as concernful Being-alongside and solicitous Being-with, it projects itself upon its ownmost potentiality-for-Being rather than upon the possibility of the they-self.'[34] The other has to die his own death *von ihm selbst,* but that does not exclude my being solicitous that he should not die alone, where a lack of such solicitude would for Levinas be tantamount to going against the spirit of the injunction 'Thou shalt not kill.' ❧ Further, the Heideggerian interpretation of Kant goes some way toward discovering in conscience and respect what it would not be entirely inappropriate to characterize as, in the phrase Levinas uses to describe ethical encounter, a passivity more passive than the passivity that is contrasted with activity in traditional thinking about faculties and powers. The voice of conscience is a middle voice, according to Heidegger, the Greek voice that he finds most appropriate to express the mood of the phenomenological thinking called for in *Being and Time,* a thinking that must be a cooperative and vigilant listening obedience.[35] 'Listening-to . . . is *Dasein*'s existential way of Being-open as Being-with for Others.'[36] Here and in the paragraph immediately following this sentence in *Being and Time* the words used are *hören* and *horchen,* where along with the idea of hearkening it is difficult not to hear overtones of heed, *gehorchen.* Here Heidegger is himself heeding the demand that phenomenology must return to the things themselves, and heeding what is said about this heed to the things themselves by Hegel when, speaking in the *Encyclopaedia* about attention or heed *(Aufmerksamkeit)*, he writes that

*it demands an effort since a man, if he wants to apprehend one particular object, must make abstraction from everything else, from all the thousand and one things going round in his head, from his other interests, even from his own person; he must suppress his own conceit which would rashly judge the subject-matter, not allowing it to speak for itself* [mit Unterdrücken seiner die Sache nicht zu Worte kommen lassenden], *must stubbornly absorb himself in the subject-matter, must fix his attention on it and let it have its say* [in sich walten lassen] *without obtruding his own reflections. Attention contains, therefore, the* negation *of* one's self-assertiveness *and also the* surrender of oneself *to the* matter in hand.[37]

The vigilance of Heidegger's attention to what Hegel says here reveals itself in the fact that in *Being and Time* conscience *(Gewissen)* is connected with certainty *(Gewissheit)*, and thus its phenomenology of conscience is by implication connected with and disconnected from the dialectic of self-certainty worked out in the *Phenomenology of Spirit* where, in the chapter on absolute knowing, Hegel writes that conscience knows that its existence as such is pure certainty of itself: *es weiss, dass sein* Dasein *als solches diese reine Gewissheit seiner selbst ist.* For Heidegger too, *Dasein*, which in *Being and Time* is always the existing of a capability (old-style 'faculty') of being, a *Seinkönnen*, is indeed capable of self-certainty, but this is the certainty of its existing toward its own death. ❧ The existed possibility which is being toward death is, Heidegger says, a possibility of impossibility. It is the possibility of nonbeing, and, because, as the 'Letter on Humanism' says, 'nihiling is the essence of Being,' this is precisely why it can open *Dasein*'s eyes to the possibility of there being more than and other than the common, universal beingness of beings like the entities that preoccupied the members of the faculty of science sitting in the Aula Maxima of the University of Freiburg when Heidegger delivered his inaugural lecture 'What Is Metaphysics?' Hence, when Heidegger says 'in anticipation *Dasein* can first make certain of its ownmost Being in its totality – a totality which is not to be outstripped,' the totality here referred to is not a well-rounded whole, but a detotalized totality, at least for authentic *Dasein*. The hermeneutic circularity in which *Dasein* is at home is one in which *Dasein* is not at home. The circle is a broken circle. The home is a broken home. Its home is supplemented by the unhomely and its sameness disseminated by alterity. *Dasein*'s enclosure is at the same time dis-closure, *Entschliessen*, and disclosure, *Erschliessen*, of the finitude of its indefinite certainty.[38] This explains the careful ambiguity of some of Heidegger's sentences about the possibility of death, as when he writes: 'The certain possibility of death, however, discloses *Dasein* as a possibility, but does so in such a way that, in anticipating this possibility, *Dasein makes* this possibility *possible (ermöglicht)* for itself as its ownmost potentiality-for-Being.'[39] As the translators John Macquarrie and Edward Robinson explain, although they have taken 'Die gewisse Möglichkeit des Todes' to be the subject of the sentence, 'das Dasein' could be taken as the subject instead. There is good reason to think that Heidegger wanted to leave open the possibility of a double reading here. Likewise in the sentence two sections further on: 'To lay bare the "upon-which" of a projection, amounts to disclosing that which makes possible what has been projected.'[40] As the translators again point out, 'what is projected,' *das Entworfene*, can be taken as subject or object of 'makes possible,' *ermöglicht*, and, as before, there is good reason to take it at one and the same time as both. In his translation of the 'Letter on Humanism,' Roger Munier draws attention to the link between *möglich*, meaning 'possible,' and *mögen*, meaning 'to like' or 'to love' (or 'to desire'?).[41] He could well have added that *aimant* means both 'loving' and 'magnet,' an association that it would be difficult to justify on etymological grounds, but one that conveys the idea expressed in the dictum that has played so significant a role in the case for the utilitarian analysis of ethics, 'Nothing is desired except *sub specie boni.*' Whatever we desire or like or love must appear attractive in some way. This idea involves a bi-directionality similar to that intended in Heidegger's notion of letting being be, except that *Seinlassen* is not a reciprocity of beings solely, hence not a neutral state intermediate between action and passion. ❦ Once more there is reason to think that there is some agreement between Heidegger and Levinas on topic, notwithstanding their disagreement over what should be said about it. They are not talking at cross-purposes all the time. Thus, we see here that they are both trying to bring out what is neither a mixture or colloid compounded of action and passion, nor an ethico-legal analogue, namely systematic justice, but the ground or *Abgrund* without which neither this classical opposition nor unviolent justice can obtain. However, one cannot help wondering whether Levinas occasionally mistakes what Heidegger says about the everyday way of being in the world for a description at the level of what makes that possible; as when, recalling what Heidegger says about the priority of readiness to hand over presence at hand, he speaks of *praxis* as though Heidegger's fundamental ontology were a transplantation to the Black Forest of Sartrian existentialism or the pragmatism of Dewey or James. Heidegger does state that 'thinking is a deed *(ein Tun)*.'[42] He adds immediately, however, that it is a deed that goes beyond *(übertrifft)* all *praxis*. Of course, by the time of the 'Letter on Humanism,' in which these statements are made and in which Heidegger explicitly distances himself from Sartre, Heidegger has come to believe that what he here means by the thinking that arises before the distinction between theory and practice should no longer be called by the traditional name of ontology, even if that name be qualified by the adjective 'fundamental,' as it is in *Being and Time*. Metaphysical ontology, including that of Kantian Criticism, is conceptual. What Heidegger now calls essential thinking attempts to think unconceptually the truth, *a-lētheia*, that is to say, the unconcealing of being. And this thinking of being is a thinking of being where the 'of' is a double genitive.[43] Heidegger also advises his reader that in spite of the dangers involved in continuing to employ the terms 'ontology' and 'ethics,' there is still room to ask the question as to the relation between ontology and ethics, the question that taxed Jean Beaufret, the recipient of the 'Letter,' provided that the question be thought in a more original way. The more original thinking called for leads Heidegger to suspend temporarily the use of the word *Ermöglichung* to express the notion of making possible. (One of his reasons for doing this may be that he feels that the prefix *er-* leans too far toward the activity side of the opposition between activity and passion, but in that case one wonders why he later resumes the use of this word. That is a question that cannot be answered without close textual comparison that cannot be undertaken here.) He does not suspend employment of the term *das Mög-liche*, with its play between the idea of possibility and *mögen*, to be disposed toward favorably. But he now introduces *Vermögen*. This word does not appear in the glossary of German expressions drawn up by Macquarrie and Robinson in their translation of *Being and Time*, nor is it listed in Hildegard Feick's index to that book. However, it reappears in what it is natural to think of as the projected third part of *Being and Time*, namely the essay published in 1969 under the heading 'Time and Being.'[44] There Heidegger refers to his statement in the 'Letter on Humanism' that 'The *esti gar einai* of Parmenides is still unthought today.'[45] It is unthought if Parmenides' saying is interpreted literally as 'Being is,' since that implies that only of a being does it hold that it is. And Parmenides' saying is still unthought if we translate *esti* only, as the 'Letter on Humanism' does, by 'It allows,' unless we pick up the *Es gibt* implicit in it which gives it the quiet force of donation and gift, as expressed by the words *kraft* and *vermöge*, in the sense of 'thanks to . . . ,' 'grâce à. . . .' Only then do we take the long route around from the psychology of faculties, potentialities, and powers of the *animal rationale* which, on a superficial understanding, are denoted by the noun *Vermögen*. ᕤ It is to be expected that in a letter on humanism one should come across the word that Kant uses of the transcendental parallels he draws to the empirical faculties that make up human nature. *Vermögen* and *Fähigkeit* are classical words for classifying man's powers. This is why what Heidegger does with the word *Vermögen* in the 'Letter on Humanism' has such wide repercussions. The term traditionally used in psychology and metaphysics for what in his earlier vocabulary Heidegger calls an ontic faculty such as the faculty of hearing or sight is being asked to perform a role in what according to that earlier vocabulary is called ontology. In the essay 'Wie wenn am Feiertage . . .' (1939–40) to which Heidegger refers the reader of the 'Letter on Humanism,' *vermögen* and *vermag* are used several times intransitively with the meaning of 'is able,' for example, pages 59, 64, 65, and 71 of the *Gesamtausgabe* edition of *Erläuterungen zu Hölderlins Dichtung*, but on page 65 the word *vermögen* is employed with the transitive meaning of 'to enable,' the meaning which, as suggested earlier, is expressed more actively perhaps by *ermöglichen*.[46] However, *ermöglichen* is employed in the same lecture (e.g., p.62) and in later works, for example in the lecture 'The Essence of Language' (1957), in conjunction with *Möglichkeit* as in the duple, reversible sentences cited from *Being and Time* earlier in this essay. ᕤ In 'The Essence of Language' Heidegger writes: 'Anything that gives us room and allows us to do something gives us a possibility, that is, it gives what enables us. 'Possibility' *(Möglichkeit)* so understood, as what enables *(das Ermöglichende)*, means something else than mere opportunity *(Chance)*.'[47] The aim here is an aim that shapes the whole of Heidegger's thinking: to find a way of saying the *lassen* of *Seinlassen* and *Gelassenheit* in which the *lassen* is audible in what the following sentences from the 'Letter on Humanism' say regarding *Vermögen* and the Element, where, it should be noted, the meanings of these two words are already stretched well beyond the meanings they have in Kant's Critical theory of the elements of knowledge: 'To enable something here means to preserve it in its essence, to maintain it in its element.'[48]

*Thinking comes to an end when it slips out of its element. The element is what enables thinking to be thinking. The element is what properly enables: the enabling. It embraces thinking and so brings it into its essence. Said plainly, thinking is the thinking of Being. The genitive says something twofold. Thinking is of Being inasmuch as thinking, coming to pass from Being, belongs to Being, listens to Being* [vom Sein ereignet, dem Sein gehört].

And, as Heidegger says, thinking 'lets that toward which it goes come toward it *(lässt das, worauf es geht, auf sich zukommen).*'[49] *Lassen*, although the word has an etymological tie with 'lassitude' (which, in view of Levinas's discussion of lassitude in *Existence and Existents,* is a matter of some import for any attempt to understand what is at stake in Levinas's response to Heidegger), is (to use another of Levinas's key words) vigilant *(ahnend)* mourning.[50] The 'let' of *lassen* is the 'let' of the optative subjunctive in the lines from 'Wie wenn am Feiertage . . .' that Heidegger quotes:

*Jezt aber tagts! Ich harrt und sah es kommen,*
*Und was ich sah, das Heilige sei mein Wort.*

But now day breaks! I awaited and saw it coming,
And what I saw, the holy may my word be.

This optative 'may' is not an imperative demand. Its mood can be expressed by a part of the verb some of whose forms we have been discussing, namely by *möge* (which has the same root as 'may'), as in 'Möge das Heilige mein Wort sein,' which is perhaps what Levinas would call a 'prière sans demande.'[51] 🍂 Heidegger's lifelong attention to the question of how to read the saying of Parmenides, *to gar auto noein estin te kai einai,* which we so quickly translate 'Thinking and Being are one,' discloses to him, if not to us, that the thinking of being that lets being be is something close to thanking and not far removed from prayer.[52]

NOTES

1. Jacques Derrida, *Glas* (Paris: Denoël/Gonthier, 1981), p.124.

2. Ibid.

3. Martin Heidegger, *Poetry, Language, Thought,* trans. Albert Hofstadter (New York: Harper and Row, 1971). Emmanuel Levinas, 'Reality and Its Shadow,' *Collected Philosophical Papers,* trans. Alphonso Lingis (Dordrecht: Nijhoff, 1987), pp.1–13.

4. Heidegger, *Poetry,* p.184.

5. Jacques Derrida, 'Mochlos; ou, le conflit des facultés,' *Philosophie* 2 (April 1984), 30.

6. John Llewelyn, 'Heidegger's Kant and the Middle Voice,' in David Wood and Robert Bernasconi, eds., *Time and Metaphysics* (Warwick: Parousia Press, 1982), p.93.

7. Immanuel Kant, *Critique of Pure Reason,* trans. Norman Kemp Smith (New York: St. Martin's Press, 1945), B 180–81, p.183.

8. Emmanuel Levinas, 'Un Dieu homme?' *Exercices de la patience* 1 (1980), 72.

9. John Stuart Mill, *Autobiography* (London: Oxford University Press, 1924), p.113.

10. Martin Heidegger, *Schelling's Treatise on the Essence of Human Freedom,* trans. Joan Stambaugh (Athens: Ohio University Press, 1985), p.92.

11. Martin Heidegger, *The Basic Problems of Phenomenology,* trans. Albert Hofstadter (Bloomington: Indiana University Press, 1982), p.133 (abbreviated hereafter as BPP).

12. Martin Heidegger, *Kant and the Problem of Metaphysics,* trans. Richard Taft (Bloomington: Indiana University Press, 1990).

13. Heidegger, BPP, p.136.

14. Immanuel Kant, *Critique of Practical Reason and Other Works on the Theory of Ethics,* ed. T. K. Abbott (London: Longmans, Green, 1889), pp.169, 18.

15. Heidegger, BPP, p.160.

16. Ibid., p.310.

17. Martin Heidegger, *Being and Time,* trans. John Macquarrie and Edward Robinson (Oxford: Blackwell, 1962), p.54 [abbreviated hereafter as BT]. Hei-

degger, *History of the Concept of Time,* trans. Theodore Kisiel (Bloomington: Indiana University Press, 1985), p.158. Heidegger, 'Letter on Humanism,' *Basic Writings,* ed. David Farrell Krell (London: Routledge and Kegan Paul, 1978), pp.231–35 (abbreviated hereafter as BW).

18. Heidegger, BPP, p.133.

19. Ibid., p.137.

20. Ibid., p.149–50, 170. Kant, *Critique of Practical Reason and Other Works on the Theory of Ethics,* pp. 18–19.

21. Heidegger, BPP, p.170.

22. Martin Heidegger, *The Metaphysical Foundations of Logic,* trans. Michael Heim (Bloomington: Indiana University Press, 1984), p.192.

23. *Kants handschriftlicher Nachlass* (Berlin and Leipzig: Walter de Gruyter, 1936), 8:30.

24. Meister Eckhart, *Sermons,* in *Meister Eckhart,* ed. Raymond B. Blakney (New York: Harper and Row, 1941), p.220.

25. Kant, *Religion Within the Limits of Reason Alone,* trans. Theodore M. Greene and Hoyt H. Hudson (New York: Harper and Row, 1960), pp.21–23.

26.Heidegger, BPP, p.138.

27. Kant, *Critique of Practical Reason and Other Works on the Theory of Ethics,* p.180. Kant, *Religion within the Limits of Reason Alone,* p.21.

28. Georg Wilhelm Friedrich Hegel, *Encyclopaedia of the Philosophical Sciences,* trans. William Wallace (Oxford: Clarendon Press, 1975), paragraph 20, supp.

29. Jean Wahl, *Le Malheur de la conscience dans la philosophie de Hegel,* 2d ed. (Saint-Pierre de Salerne: Montfort, 1951), pp.26–27. Kant, *Critique of Practical Reason and Other Works on the Theory of Ethics,* p.180. Only the word 'humanity' is emphasized by Kant.

30. Martin Heidegger, BT, p.275.

31. Emmanuel Levinas, *En découvrant l'existence avec Husserl et Heidegger* (Paris: Vrin, 1982), p.174.

32. Kant, *Critique of Practical Reason and Other Works on the Theory of Ethics,* pp.78, 81.

33. Heidegger, BT, p.120.

34. Ibid., pp.264, 263.

35. See Llewelyn, 'Heidegger's Kant,' and Charles E. Scott, 'The Middle Voice in *Being and Time*,' in *The Collegium Phaenomenologicum: The First Ten Years*, ed. John C. Sallis, Giuseppina Moneta, and Jacques Taminiaux (Dordrecht: Kluwer, 1988), pp.159–73.

36. Heidegger, BT, p.163.

37. Hegel, *Encyclopaedia*, paragraph 448, supp., emphasis added.

38. 'Letter on Humanism,' in Heidegger, BW, p.238. Heidegger, BT, p.265.

39. Heidegger, BT, p.264.

40. Ibid., p.324.

41. Heidegger, *Questions III* (Paris: Gallimard, 1966), p.78.

42. Heidegger, BW. p.299.

43. Ibid., p.196.

44. Richard Kearney, *Poétique du possible* (Paris: Beauchesne, 1984), chap.6. Martin Heidegger, *Zur Sache des Denkens* (Tübingen: Niemeyer, 1969), pp.1–25; Heidegger, *On Time and Being*, trans. Joan Stambaugh (New York: Harper and Row, 1972).

45. Heidegger, BW, p.215.

46. Martin Heidegger, *Erläuterungen zu Hölderlins Dichtung* (1936–68) in *Martin Heidegger Gesamtausgabe* (Frankfurt: Klostermann), vol.4.

47. Martin Heidegger, *On the Way to Language*, trans. Peter D. Hertz and Joan Stambaugh (New York: Harper and Row, 1971), p.92–95.

48. Heidegger, BW, p.197.

49. Ibid., pp.196, 237.

50. Emmanuel Levinas, *Existence and Existents*, trans. Alphonso Lingis (The Hague: Martinus Nijhoff, 1978). *Martin Heidegger Gesamtausgabe*, 4:57.

51. Heidegger, *ibid.* Emmanuel Levinas, 'De la prière sans demande,' *Etudes philosophiques* 38 (April–June 1984), 157–63.

52. For a continuation of the discussion begun in this essay see John Llewelyn, *The Middle Voice of Ecological Conscience: A Chiasmic Reading of Responsibility in the Neighbourhood of Levinas, Heidegger and Others* (London: Macmillan, 1991), especially chapter 5.

# 7

The Philosophy of Electrical Science

*by Alan Bass*

*The results connected with the different conditions of positive and negative discharge will have a far greater influence on the philosophy of electrical science than we at present imagine.* – M. Faraday, 1838

How might Freud have read *The Conflict of the Faculties?*[1] 🞙 We know of Kant's appeal to Freud from scattered, but significant, references throughout the Freudian corpus.[2] In well-known passages Freud compares the unconscious to the unknowability of the thing in itself ('The Unconscious,' SE, 14:171), the super-ego to the categorical imperative ('The Economic Problem of Masochism,' SE, 19:167), the timelessness of the unconsciousness to time and space as necessary forms of thought (*Beyond the Pleasure Principle,* SE, 18:28). He mentions Kant in the posthumous reflections that appear at the very end of the *Standard Edition* (23:300). Moreover, in *The Conflict of the Faculties* Kant raises several points that could touch upon psychoanalysis as an institution and as a theory. The remarks on the conflict between the medical and philosophical faculties are obviously relevant to the institutional history of psychoanalysis; the references to dreaming and mental energy call for comparison with basic Freudian concepts. My purpose here will be to demonstrate the relevance of Kant's remarks about *energy* in the final section of *The Conflict of the Faculties* to problems that beset psychoanalysis as an institution. 🞙 This demonstration will proceed in several stages. The first compares *The Conflict of the Faculties* to one of Freud's papers on psychoanalysis as an institution; the second is a review of some of Freud's familiar remarks about the relations among psychoanalysis, philosophy, and paranoia; the third, a closer look at the less familiar history of Freud's ideas about paranoia, philosophy, and psychoanalysis; and the fourth is an examination of one of Freud's unfamiliar papers on paranoia. Although Freud's major text on paranoia, the Schreber case, will not be my focus, I will have occasion to make some remarks about it, and about Lacan's reading of it. Before launching into the details of my analysis, I do want to state that the thread I will be following throughout is the question of the central defense mechanism in paranoia. Lacan, of course, rereads the Schreber case in order to propose *foreclosure* as the major defense in paranoia, and justifies his reading via reference to Freud's own doubts about the role of *projection.* What I want to show here is that there are some unfamiliar chapters in Freud's thinking about paranoia and defense, and that they touch upon some points at which institutional and clinical questions, the interdisciplinary or intrapsychic conflicts intrinsic to psychoanalysis, are transformed. In tracing the implications of Freud's ideas about energy and defense in paranoia, I hope to justify the transformation of institutional and clinical questions via a reversal of prefixes: interdisciplinary and intrapsychic conflicts will be recast as *intra*disciplinary and *inter*psychic ones.

### FACULTIES AND RESISTANCES

Freud's short paper 'The Resistances to Psychoanalysis' (1924, SE, vol.19) can be read as his own version of *The Conflict of the Faculties.* It is mainly concerned with why the medical and philosophical faculties *resist* – and Freud indeed uses the psychoanalytic term – psychoanalysis. It provides several answers to the question of how Freud might have read Kant on the university. ◆ Most of the paper is concerned with why official medicine and philosophy reject new ideas, that is, Freud's own, even though these new ideas subscribe to the same doctrine of truth as the old. Freud begins with medicine, because of the (supposed) origin of psychoanalysis as a clinical procedure. The neuroses, the starting point of psychoanalysis, Freud says, '. . . must necessarily be put alongside the intoxications and such disorders as Graves' disease.' In other words, the neuroses belong to the realm of medicine, to the investigation of *bodily* processes. Freud then repeats the familiar account: Charcot and Breuer showed that 'the somatic symptoms of hysteria are psychogenic too' (19:214). The somatic symptoms of hysteria can be removed 'artificially,' that is, without direct physical intervention, by hypnosis. ◆ Once psychoanalysis began to investigate the psychical processes that produced physical results, it ran into the resistances of official medicine. Freud puts it this way:

*The direction taken by this enquiry was not to the liking of the contemporary generation of physicians. They had been brought up to respect only anatomical, physical and chemical factors. They were not prepared for taking*

*psychical ones into account and therefore met them with indifference or an-*
*tipathy. They obviously had doubts whether psychical events allowed of any*
*exact scientific treatment whatever. As an excessive reaction against an ear-*
*lier phase during which medicine had been dominated by what was known*
*as the 'philosophy of Nature,' they regarded such abstractions as those with*
*which psychology is obliged to work as nebulous, fantastic and mystical. . . .*
*During this materialistic, or, rather, mechanistic period, medicine made*
*tremendous advances, but it also showed a short-sighted misunderstanding*
*of the most important and most difficult among the problems of life.*
*(19:215–16)*

Would Freud have read *The Conflict of the Faculties* as prescribing just
the kind of relation between medicine and philosophy that the materialistic or mechanistic medical establishment of his day rejected? Kant
does stress that the higher faculties must not enter into a misalliance
with the philosophy faculty in order to avoid mixture of the a priori and
the empirical. But the 'misalliance' that theology and philosophy must
avoid is just what medicine and philosophy cannot avoid. Unlike theology and law, Kant claims, the rules of medicine come not from the 'orders of authorities,' but from 'the nature of things themselves, so that its
teachings must have also belonged originally to the philosophy faculty,
taken in its widest sense' (*Conflict of the Faculties*, p.41). Freud could certainly read this passage in relation to psychoanalysis. The physicians'
credo is that medicine had to liberate itself from philosophy in order to
become scientific. Curiously, however, this leaves the physicians in exactly the state that Kant describes. Given that the content of medical instruction has to derive from the 'nature of things,' and not rules, the
medical faculty, Kant says, is *freer* than the theological and legal faculties.
In this freedom to judge its own rules, it is most *like* the philosophy faculty. Certainly the government has the right to *regulate* medical practice,
just as it can prevent philosophers from misusing their positions. But
the government has no authority over medical learning, just as it has no
authority over philosophical debates. Kant's text confronts the physician
– and the psychoanalyst-physician – with a double bind: as soon as he
claims independence from philosophy, he endorses Kant's idea about the
philosophical origin of medicine.[3] And of course no direct knowledge of
Kant is necessary for this bind to exert its effects. ❧ I think that the
shadow of this paradox is evident in Freud's remarks about the *philosophical* resistances to psychoanalysis. Given the physicians' materialist

approach to the mind, he writes, one would have thought that the philosophers, unlike their medical colleagues, would have embraced the
new psychology. But no, for the

*philosophers' idea of what is mental was not that of psychoanalysis. The
overwhelming majority of philosophers regard as mental only the phenomena of consciousness. . . . Or, more strictly speaking, the mind has no
contents other than the phenomena of consciousness, and consequently psychology, the science of the mind, has no other subject-matter. . . . What,
then, can a philosopher say to a theory which, like psychoanalysis, asserts
that on the contrary what is mental is in itself unconscious and that being
conscious is only a quality . . . ? He will naturally say that anything both
unconscious and mental would be an impossibility.* (SE, 19:216)

Freud goes on to say that the philosophers, like the physicians, simply
take no account of the phenomena that compel a new conception of
mind (hypnosis, dreams, obsessions, delusions). Nor do the analysts fall
into the trap of predicating the unconscious; they 'refuse to say what the
unconscious is,' contenting themselves with demonstrating why it has to
be inferred. Up to this point, one could interpret that Freud is opposing
a materialist (medical) tradition to an idealist (philosophical) tradition;
he wants to demonstrate the shared presuppositions that make both see
psychoanalysis as a threat, and justifiably so. Such is his conclusion:

*So it comes about that psychoanalysis derives nothing but disadvantages
from its middle position between medicine and philosophy. Doctors regard
it as a speculative system and refuse to believe that, like every other natural
science, it is based on a patient and tireless elaboration of facts from the
world of perception; philosophers, measuring it by the standard of their
own artificially constructed systems, find that it starts from impossible
premises and reproach it because its most general concepts (which are only
now in process of evolution) lack clarity and precision.* (19:217)

However, Freud had made a curious statement about philosophy that
cannot simply be reconciled with this interpretation. On the point that
observation compels the inference of the unconscious, he had written
that analysts '. . . can indicate the domain of phenomena whose observation has obliged them to assume its existence. Philosophers, who know
no kind of observation other than self-observation, cannot follow them
into that domain' (19:217). ﹖ The reading of this last sentence that

Freud most likely intends is consonant with his line of reasoning. The philosopher, unlike the physician-scientist, does not observe external phenomena, but internal ones; since his observation is restricted to conscious events, the realm of psychoanalysis is barred to him. However, I think that this reading is a weak one. It corresponds to Freud's frequent attempts to give psychoanalysis a natural science genealogy in *opposition* to a philosophical genealogy. In a sense this corresponds to Kant's intent to separate the empirical from the a priori; Freud wants to leave the a priori to the philosophers, and claim the empirical for his own. He can do so, however, only by smoothing out his own history. At the very least, one can say that the founding of psychoanalysis through Freud's self-analysis does not exactly fit into the categories Freud wants to use here: self-observation-idealism versus empirical-observation-materialism. And then, as soon as Freud goes on to discuss the resistances to psychoanalysis due to its emphasis on sexuality, he cites – as on many other occasions – Schopenhauer and Plato as his 'illustrious forerunners' (19:218). ❧ Again, then, the claim of independence from philosophy leads to a simultaneous erasure of philosophical origins – self-observation – in order to claim another philosophical origin that is the same. To keep to the usual, and questionable, categories, we might say that Freud selectively affirms the 'idealist' tradition he wants to distance himself from. Now, to make a quick jump, this is precisely the paranoid person's dilemma: the more he attempts to expel the other who is everything that he rejects, the more he finds himself enmeshed with this other. And although I am treating 'psychoanalysis' as if it had a definable border with 'philosophy' outside it and then tormenting it from within, I think that the same (paranoid) structure holds for the relations between the philosophy of consciousness and psychoanalysis. For Freud is certainly right about the rejection of psychoanalysis by medicine and philosophy in general; my point is that he is right in order to blind himself to certain paradoxes within psychoanalysis. Now, one can readily imagine Freud reading Kant's chapter on the conflict between the medical and philosophical faculties, and saying something like this: Kant's plan for the university is precisely the one that has to exclude psychoanalysis for many reasons, both political and theoretical. But then what does Kant discuss when he wants to provide the philosophical rationale for what he calls a regimen? How to make reason the master of the senses without drugs or surgery. Is this not *the* psychoanalytic problem, both in the narrow sense of its (supposed) origin in using psychic means to treat the 'physical' disorders of hysteria, and in the general sense of being the therapy in which 'the inefficient method of suppressing [the drives] by means of repression should be replaced by a better and securer procedure' (19:220)? Furthermore, Freud could ask with ironic satisfaction, to what phenomena is Kant's attention drawn in this discussion? Mental energy and dreams. Certainly, Freud could say, Kant treats these phenomena in the same way that 'men in the mass behaved to psychoanalysis,' that is, 'precisely the same way as individual neurotics under treatment for their disorders' (19:221). In other words, they are preoccupied with the same problems, but propose defensive solutions to them, whence their *resistances*. For Freud could easily read Kant as proposing a typically hysterical solution to sexual conflicts: either simple displacement of the conflict to another activity and consequent hypercathexis of this activity, as in Kant's remarks about the benefits of puttering, or defensive displacement and then secondary defensive hypercathexis away from the displacement, as in Kant's remarks about *diverting* his attention from the ailments and deficiencies of old age. The epitome of neurotic or philosophic looking without seeing, Freud could say, is to be found in Kant's brief remarks about dreams. Kant quite accurately (from the Freudian perspective) notes the inhibition of muscular activity in dreams – 'an admirable device of our animal organization by which the body is relaxed for animal movement' – but then wants to treat them as related only to somatic processes – 'but stimulated within for vital movement' (*The Conflict of the Faculties*, pp.191–93). Again, Freud could say, the philosopher's self-observation, like the neurotic's, fails to observe the psychic conflict over a *vital* process that occasions dreams and symptoms. ✿ But this imagined Freudian reading cuts both ways, and can immediately be turned against itself. I only want to say as an introduction to my reading of Freud on paranoia, philosophy, and psychoanalysis, that Kant on the diversion of energy can be read as an 'illustrious forerunner' as much as Plato on Eros and Schopenhauer on sexuality – provided that one keep in mind the double bind of the relations between psychoanalysis and philosophy. And I will state dogmatically what I hope to demonstrate: that Freud's less well-known ideas about paranoia provide the means to conceptualize this paradoxical relation. ✿ Before some final remarks on Freud and Kant on institutional questions, I do wish to indicate where Derrida's reading of Kant in

'Mochlos' intersects with my analysis of Freud.[4] Derrida justifies the strange title of his text ('Mochlos') in his concluding citation of Kant. He is concerned, he says, with the question of the lever, the fulcrum, the specific means of displacement – *mochlos* in Greek – for the foundation of a new academic responsibility, a responsibility that would no longer answer to the ideal of decidability. And he concludes his essay with the citation of Kant's quirky footnote on the advantages of the right side of the body over the left. Arguing in favor of the innate superiority of the right over the left, Kant notes that even the Prussian infantryman who starts to cross a ditch with his left foot actually uses it as a *fulcrum*, a *hypomochlium* – whence Derrida's citation – in order to attack with the right foot. Now, the context of Kant's footnote on the fulcrum is precisely his discussion of dreams, energy, and diversion. He has asserted that 'the nervous energy that proceeds from the brain, the seat of representations' works 'in unison with the muscular power of the viscera' (*Conflict of the Faculties*, p.193): thus, we dream as our viscera continue to work in our sleep. However, anyone can suffer insomnia, which is accompanied by brain cramps on the weaker, left side. As one ages and grows weaker, so insomnia and *left*-side cramps increase. And here Kant appends the note on the *hypomochlium*, in order to support the argument that the left side weakens first due to its innate inferiority. What, then, is the *philosopher* to do if he does not wish an empirical, medical solution to the disturbance of his sleep? He is to hold fast to his general principle of *diverting* (*ablenken*) his attention from any thoughts that come to mind while he lies awake by concentrating on a 'neutral object' with many associated ideas. And he will sleep, even though the inflammation of the toes of his *left* foot that he finds upon awakening will convince him that his pains were *not* imaginary. (I hear Freud's sardonic chuckle here, and a reference to hysterics' imaginary maps of the nervous system, constructed for precisely Kant's reason: to convince themselves that their pains are not imaginary.) But despite the humor of the description, we cannot forget that Kant proposes his principle of energy diversion as the *truth* of the conflict between the medical and philosophical faculties. And the question of energy *diversion (ablenken)* will be *my* fulcrum, *mochlos,* for analyzing the 'conflicts' between psychoanalysis and philosophy. ❧ Returning to some more overtly institutional questions, Freud raises the Kantian question of regulation. Recall that he wants to include psychoanalysis within the empirical disciplines. Kant proposes that although the government cannot *sanction* medical learning, it can *police* the medical profession so that physicians are trained without harming the people. I think that Freud would subscribe to these ideas as long as psychoanalysis is granted equal rights as an empirical enterprise whose practitioners then would have to be policed in the way Kant suggests. Since this cannot be done in the (Kantian) university, it will have to be done in the parallel system of the psychoanalytic institutes. Thus Freud asserts the *freedom* for psychoanalysis that Kant gives to medicine. Freud writes, 'It is not easy to arrive at an independent judgment upon matters to do with analysis without having experienced it oneself or practiced it on someone else' (SE, 19:222). In other words, since psychoanalysis derives from 'the nature of things,' only the psychoanalytic 'faculty' can decide on psychoanalytic questions. Freud then proposes the parallel institutions that provide the necessary policing: 'Until recently there was no easily accessible means of learning psychoanalysis and its technique. This position has now been improved by the foundation (in 1920) of the Berlin Psychoanalytic Clinic and Training Institute, and soon afterwards (in 1922) of an exactly similar institute in Vienna' (19:222). (And one wonders: why Berlin first? What role does the University of Berlin play here?) Once again, though, a paradox has to be noted. It is the one raised by Derrida in 'Mochlos.' Kant wants to analyze the properly *internal* academic conflicts. What about those specialized institutions *outside* the university – and today the psychoanalytic institutes, even those formally attached to universities, are such a body – that maintain with the *inside* of the university 'a relation of resemblance, of participation, and of parasitism'?[5] Certainly the psychoanalytic institutes do *not* have the kind of research relations to the government that Kant and Derrida envisage. However, what Derrida says, reading Kant, certainly does hold for psychoanalysis: 'When regions of knowledge can no longer occasion properly academic training and evaluation, then the entire architectonics of *The Conflict of the Faculties* finds itself threatened. . . . As soon as the university, for structural reasons or due to attachment to the old representations, can no longer open itself to certain investigations, participate in them or transmit them, it feels itself threatened in certain parts of its own body: threatened by the development of the sciences, or a fortiori by the questions *of* science or *about* science, threatened by what it considers to be an invasive margin.' The university is 'threatened by an invasive margin because the nonacademic, public, official or not, research societies can also form pockets in the university campus. Certain members of the university can take part in them and can irritate the inside of the teaching body like parasites. In tracing the system of the pure limits of the university, Kant wants to hunt down all possible parasitism.'[6] ﷯ Recall Freud's famous words about being invited to lecture at Clark University: 'They do not know that I am bringing them the plague.' In other words he was carrying a dangerous parasite. And although there can be no question that psychoanalysis generally *has* been treated like a dangerous parasite by the university, there is another, evident paradox. Since psychoanalysis claims for itself the same rights as medicine, the formation of the institutes, with their necessary policing function, has also led to a strangely similar situation within them. An inside and an outside of psychoanalysis are proclaimed, autonomy is asserted, and irritating parasites are not tolerated. The institutes then suffer from their own plagues, which gnaw at them from within the more the parasites are hunted down in Kantian fashion. I know of no institute that considers it worthwhile or important to give its candidates any philosophical training. Thus they suffer from the paranoid double bind alluded to earlier. ﷯ At this point I want to make a few remarks about an enormous question raised briefly, too, by both Kant and Freud – the role of the Jews in the university. Significantly, Freud's text first appeared in French translation in *La Revue Juive*, a Swiss journal with Freud's name on its editorial committee, as Strachey tells us in the *Standard Edition*. Freud relates the resistances to psychoanalysis to anti-Semitism only in his final paragraph, but the initial appearance of this text in a journal of Jewish affairs makes anti-Semitism its general frame. There is nothing new in Freud's remarks here. He states, as on many other occasions, that the identification of psychoanalysis with himself as 'a Jew who has never sought to disguise the fact that he is a Jew' probably has 'a share in provoking the antipathy of his environment to psychoanalysis.' And again, as on many other occasions, he states that it is not 'entirely a matter of chance that the first advocate of psychoanalysis was a Jew,' given the Jew's familiarity with what Freud calls the 'situation of solitary opposition' (SE, 19:222). ﷯ At first glance then, it is not difficult to surmise that had Freud read Kant on the conflict of the philosophy faculty with the theology faculty he would have said: anti-Semitism. I do not think that Freud would have misread Kant as grossly anti-Semitic. Kant clearly wants to find a way to recognize the Jews 'as an educated and civilized people who are ready for all the rights of citizenship and whose faith could also be sanctioned by the government' (*Conflict of the Faculties*, p.95). But what does Kant propose? He suggests that the Jews maintain their identity while publicly adopting the religion of Jesus. Kant here lauds his (Jewish) disciple Lazarus Ben David who endorsed such an idea – a familiar one at the time. (Interestingly, a translator's note tells us that Ben David 'was noted for his role in propagating Kant's philosophy in Vienna' from 1794 to 1797; p.217, n.17.) The logic of Kant's argument is that a Jew who did not also adopt the religion of Jesus could have no place on the philosophy faculty. And a self-proclaimed Jew on the theology faculty, to follow Kant's logic, would be in a position to engage in what Kant calls an *illegal* conflict, since as a Jew, he would have to use his position in either the magical or businesslike ways Kant condemns (cf. p.51). So, Freud could say that in the name of truth and philosophy Kant would exclude Freud and psychoanalysis from the university – as usual. ❧ As is so well known, however, persecution does not exclude paranoia. I hear an allusion to this problem in Freud's final paragraph on anti-Semitism. Speaking of the rejection of psychoanalysis due to its identification with himself as a Jew, Freud writes that one does not often speak aloud about such questions. 'But we have unfortunately grown so *suspicious* that we cannot avoid thinking that this factor may not have been quite without its effect' (SE, 19:222). I emphasize the word *suspicious* both because of its link to paranoia, and because of Freud's obvious attempt to say here that despite the paranoid flavor of such remarks, he thinks that they are well founded. ❧ Yet Freud's relations with academic anti-Semitism were far from simple. As powerful as such anti-Semitism was, we know from *The Interpretation of Dreams* and the letters to Wilhelm Fliess that Freud himself was only too ready to construct a neurotic symptom around it. I cannot trace here the entire story of Freud's eventual university appointment in relation to his long-held belief that his Judaism would make such an appointment impossible. We could turn here to one of Freud's dreams ('Uncle with the yellow beard') which he analyzes in terms of his own *identification* with an anti-Semitic Minister of Education. Given the enormous role of Freud's self-analysis in the foundation of psychoanalysis, no consideration of its institutional history can neglect the complexities of Freud's 'official' and 'personal' relations to the university. The question of academic anti-Semitism runs throughout the self-analysis; it is in no way exempt from the general question about the relations between Freud's 'personal' and 'official' life that Derrida asks in *The Post Card:* 'How can an autobiographical writing, in the abyss of an unterminated self-analysis, give to a worldwide institution *its* birth?' And, in partial answer to this question, Derrida writes, concerning Freud's legacy: 'No legacy without transference. Which also gives us to understand that if every legacy is propagated in transference, it can get underway only in the form of an inheritance of transference.'[7] 🪶 I am suggesting then, that Freud's well-founded suspicions about academic anti-Semitism are also part of the inheritance of transference, and are as specifically related to the problem of paranoia as they are to the role of psychoanalysis in the university. The question of identification with the unacceptable 'other' is the 'red thread' that runs throughout. 'Clinically,' this question is central to the defensive process in paranoia.

SUCCESS

As briefly as possible, I now wish to provide the framework for my reading of the byways of Freud on paranoia. I will cite some well-known passages on the institutional and personal relations between psychoanalysis and paranoia and comment on them sparingly. These citations all concern the analogies of psychoanalysis and paranoia, and philosophy and paranoia on the institutional level; and the question of Wilhelm Fliess, and his alleged paranoia on the personal level.[8] 🪶 The groundwork for the institutional analogy is laid in a famous passage from *The Psychopathology of Everyday Life.* In the chapter on 'Determinism and Superstition' Freud compares himself, as psychoanalyst, to the superstitious person. The interplay of the institutional and the interpersonal is crucial here. The particular superstitious person in question, of course, is Fliess, as we know from Freud himself. At the time of the publication of *The Psychopathology of Everyday Life,* Freud had written to Fliess, on 7 August 1901:

*There is no concealing the fact that the two of us have drawn apart to some extent . . . you too have come to the limit of your perspicacity: you take sides against me and tell me that 'the reader of thoughts merely reads his own thoughts into other people,' which renders all my efforts valueless. If that is what you think of me, just throw my* Everyday Life *unread into the wastepaper basket. It is full of references to you – manifest ones, for which you supplied the material, and concealed ones, for which the motivation goes back to you. . . . Apart from anything that might remain of the content, you can take it as a testimonial to the role you have played for me up to now.*[9]

I will return to this letter. For now, I want to underline its paranoid *tone* – the feeling that the former friend is no longer on Freud's side, and has become an enemy, the vehement denial of projection. (I am leaving aside the question of whether or not Fliess was already suffering from paranoia in his last meeting with Freud in August 1900. Fliess at the time was convinced that Freud wanted to murder him.) For the moment, I want to juxtapose this passage with the more detached comments from *The Psychopathology of Everyday Life.* I am stressing the parallelism between the Freud-Fliess relationship and the relationship between psychoanalysis and superstitious determinism:

*The differences between myself and the superstitious person are two: first, he projects outward a motivation which I look for within; secondly, he interprets chance as due to an event, while I trace it back to a thought. But what is hidden from him corresponds to what is unconscious for me, and the compulsion not to let chance count as chance but to interpret it is common to both of us.* (SE, 6:257–58)

Recall, here, Lacan's *bon mot* that psychoanalysis is a 'guided paranoia.' The psychoanalyst *resembles* the strict determinist. They differ on the provenance of determinism: from within for the psychoanalyst, from without for the superstitious person. To paraphrase: I, Freud, the psychoanalyst, acknowledge my resemblance to him, Fliess, the superstitious determinist, but my concept of *unconscious* determinism makes my interpretive compulsion scientific – his is mad. ❧ And then Freud widens his angle, enlarges the analogy between psychoanalysis, superstition, and paranoia:

Because *the superstitious person knows nothing of the motivation of his own chance actions, and* because *the fact of this motivation presses for a place in his field of recognition, he is forced to allocate it, by displacement, to the external world. If such a connection exists, it can hardly be limited to this single application. In point of fact I believe that a large part of the mythological view of the world, which extends a long way into the most modern religions,* is nothing but psychology projected into the external world. *The obscure recognition (the endopsychic perception, as it were) of*

*psychical factors and relations in the unconscious is mirrored* – it is difficult to express it in other terms, and here the analogy with paranoia
must come to our aid *[my emphasis]* – *in the construction of a* supernatural reality, *which is destined to be changed back once more by science
into the psychology of the unconscious. One could venture to explain in this
way the myths of paradise and the fall of man, of God, of good and evil, of
immortality, and so on, and to transform* metaphysics *into* metapsychology.

Here, an editor's note tells us that this is the first published appearance
of the word 'metapsychology.' It had originally appeared in the letter to
Fliess of 13 February 1896. Freud continues, saying that the 'gap between
the paranoiac's displacement and that of the superstitious person' is not
as wide as it 'appears at first sight.'

*When human beings began to think, they were, as is well known, forced to
explain the external world anthropomorphically by means of a multitude
of personalities in their own image; chance events, which they interpreted
superstitiously, were thus actions and manifestations of persons. They behaved, therefore, just like paranoiacs, who draw conclusions from insignifi-
cant signs given them by other people, and just like all normal people, who
quite rightly base their estimate of their neighbors' characters on their
chance and unintentional actions. It is only in our modern, scientific but as
yet by no means perfected* Weltanschauung *that superstition seems so very
much out of place; in the* Weltanschauung *of pre-scientific times and peoples it was justified and consistent.* (6:258–59)

Before psychoanalysis, knowledge of the unconscious as internal reality
was impossible. But internal reality existed, and made itself felt as something unacceptable. Thus it was projected into the external world, which
then reflected back the projections in the form of the supernatural. The
paranoid does the same: he is necessarily unaware that he magically
creates in others the signs of the internal reality he defends against. And
on a larger scale, religion and metaphysics also do the same: they are systematic, defensive creations of a magic realm beyond the empirical that
mask an unacceptable inner reality. To change registers, one can read
Freud as saying that Fliess's mathematical determinism is a reflection of
Freud's psychological determinism, which Fliess no longer can tolerate,
given his essentially paranoid, religious, metaphysical view of the world.
But Freud is claiming something further; he is saying something like

this: 'I am not paranoid like you, Wilhelm. When I wrote to you about your role in *The Psychopathology,* I expressed anger at your telling *me* that *my* theory consisted of projections. But you see that in print I am *not afraid* of the analogy between my psychology and a paranoid system. My system, my metapsychology, my agencies and energies, coherently explain the relations between inner and outer reality. *I* am the scientist. In fact, I am more the scientist than the majority of scientists who in rejecting my theories fall back into metaphysics – and paranoia. Only he who *does not fear* his resemblence to the paranoid escapes paranoia – and metaphysics.' ❧ The use of a fearless confrontation with the 'paranoid' aspects of psychoanalytic theory to guarantee its scientificity also informs another well-known passage, this time from the Schreber case. We know from the letters to Jung that Fliess is no less a presence in the Schreber text than he was in *The Psychopathology of Everyday Life.* On 18 December 1910, Freud had written to Jung: 'My Schreber is finished. . . . The piece is formally imperfect. . . . I am unable to judge its objective worth as was possible with earlier papers, because in working on it I have had to fight off complexes within myself (Fliess).'[10] Here is the passage from the Schreber study. Freud's reasoning resembles that in the passage from *The Psychopathology of Everyday Life:*

*Since I neither fear the criticism of others nor shrink from criticizing myself, I have no motive for avoiding the mention of a similarity which may possibly damage our libido theory [I interpolate: our metapsychology] in the estimation of many of my readers. Schreber's 'rays of God,' which are made up of a condensation of the sun's rays, of nerve fibres, and of spermatozoa, are in reality [my emphasis] nothing else than a concrete representation and projection outwards of libidinal cathexes; and they thus lend his delusions a striking conformity with our theory. His belief that the world must come to an end because his ego was attracting all the rays to itself, his anxious concern at a later period, during the process of reconstruction, lest God should sever His ray-connection with him, – these and many other details of Schreber's delusional structure sound almost like endopsychic perceptions of the processes whose existence I have assumed in these pages as the basis of our explanation of paranoia. I can nevertheless call a friend and fellow-specialist to witness that I had developed my theory of paranoia before I became acquainted with the contents of Schreber's book. It remains for the future to decide whether there is more delusion in my theory than I should like to admit, or whether there is more truth in*

*Schreber's delusion than other people are as yet prepared to believe.* (SE, 12:78–79)

Whether the metapsychology is delusional, or Schreber's rays are scientific, the psychoanalyst and the paranoid are joined in their attempts to provide a systematic explanation of mental energy. As in the passage from *The Psychopathology of Everyday Life*, the dividing line between the metaphysician and the psychoanalyst is the use of projection as a defense: Schreber projects outward his perception of libidinal cathexes, while the psychoanalyst internalizes them to construct a new picture of inner reality. One could say schematically that Fliess (strict determinism) plus Schreber (preoccupation with energy) minus projection equals Freud. What would happen to the relations between psychoanalysis and paranoia if one could not *simply* subtract projection from the formula? ❧ The success of psychoanalysis would certainly be at stake. Freud assured himself of this success in a letter to Sandor Ferenczi of 6 October 1910, again from the period when he was working on Schreber:

*You not only noticed, but also understood, that I no longer have any need to uncover my personality completely, and you correctly traced this back to the traumatic reason for it. Since Fliess' case, with the overcoming of which you recently saw me occupied, that need has been extinguished. A part of the homosexual cathexis has been withdrawn and made to enlarge my own ego. I have succeeded where the paranoiac fails.*[11]

Again, the interpersonal and the institutional are inextricably entwined here. Certainly, Freud is making a self-analytic point. The paranoid, according to his theory, pathologically defends against his homosexuality. Fliess's paranoia is due to his inability to integrate his homosexual feelings for Freud into his ego. If Freud is not to follow the same path, he has to acknowledge the homosexuality without defense. He is then free to accomplish a healthy, narcissistic expansion. But note immediately that paranoia is the 'theoretical disease' *par excellence*. The cure for Freud is not only in the establishment of a healthy ego ideal, instead of delusions of persecution, it is also in the construction of a theory that is deterministic without being superstitious, religious, or metaphysical. For Freud, the *philosophy* implicit in paranoia is as much a part of its *failure* as are its delusions of persecution. As he famously put it in *Totem and Taboo* (1913): '. . . a paranoiac delusion is a caricature of a philosophical system' (SE, 13:73). Without the 'overcoming' of the Fliess case, could not Freud's enterprise also have developed into the caricature of a philosophical system, like Fliess's mathematical theory of development? Is not Freud implying that the *criterion* of not resorting to the defense of projection explains Fliess's personal and intellectual failures? And what if the criterion changed?

ARRIVAL

I now want to present evidence that eventually the criterion *did* change, and that this change implies reconceptualization of the relations between philosophy and psychoanalysis. I will again be proceeding in the style of a collage of citations, ranging over the years from 1894 to 1922. Such an accumulation and juxtaposition of citations is quite dense, but we are dealing here with the entire history and implications of Freud's *energic* thinking. ❧ The first citation is from an early paper, 'The Neuro-Psychoses of Defense,' written in January 1894. In considering what is to follow, note that Breuer and Freud published their 'Preliminary Communication' in 1893 and that the *Studies in Hysteria* was published in 1895. I am citing this passage because it contains perhaps the first published assertion that a theory of mental energy underpins the Freud and Breuer theory of hysteria. Freud concludes this clinical paper by saying,

*I should like, finally, to dwell for a moment on the working hypothesis which I have made use of in this exposition of the neuroses of defense. I refer to the concept that in mental functions something is to be distinguished – a quota of affect or sum of excitation – which possesses all the characteristics of a quantity (though we have no means of measuring it), which is capable of increase, diminution, displacement and discharge, and which is spread over the memory-traces of ideas somewhat as an electric charge is spread over the surface of a body. This hypothesis, which incidentally, already underlies our theory of 'abreaction' in our 'Preliminary Communication' (1893), can be applied in the same sense as physicists apply the hypothesis of a flow of electric fluid. (SE, 3:61)*

Eventually, of course, this quantity was to be called 'libido.' ❧ Now, in his Editor's Introduction to *The Studies in Hysteria* Strachey has pointed out a 'remarkable paradox' concerning the role of this idea in Breuer and Freud's relations.[12] The paradox, as Strachey notes, is that Breuer, in his theoretical chapter of *The Studies in Hysteria*, states his intention of treating hysteria in exclusively psychological terms, but winds up tracing the 'parallels between the nervous system and electrical installations' (SE 2:xxiv). Breuer acknowledges, as does Freud in the passage just cited, that the 'Preliminary Communication' already assumed an energic explanation of abreaction. Breuer winds up using the electrical analogies Freud had used in 'The Neuro-Psychoses of Defense,' despite his stated intent of adhering to the psychological. For example, Breuer writes that we can compare a cerebral path of conduction to a

*telephone line through which there is a constant flow of galvanic current and which can no longer be excited if that current ceases. Or better, let us imagine a widely-ramified electrical system for lighting and the transmission of motor power; what is expected of this system is that simple establishment of a contact shall be able to set any lamp or machine in operation. To make this possible, so that everything shall be ready to work, there must be a certain tension present throughout the entire network of lines of conduction, and the dynamo engine must expend a given quantity of energy for this purpose. In just the same way there is a certain amount of excitation present in the conductive paths of the brain when it is at rest but awake and prepared to work.* (2:193–94)

In a footnote to this passage Breuer goes on to say that there are two kinds of excitation: potential, quiescent energy and immediately dischargable, kinetic energy. Strachey adds an editor's note explaining that this passage was the source of Freud's fundamental metapsychological distinction between bound and free energy, which he always attributed to Breuer. ❧ I wish to make two conjoined points here. First, we have seen Freud's willingness, in the Schreber text, to compare his libido theory with paranoid delusions about rays and energies. Nor is Schreber in any way atypical; the paranoid person is generally preoccupied with rays, energies, and apparatuses.[13] My contention here is that as soon as Freud begins to formulate a theory of mind based on analogies to electrical processes, he has unwittingly installed the problematic of paranoia at the heart of psychoanalysis. By extension, and again reading backward, if paranoia is *also* the pathology most closely related to metaphysics, then the electrical analogies also install philosophy at the heart of psychoanalysis. When libido theory transforms metaphysics into metapsychology, according to the program of *The Psychopathology of Ev-*

*eryday Life*, it becomes the philosophy of electrical science. Second, I think that the paradox of Breuer's veering off into Freud's electrical analogies is not coincidental. I think, rather, that it is related to the paradoxes of identification mentioned earlier in the discussion of *The Conflict of the Faculties*. When Breuer speaks about an electrical system for lighting and transmission of motor power, I read him to be alluding, blindly, to the problem of collaboration and boundaries in psychoanalysis as theory or therapy. If one person or discipline makes *contact* with another are they separate or joined? And if the 'simple establishment' of contact joins two 'people' or 'two disciplines,' can they be said to be entirely separate should the current be turned off? If the telephone line is no longer excited when the current ceases, as Breuer mentions, it does not mean that the apparatus has withdrawn from the circuit. Indeed, the possibility of electrical circuitry implies that energy can be transmitted from anywhere to anywhere, provided that the system is not overloaded. This possibility changes our ideas about voluntary inclusion or exclusion, and also has to be taken into account by the philosophy of electrical science. And it is a typically paranoid problem. ❧ Of course, I am interpreting Freud and Breuer here; these passages are not directly concerned with paranoia. Let us look at some of the discussions of paranoia from the Fliess correspondence. These discussions throw new light on the question of projection; eventually I will link them to the 1922 paper called 'Some Neurotic Mechanisms in Jealousy, Paranoia and Homosexuality.' In a related analysis of the Freud-Jung correspondence, Borch-Jacobsen succinctly asks the questions that necessarily haunt this material. He notes the 'great proximity' between the 'knowledge of paranoia and paranoid knowledge,' and says that

*the matter is indissociably of practical and theoretical importance. Such is the singular 'practice-theory' of psychoanalysis, such also the singular implication of the subjects 'themselves' in this theory of the subject, that the failure of the empirical relation with Jung (or with Fliess . . .) simultaneously signs a failure of the analysis of this relation. Let us simplify the question. It amounts to wondering about the validity of a theory of madness (Fliess' madness, for example . . .) when there is every indication that the theory is elaborated in a relation or correspondence that contributes to provoking the phenomenon of which it treats. . . . Can it account for that in which it participates. . . ? And is there not here an unanalyzed aspect of Freud, all the more unanalyzed in that it touches upon his very active par-*

*ticipation in the scene that he appears to describe 'objectively,' from the out-side?*[14]

The first, and perhaps most astonishing, reference to paranoia in the Freud-Fliess correspondence is in the letter of 24 January 1895. This is one year after the electrical metaphors of 'The Neuro-Psychoses of Defense,' and one year before the 'Further Remarks on the Neuro-Psychoses of Defense,' which was to contain a case history of paranoia and the first *published* mention of projection. As Strachey notes (SE, 3:184, n. 1), this letter in fact contains a fuller description of projection than the 'Further Remarks.' Strachey, of course, did not have the uncensored text of the letter at his disposal, and could not analyze the *context* in which the idea of projection first appears. That context is my emphasis here:

*Dearest Wilhelm: I must hurriedly write to you about something that greatly astonishes me; otherwise I would be truly ungrateful. In the last few days I have felt quite unbelievably well . . . a feeling . . . I have not known for ten months. Last time I wrote you . . . that a few viciously bad days had followed [a good period] during which a cocainization of the left nostril had helped me to an amazing extent. I now continue my report. The next day I kept the nose under cocaine, which one should not really do; that is, I repeatedly painted it to prevent the renewed occurrence of swelling; during this time I discharged [emphasis added;* entleeren, *meaning to evacuate, to empty out, as in a bowel movement] what in my experience is a copious amount of thick pus; and since then I have felt wonderful. . . . I am postponing the full expression of my gratitude and the discussion of what share the operation [by Fliess on Freud's nose] had in this unprecedented improvement until we see what happens next. In any event, I herewith dedicate to you [my emphasis] a new insight which is upsetting my equilibrium more than much that happened before and to which I have not yet become indifferent. It is the explanation of paranoia . . . chronic paranoia in its classical form is a pathological mode of defense, like hysteria, obsessional neurosis, and hallucinatory confusion. . . . The purpose of paranoia is thus to ward off an idea that is incompatible with the ego, by projecting its substance into the external world. . . . Whenever an internal change occurs, we have the choice of assuming either an internal or an external cause. If something deters us from the internal derivation, we naturally seize upon the external one. Second, we are accustomed to our internal states being be-*

*trayed (by an expression of emotion) to other people. This accounts for nor-*
*mal delusions of observation and normal projection. . . . If we forget (that*
*we project) and are left with only the leg of its overvaluation of what people*
*know about us and of what people have done to us. What do people know*
*about us that we know nothing about, that we cannot admit? It is therefore*
*abuse of the mechanism of projection for the purposes of defense.*[15]

'Dear Wilhelm,' I paraphrase with hindsight, 'what the future is to bring
imparts a vertiginous irony to this letter. The official version of my relation with you is not entirely wrong. In 1895 I was still two years away
from the period of intensive self-analysis that eventually was to help me
understand my neurotic idealization of you. How hysterical I sound in
this letter! I feel ill and I want a physician magically to rid me of my
pains. And should a sufficient erotic transference be present, he will succeed, and will win increased love and gratitude from the patient. So,
Wilhelm, I was only too eager to accept your theories about the nasal
origins of many maladies, especially mine. Nor could I see that I used
cocaine more than one should as another magical remedy. Instead I
combined the effects of drugs and transference, and temporarily felt
wonderful. Had I read *The Conflict of the Faculties* I might even have noticed that I sound exactly like the people, according to Kant, the non-
philosophers who make the practitioners of the higher faculties into
magicians. Certainly I was not capable at the time of the philosophical
approach to real or imagined problems that Kant recommends: a self-
imposed rechanneling of energies. But finally, my self-analysis made this
possible. I succeeded where you were to fail, Wilhelm. I helped myself to
divert the energy directed toward you, the homosexual libido so apparent in my gratitude for your ministrations. ❧ 'But, Wilhelm, looking
backward I cannot fail to be impressed by the irony of my dedicating to
you – of all people! – the insight that paranoia is a pathological means of
defense characterized by projection. Can one not ask oneself whether
this letter indicates some foreknowledge, some dim perception of your
paranoia? What is it that makes me feel so wonderful that my mind
clears, and I gain new insight into paranoia? Discharge! Expelling into
the external world that which I believed to have been tormenting me
from within, pus. Does this not sound like the hysterical version of projection? (A libidinized, bodily *flow* is eliminated bringing great relief.)
And we know Wilhelm, that what sexual energy is for me, the nose and
its problems, are for you, specifically as concerns sexuality. So it is not so

far-fetched to compare the discharge of pus to the expulsion of unwanted libido. But of course, I did not yet understand the specific role of homosexual conflict in paranoia. Only while thinking about you once again while working on Schreber was this to become clear to me. But still, Wilhelm, what a convoluted parallelism we have here – if it makes any sense at all to speak of convolution and straight lines together.'

One year later on 1 January 1896, Freud writes another letter to Fliess that mentions paranoia in a context that is crucial for my purposes. This time I will interrupt the citation with commentary:

*How much I owe you: solace, understanding, stimulation in my loneliness, meaning to my life that I gained through you, and finally even health that no one else could have given back to me. It is primarily through your example that intellectually I gained the strength to trust my judgment, even when I am left alone – though not by you – and, like you [my emphasis] to face with lofty humility all the difficulties that the future may bring. For all that accept my humble thanks.* (Masson, p.158)

We have here, again, the question of identification. The hysteric in the thralls of devotion to the healer, identifies with him, takes on his admired attributes. And of course Freud will teach us that there is no such identification without a component of aggressive rivalry. The paradoxes of erotic-aggressive identification are then taken onto the interdisciplinary institutional level in the next paragraph of this letter. By now, I hope it is clear that the usual opposition of the personal and the institutional as the internal and the external cannot account for what I just called the convoluted parallelism of identifications. Freud continues:

*Even if you had not said so explicitly, I would have noticed that your confidence in your [nasal] therapy was finally borne out in your own case as well. Your letters, as again the last one, contain a wealth of scientific insights and intuitions, to which I unfortunately can say no more than that they grip and overpower me. The thought that both of us are occupied with the same kind of work [and are inevitably rivals] is by far the most enjoyable one I can conceive at present. I see how, via the detour of medical practice, you are reaching your first ideal of understanding human beings as a physiologist; just as I most secretly nourish the hope of arriving, via these same paths, at my initial goal of philosophy.* (Masson, p.159; my emphasis)

This passage should not be read in the naive mode that would simply find the conflicted wish that gave rise to all of Freud's well-known ambivalence about philosophy, his defensive avoidance of some philosophers, and his perhaps equally defensive embracing of others. In his next sentence, Freud indeed refers to wishes from his earlier life: 'For that [i.e. philosophy] is what I wanted originally, when it was not yet at all clear to me to what end I was in the world' (p.159). One can always find evidence of Freud's conflicted childhood and adolescent wishes, and then argue that psychoanalysis for him is the compromise formation that contains the return of the repressed wish and the defense against it. As soon as psychoanalysis is reduced to philosophy on the basis of Freud's conflicted philosophical ambitions, his assertion that even the philosophers he approvingly cites had no conception of an unconscious mental life regains its force. What I want to stress here is the similarity, the institutional identification that Freud wants to establish between himself and Fliess. Here we both are, physicians, he seems to be saying, physicians so that we can make our way in the world that offers precious few rewards to those who want to hold to their *ideals,* and to unearth the secrets of body (physiology) and mind (philosophy, in the broadest sense, including psychology in the division of the faculties in Freud's day, and until fairly recently). Medicine Freud is obviously saying, is but a detour from our loftier goals. ❧ But, given the complexities of identification between lonely fellow travelers, how are we to interpret Freud's statement of his philosophical goals in the rest of the letter? He continues,

*For that [philosophy] is what I wanted originally, when it was not yet at all clear to me to what end I was in the world. During the last weeks I repeatedly tried to give you something in return for your communications, by sending you a short summary of my most recent insights into the neuroses of defense, but my capacity to think so exhausted itself in the spring that now I can accomplish nothing. Nevertheless, I have prevailed upon myself to send you the fragment. A gentle voice has counseled me to postpone the account of hysteria since there are still too many uncertainties in it. You probably will be satisfied with the obsessional [neurosis]. The few notes on paranoia come from a recently started analysis which has already established beyond any doubt that paranoia is really a neurosis of defense. [Thus, a reassertion of the insight gained a year before, indicating continued work on it.] Whether this explanation also has therapeutic value remains to be seen. Your remarks on migraine have led me to an idea, as a*

*consequence of which all my theories would need to be completely revised –*
*something I cannot venture to do now. I shall try to give you some idea of*
*it, however. I begin with the two kinds of nerve endings. The free ones re-*
*ceive only quantity and conduct it by summation.* (p.159)

There follow two paragraphs on the subject of quantity and quality, energy and perception. These paragraphs are in the style of *The Project for*
*a Scientific Psychology*, the neurophysiological text, enthusiastically written by Freud, and just as quickly criticized by him only a few months
before – the *psi, phi, omega* neural scheme. In fact, these paragraphs are
Freud's answers to some of his own criticisms of *The Project*, as Strachey
notes (SE, 1:230). But why the fresh approach to what Freud had referred
to only a month before in the following terms: 'I no longer understand
the state of mind in which I hatched the psychology; I cannot conceive
how I could have inflicted it on you. I believe you are still too polite; to
me it appears to have been a kind of madness' (29 November 1895; Masson, p.152)? Freud says that Fliess's remarks on migraine provided the
impetus for new ideas about the conduction of mental energy. And what
new conclusions does Freud reach? That the *psi* pathways for sexual energy are themselves unconscious, and become conscious only sec-
ondarily by linkage with processes of discharge and perception. Thus,
Freud concludes his neurophysiological gift to Fliess, 'It is much easier
today to understand the rule of defense, which does not apply to perceptions but only to processes' (p.160). We have here fundamental Freudian
principles: the unconscious is characterized by energic displacements
which in themselves can never become conscious; this is where the defensive struggle is crucial to pathogenesis. But, note that it is Freud's
*identification* with Fliess's goal of using medicine to reach basic truths,
that leads him first to refer to philosophical ambitions, and then to
speak of energic displacements. Such, again, is what I am calling the philosophy of electrical science. And in the performance of this letter, the
sequence is roughly this: arrive at philosophy – exposition of the neuroses as a return gift to Fliess – hysteria still uncertain, obsessional
neurosis secure, paranoia newly and clearly acquired – return to neurophysiological and energic questions. In other words, read in terms of
contiguity, paranoia is the transition between philosophy and energy.
And such is my theme here. ❧ Freud enclosed with this letter the draft
of a text on the neuroses of defense. (This draft was to become the 'Further Remarks on the Neuro-Psychoses of Defense.') In it, he makes gen-

eral theoretical remarks about neurosis, and goes on to dissect obsession, paranoia, and hysteria. He contrasts the latter two in a way that he will develop further:

*The determining element of paranoia is the mechanism of projection involving the refusal of belief in the self-reproach. Hence the common characteristic features of the neurosis: the significance of the voices as the means by which other people affect us, and also of gestures, which reveal other people's emotional life to us; and the importance of the tone of remarks and allusions in them – since a direct reference from the content of remarks to the repressed memory is inadmissible to consciousness. . . . Hysteria necessarily presupposes a primary experience of unpleasure – that is, of a passive nature. The natural sexual passivity of women explains their being more inclined to hysteria. Where I have found hysteria in men, I have been able to prove the presence of abundant sexual passivity in their anamneses. . . . Hysteria begins with the overwhelming of the ego, which is what paranoia leads to.* (Masson, pp.168–69; my emphasis)

Thus hysteria and paranoia are placed in a relation of temporal opposition. Freud is attempting to explain why he thinks that hysteria has the earliest onset of the neuroses, and paranoia the latest. Even though he was to abandon this early explanation of the choice of neurosis, Freud did continue to see a relation of *opposition* between hysteria and paranoia, an opposition that produced an interesting discussion of the processes of identification. ❧ Almost four years later, when much has changed in his theories, Freud picks up the question of this *opposition*. On 9 December 1899, he writes to Fliess:

*I may recently have succeeded in gaining a first glimpse of something new. The problem confronting me is that of the 'choice of neurosis.' When does a person become* hysterical instead of paranoid? *In my first crude attempt . . . I thought it depended on the age at which the sexual trauma occurred. . . . That I gave up long ago; but then I was left without a clue until a few days ago, when I saw a connection with the sexual theory. The lowest of the sexual strata is autoerotism, which dispenses with any psychosexual aim and seeks only locally gratifying sensations. It is then succeeded by alloerotism (homo- or heteroerotism), but certainly continues to exist as an undercurrent. Hysteria (and its variant, obsessional neurosis) is alloerotic, since its main path is identification with the loved one. Paranoia again dissolves the identification, reestablishes all the loved ones of childhood who have been abandoned . . . , and dissolves the ego itself into extraneous persons. So I have come to regard paranoia as a forward surge of the autoerotic current, as* a return to a former state. (Masson, p.390, my emphasis)

Unlike his rejection of many other early formulations, Freud retained this relatively unfamiliar idea. He repeats it briefly in the official record of his long history of reflection on paranoia, the Schreber case: 'Paranoia decomposes just as hysteria condenses. Or rather, paranoia resolves once more into their elements the products of the condensations and identifications which are effected in the unconscious' (SE, 12:49).
Again, we cannot help but be struck by the foresight contained in the 1899 letter. Paraphrasing, it can be read as asserting the following: 'Wilhelm, I will be able to take you in, but you will not be able to take me in. Alloerotically, I will identify; autoerotically you will disidentify. You will have to see me as a threat to you, as I become the screen for the erotic feelings for men that you cannot tolerate. I, on the other hand, suffer neurotically, but like the neurotic I will suffer from a love that I can contain within myself; I will condense it unconsciously. That is why I *must not* be afraid of the analogy between psychoanalysis and paranoia: to run away from such an analogy would be autoerotic, regressive, while to embrace it is alloerotic, progressive. Thus, eventually, I will achieve *success,* and you will fail. So, Wilhelm, I will love the analytic, interpretive aspects of paranoia, as part of my hysteria; as a paranoid, you will have to see my interpretive capacities as a threat. No wonder that you will come to accuse me of projection and will call me a thought reader.'
 There is also a subtler, more difficult issue that Freud probably could not have raised, but it is implicit in the contrast between hysteria and paranoia as concerns identification. Many other passages could be cited to justify Freud's diagnosis of himself as hysteric, and Fliess as paranoid. On the basis of Freud's question – when does one become hysterical *instead* of paranoid? – we can ask what happens to the hysteric (Freud) who has to identify with his opposite, the paranoid (Fliess)? How far does the identification go? Does it include not only the amorous-rivalrous identification on the personal and intellectual levels, but also identification with the paranoid's tendency toward a breakdown of identifications, toward disidentification? In Freud's case, one could certainly say that his therapeutic procedure includes the 'paranoid' process he describes in the letter just cited: dissolution of identifications, their subsequent reestablishment (in the transference to the analyst), the necessary

forward surge of the accompanying autoerotic current, and the equally necessary dissolution of the ego itself into extraneous persons. And the psychoanalyst could say here that this is why every patient experiences effective analysis as madness; again, psychoanalysis as a 'guided paranoia.' But despite the validity of this observation, it does not address the 'institutional' question of a discipline founded on identification with disidentification. When one conceives psychoanalysis in this way, its autonomy is threatened. It becomes the 'hysterical-paranoid' process of both alloerotic identification and autoerotic disidentification, of 'taking in' and 'expelling,' in which the taking in, the identificatory love, and the expelling, the disidentificatory interpretive compulsion, are joined so that the one 'is' the other. 'Hysterical,' identifying psychoanalysis 'is' philosophical, energy-obsessed 'paranoia,' the one process always turning into the other. Metapsychology, viewed not as a closed system, but as text, performs this identification-disidentification with other disciplines, so that strictly speaking psychoanalysis cannot be said to be either an independent discipline or the branch of another one, such as medicine or philosophy. Perhaps we might say that psychoanalysis is the intradisciplinary fold that yields the resemblance between philosophy and medicine noted by Kant, but that simultaneously subverts the possibility of a regulated autonomy. I began by stating that I hoped to justify the transformation of interdisciplinary and intrapsychic problems into intradisciplinary and interpsychic ones. I hope to have made clear by now that metapsychology, read as the philosophy of electrical science, is so interlaced with the Freud-Fliess relationship, with the identification with disidentification, that the personal has to be read in terms of the interdisciplinary, and the institutional in terms of the intrapsychic. ❧ I find further striking evidence of this assertion when one juxtaposes the letter just cited with another major metapsychological hypothesis. Those familiar with *Beyond the Pleasure Principle*, and all the debates it has occasioned, cannot fail to be struck by the similarity between the description of paranoia and the controversial definition of the drives in *Beyond the Pleasure Principle*: the impulsion to 'return to a former state,' 'to restore an earlier state,' to cite the letter of December 1899 and *Beyond the Pleasure Principle* together. Moreover, I think that this parallel description of paranoia and the drives obeys the logic of thinking identification and disidentification together. Recall that in *Beyond the Pleasure Principle*, as so many have noted, the description of the drives as the urge to restore a former state is linked to the death drive, as the tendency toward dissolution, decay. Whether one reads *Beyond the Pleasure Principle* in terms of the logical necessity for an account of the drives that includes a regressive principle, as Sulloway does; or in terms of the chiasmatic structure of the life and death drives, as Laplanche does (in *Life and Death in Psychoanalysis*); or in terms of the impossibility of opposing life and death and of isolating a singular thesis in *Beyond the Pleasure Principle*, as Derrida does (in *The Post Card*), one arrives at the point at which the metapsychological principles of progression and regression are intricated in the same way as hysteria and paranoia are intricated at the heart of psychoanalysis.[16] ❦ In a sense this is obvious: Freud, in the 1899 letters, is contrasting alloerotism and autoerotism as progression and regression. What is not obvious is that the paradoxical metapsychology that issues from *Beyond the Pleasure Principle*, in which life and death are intertwined, has a structural similarity with the paranoia-philosophy, paranoia-psychoanalysis interlacings, with paranoia as the switchpoint that makes an opposition, a clear-cut boundary, between psychoanalysis and philosophy impossible. To force the material I have been compiling, one could say that if Freud wants to arrive at philosophy via psychoanalysis as the energics of neurosis, then (1) as I have been emphasizing, he will also arrive at paranoia; (2) his system then will have to include a principle of disintegration at the heart of its principles of integration; and (3) such a principle also will have to define the unstable boundaries between psychoanalysis and other disciplines, just as it applies to the unstable boundaries between Freud and Fliess. As a footnote to all the debates on *Beyond the Pleasure Principle*, I am also alleging that the speculativeness Freud so insists upon in that work, is prepared by the twisting specularity of identification with disindentification that I have been analyzing here.

CIRCUIT ACTION

But we have not yet dealt with the question of *projection*, which in a sense is the safety device, quite specifically the *circuit breaker* for these shifting, highly charged, reflections. The image of the circuit breaker is particularly apt here, if one recalls, for example, Breuer's analogies to a 'widely ramified electrical system' in interdisciplinary terms. The circuit breaker stops the 'transmission of motor power' and the 'establishment of a contact' when it is necessary to eliminate some apparatus from an overloaded circuit. Projection serves just such a function, whether as the central defense in paranoia, when the overload of homosexual libido is 'expelled,' so to speak, or in the relations between metaphysics and meta-psychology, where metaphysics is construed as expelling, as projecting, unacceptable internal truths. Over and over again, we have seen, Freud guarantees the truth of psychoanalysis in terms of its refusal to employ the paranoid mechanism of projection. This is why a change in his con-ception of projection would have major consequences for the entire sys-tem, especially as concerns what might be called the flattening effect that occurs when boundaries break down, when outside and inside are no longer adequate to describe interdisciplinary relations. As the electrical system expands, the circuit breaker becomes relatively less necessary; more apparatuses can stay on the circuit with less threat to the system.

&. For several reasons, I want to introduce this discussion via reference to Lacan's remarks about projection from the 'Question Preliminary to Any Possible Treatment of Psychosis.' In this text, of course, Lacan re-reads Freud on Schreber and introduces the concept of foreclosure. Lacan writes: 'Present theories are noteworthy for the totally uncritical way in which the mechanism of projection is used. The objections against such a use are overwhelming, yet this seems to deter no one, and this despite all the clinical evidence that there is nothing in common be-tween affective projection and its supposed delusional effects. . . . Espe-cially as Freud in this text [Schreber] expressly dismisses the mechanism of projection as insufficient to account for the problem.'[17] Now, Lacan is correct about this. As we listen to Freud express his doubts about the role of projection, we must keep in mind the long development of his thinking on the subject, along with the metaphysical, Fliessian, electrical components that are implied in every psychoanalytic discussion of para-noia. The Schreber text comes fifteen years after Freud's initial insight about projection. The passage that speaks most to Lacan's point is the following, in which Freud says,

*The most striking characteristic of symptom-formation in paranoia is the process which deserves the name of projection. An internal perception is suppressed, and, instead, its content, after undergoing a certain kind of dis-tortion, enters consciousness in the form of an external perception. . . . We should feel tempted to regard this remarkable process as the most important element in paranoia and as being absolutely pathognomonic for it, if we were not opportunely reminded of two things. In the first place, projection does not play the same part in all forms of paranoia; and, in the second place, it makes its appearance not only in paranoia but under other psychological conditions as well, and in fact it has a regular share assigned to it in our attitude towards the external world. For when we refer the causes of certain sensations to the external world, instead of looking for them . . . inside ourselves, this normal proceeding, too, deserves to be called projection. Having thus been made aware that more general psychological problems are involved in the question of the nature of projection, let us make up our minds to postpone the investigation of it (and with it that of the mechanism of paranoiac symptom-formation in general) until some other occasion.*

Here, Strachey adds an editor's note: 'There seems to be no trace of any such later discussion' (SE, 12:66). ❧ The fact that Strachey's note is atypically wrong gives added force to Lacan's statement concerning the uncritical use of the idea of projection: Freud specifically returns to the topic in his 1922 paper 'Some Neurotic Mechanisms in Jealousy, Paranoia and Homosexuality.' If one believes that Freud never really did modify his ideas about projection, despite reservations expressed in one or two places, then projection becomes dogma. Why should this be so, and why should such an obvious error remain in the *Standard Edition*? Does projection need protection from Freud's further discussion of the problem in the 1922 paper? And what about Lacan here? Certainly he uses Freud's doubts about projection to authorize his introduction of the concept of foreclosure. Indeed Lacan seems to be stepping into the space opened by Freud in the passage from Schreber in his 'Question Preliminary to Any Possible Treatment of Psychosis.' Thus it is tempting to think that Lacan is also eliminating reference to the 1922 paper, in order to bolster *his* modification of the theory of projection, but as we shall see the situation is more complicated. ❧ First, Lacan himself translated 'Some Neurotic Mechanisms in Jealousy, Paranoia and Homosexuality.' The translation appeared in the *Revue Française de Psychanalyse,* 1932, Number 3. Lacan refers to Freud's text in his own translation, in his thesis on paranoia, also published in 1932.[18] But the article is not cited or even mentioned in the 'Question Preliminary to Any Possible Treatment of Psychosis,' which is concerned with so much of the analytic literature on paranoia. So it becomes even more tempting to think that Lacan was insisting on his own revision of the theory of projection, without citing Freud's revision. But as my use of the word 'tempting' indicates, I do not think that this contention is completely true. Close reading shows an indirect, but unmistakable reference to Freud's 1922 reconsideration of projection in Lacan's text. In fact, an important passage of the 'Question Preliminary' becomes much more comprehensible when it is read in conjunction with 'Some Neurotic Mechanisms.' I will cite this passage after explicating the crucial material from Freud. But the fact remains that Lacan's reference to Freud's paper is indirect. ❧ Freud begins his discussion of paranoia in the 1922 paper with a gesture of reticence and the announcement of an advance: 'Cases of paranoia are for well-known reasons not usually amenable to analytic investigation . . .' (I interpolate: although I have been thinking about paranoia for twenty-seven years now). 'I have recently been able, nevertheless, by an intensive study of two paranoiacs, to discover something new to me' (SE, 18:225). (And, I note, it is still news that projection ever budged from the center of Freud's thinking on paranoia.) The first patient is a man delusionally jealous of his wife. Even though the wife was 'impeccably faithful,' according to Freud, the patient was correct in his inference, derived from 'observation of minute indications,' of the wife's *unconscious* wish to be unfaithful (as always, the paranoid as analyst). Freud contends that his patient's intense preoccupation with his wife's unconscious wishes was a defense against his own homosexual impulses which were repressed rather than sublimated. His acute consciousness of his wife's sexual wishes for men served to keep his own similar wishes unconscious. (Here is an echo of the letter to Ferenczi about the paranoid's failure, and Freud's success.) And then Freud makes a point about projection, a point that refines the parallelism between paranoia and psychoanalysis: 'We begin to see that we describe the behavior of both jealous and persecutory paranoiacs very inadequately by saying that they project outwards on to others what they do not wish to recognize in themselves.' (Thus, this is a reconsideration of the problem of projection as begun in the Schreber text.) Freud continues, 'Certainly they do this; but they do not project into the blue, so to speak, where there is nothing of the sort already. They let themselves be guided by their knowledge of the unconscious, and displace to the unconscious minds of others the attention which they have withdrawn from their own.' (18:226). Interpersonally, then, the paranoid follows Kant's suggestion: he diverts energy away from the problem, and increases his attention elsewhere. ❧ The discussion of the second patient leads Freud to use the word toward which I have been leading all along. This patient, Freud says, would not have been classified as paranoid 'apart from analysis.' In his analysis, however, 'classical persecutory ideas . . . flashed up occasionally' (18:226). The patient himself scoffed at these ideas, but their presence leads Freud to think of him as a candidate for a severe persecutory paranoia (the shadow of Fliess here?). Discussion of this patient yields a meta-psychological expansion of what Freud called his 'new' idea in the discussion of the first patient. Concerning the second patient's likely future paranoia, Freud writes:

*It seems to me that we have here an important discovery – namely, that the qualitative factor, the presence of certain neurotic formations, has less practical significance than the quantitative factor, the degree of attention or, more correctly, the amount of cathexis that these structures are able to attract to themselves [Kant's problem, again]. Our consideration of the first case, the jealous paranoia, led to a similar estimate of the importance of the quantitative factor, by showing that there also the abnormality essentially consisted in the hypercathexis of the interpretations of someone else's unconscious. . . . Thus as our knowledge grows we are increasingly impelled to bring the* economic *point of view into the foreground. I should also like to throw out the question whether this quantitative factor that I am now dwelling on does not suffice to cover the phenomena which Bleuler and others have lately proposed to name 'switching.' One need only assume that an increase in resistance in the course taken by the psychical current in one direction results in a hypercathexis of another path and thus causes the flow to be switched into that path.* (18:226–27)

Projection has now been rethought in terms of the philosophy of electrical science as 'switching.' The German text, in fact, has subtler electrical resonances than are captured in the English translation. Bleuler's word, cited by Freud, is *Schaltung*, from the verb *schalten*. *Schalten* can mean to direct, to govern, to rule, to put in the circuit, to insert, to connect, to switch. The noun *Schaltung* can mean circuit, connection, gear-change. Now, when Freud describes his quantitative, new idea – to wit that internal resistance to one direction of energic flow leads to a hypercathexis of another, related pathway – he changes Bleuler's *Schaltung* into *Einschaltung*. *Einschalten* has the senses of to interpolate, to put in, to insert, to intercalate, to switch on, to connect, to plug in. *Einschaltung* most frequently has the sense of an insertion, an intercalation, a parenthesis.

Freud's inflection of Bleuler's term admirably and subtly suits his purpose. He wants to describe a 'switching on' that also *resembles* projection, namely, a switching on of the path into someone else's unconscious
mind such that one finds there what one does not want to see in one's
own unconscious; this process, then, *deceptively* resembles the simple *insertion* of one's own thoughts into someone else's mind. On one level, we
can understand Freud to say here, as always, that there is a grain of truth
in every delusional idea, even if the grain of truth is the defensively accu-
rate perception of someone else's unconscious wishes. But the entire
stock of electrical metaphors that supports the economic, quantitative
reasoning Freud always prefers, *also* leads him to use a word that describes something that looks like a projection, with its simple demarcation of outside and inside, but *is not.* At the very least, the concept of
'switching,' as it more accurately describes the defense used in paranoia,
joins the paranoid person and the 'other' *on the same circuit.* ❧ Lacan's
1932 translation of the crucial sentences captures these points quite well.
It reads:

*J'aimerais aussi soulever le point de savoir si cette instance quantitative, sur
quoi j'insiste ici, ne tend pas à recouvrir les phénomènes pour lesquels
Bleuler et d'autres recemment veulent introduire le concept d' 'action de
circuit.' Il suffirait d'admettre que d'un surcroît de résistance dans une direction du cours psychique s'ensuit une surcharge d'une autre voie, et par là
sa mise en circuit dans le cycle qui s'écoule.*[19]

Thus, Lacan has felicitously translated Bleuler's *Schaltung* as *circuit action,* and has followed Freud's inflection of the term (with its combined
senses of putting onto and *into* the circuit) by using *mise en circuit. Mise
en circuit,* putting into the circuit, also corresponds more closely to
Freud's use of the gerund *Einschaltung.* ❧ Earlier, I suggested that Lacan
indirectly alludes to the recasting of projection as switching in the
'Question Preliminary.' Lacan's allusion occurs in the paragraph immediately following the passage cited previously, from *Ecrits,* in which
Lacan speaks of the 'totally uncritical' use of the concept of projection.
The English translation of the *Ecrits,* in fact, uses the word 'switching' in
the sentence that I think contains the allusion: 'Freud, in his essay of interpretation of the Schreber case, which is read so badly that it is usually
reduced to the rehashings that followed, uses the form of a grammatical
deduction in order to present the *switching* [my emphasis] of the rela-

tion to the other in psychosis, namely, the different ways of denying the proposition, "I love him." . . .'[20] On first reading, Lacan seems to be discussing only the famous passage in the Schreber text in which Freud shows how *projection* can operate on every word in the sentence 'I love him' (assuming the subject to be a man). But since Lacan both wants to maintain the emphasis on what he calls the 'logical problems' implicit in Freud's grammatical discussion, *and* wants to show that projection cannot account for these problems, he also *alludes* to the concept of 'switching,' which Freud introduces in order to account for the relation between homosexuality and paranoia. What is interesting for my purposes is that Lacan does not literally use his translations of *Schaltung* and *Einschaltung* as *action de circuit* and *mise en circuit* in the original French of the 'Question Preliminary.' What the English translation of the *Ecrits* accurately gives as 'switching' is '*aiguillage*' in Lacan's original: 'l'aiguillage de la relation à l'autre dans la psychose' (*Ecrits*, p.55). My question: is *aiguillage* here a re-translation of *mise en circuit? Aiguillage* certainly has the sense of 'switching direction,' but in a *railroad* sense of switching onto one set of tracks from another. It does not have the *electrical* connotations so crucial to Freud, but perhaps not to Lacan, since he wants to solve Freud's logical problems via the 'economy of the signifier' (p.200) in general, and via the 'evocation of the paternal metaphor in the subject's imaginary' (p.199), specifically in the paranoid's 'imaginary.' And, of course, Lacan's allegation is that to rethink Freud in these terms avoids the scientism of the metapsychology. Even if 'aiguillage' is not a retranslation of 'circuit action' as soon as *aiguillage* is used we know that the description is 'metaphorical,' and not literal, in the traditional senses: only a psychotic would think literally of railroad tracks from one unconscious to another. But, and this is my point here, Freud most certainly *does* want us to think of the literal flow of energies between one unconscious and another. ❧ And what if we reapply this energic refinement of projection to all the passages in which the analogy between paranoia and psychoanalysis is as inescapable as the analogy between paranoia and metaphysics? In all these analogies, as I have stated, 'projection' plays the role of 'circuit *breaker*': metaphysics is *outside* psychoanalysis, not on the same circuit, because it places *outside* itself the truths that psychoanalysis keeps *inside* itself. But, as Freud has insisted, this psychoanalytic explanation is not adequate; libido theory can be modified to account for the paranoid's experience of literally being on the same circuit – the 'same wavelength' – as the other. Thus, another 'logical problem' implicit in keeping to Freud's energic literalism is that we cannot use the concept of projection to break the circuit between psychoanalysis and philosophy and paranoia. They switch each other on and off without one being outside the other; thus circuit action has the 'flattening effect' mentioned earlier. As always, when paranoia is in question, the institutional implications are massive. Again, to keep to the 'projective' relation between psychoanalysis and philosophy is at very least not to follow rigorously Freud's introduction of the concept of switching. And if it is objected that 'switching' is a quirk of Freud's natural science insistence on economic, energic reasoning, I would reply that we are still compelled to *read* metapsychology as 'the philosophy of electrical science,' and to pursue the consequences of such a reading. Here, we come back to the paradox delineated in the contrasting of 'The Resistances to Psychoanalysis' to *The Conflict of the Faculties*. The paradox was that as soon as Freud argued for the autonomy of psychoanalysis, due to the resistances of medicine and philosophy, he reaffirmed Kant's emphasis on the autonomy of medicine due to its *philosophical* origins. Obviously, I am not arguing for a resolution of this paradox, in the usual sense of resolution, but for a deconstruction of psychoanalytic autonomy via the notion of switching. In fact, returning to points made earlier, one might say that as soon as Kant uses energic concepts and the notion of diversion of energy as a philosophical argument, psychoanalytic 'autonomy' has been rendered impossible in advance. ❧ In conclusion, I want to switch switching onto two other paths, thereby further 'ramifying' (Breuer) the circuit. One path is directly mentioned in Freud's discussion of switching and the other is part of its context. I will only sketch out these paths, and am calling them 'two' as a provisional convenience. ❧ The first takes us back to hysteria, and to the oscillating theory in which it is possible for paranoia and hysteria to 'become' one another. In citing the passage on switching I elided the following sentences: 'We have long known of an analogous fact in the analysis of hysteria. The pathogenic phantasies, derivatives of repressed instinctual impulses, are for a long time tolerated alongside the normal life of the mind, and have no pathogenic effect until by a revolution in the libidinal economy they receive a hypercathexis; not until then does the conflict which leads to the formation symptoms break out' (SE, 18:228). What Freud means here is that the situation that obtains between the paranoid

and the other, such that the paranoid takes cognizance of something unconscious in the 'other,' also obtains internally for the hysteric. There
has to be a diversion of energy (Kant again!), a hypercathexis of something previously considered too minute to deserve attention in order for
hysterical symptoms to arise. And again, there is a long history of Freudian reflection on just how this process occurs in *hysteria*, a history that
these sentences carry along with them. These reflections concern the
role of what are called in English '*switch* words'; Freud, in fact, consis-
tently uses *Wechsel* to describe switch words in hysteria and dreams. One
brief discussion of switch words, in the Dora case, even compares them
to switch points on railroad tracks (SE, 7:65, n.1). One could certainly
cite this comparison in order to justify Lacan's use of *aiguillage*. I think,
however, that Freud would prefer the energic, electrical, circuitry model
for switch words, and that he once more brings a comparison with hysteria into a discussion of paranoia for just this reason. Freud would also
say that the analogy with hysteria holds *only* to the extent that the energic displacements that occur *between* the paranoid and another person
occur *internally* for the hysteric. But if we take Freud in the literal way I
have been emphasizing here, and think of 'real' energy displacements,
then the *quantitative* processes are the same, there is the *same* expansion
of the circuit: such is Freud's point. Metapsychologically there may be
differences between the paranoid and the hysterical hypercathexis of the
trivial, but they are not *opposed*. The familiar notion of switch words,
and the use of *Wechsel*, then, needs further comparison with *Einschaltung*, and with the fluctuating relations between hysteria and paranoia in
Freud's theory. ❧ I will indicate the second more contextual pathway
with a citation from Ernest Jones's biography of Freud. In September
1921, Freud, Jones, and the rest of the secret committee took a joint vaca-
tion in the Harz Mountains. Jones writes about the event: 'Freud read to
us two papers he had specially written for the occasion, the only time he
ever did this. One was on telepathy, which he had begun to write at the
end of July and had finished in three weeks. . . . The other paper he read
to us is better known, since it was published in the following year. Freud
had announced in the previous January that he had suddenly obtained a
deep insight, "as to the hewn rock," into the mechanism of paranoiac
jealousy.'[21] Perhaps you had foreseen that the paper on homosexuality,
jealousy, and paranoia has the debate on telepathy as its context. In the
*Standard Edition* the papers on telepathy immediately precede it. And

perhaps you will have noticed that the Kantian question of the diversion of energy is precisely the explanation of what Freud calls thought-transference. In other words, there is the same *economic* explanation of telepathy or rather 'thought-transference' (to keep to Freud's category), as of paranoia. Again, I am not saying that the economic processes Freud describes are identical, but they are structurally similar; Freud's sudden insight into paranoia cannot be divorced from the question of telepathy. ᨠ In the posthumous paper 'Psychoanalysis and Telepathy,' Freud relates the story of a patient who consulted a well-known fortune-teller in Munich. This fortuneteller asked only to be supplied with a date, which she used for 'astrological calculations,' in order then to make her prediction. She predicted that Freud's patient's brother-in-law would die the next July or August of shellfish poisoning. The patient was thunderstruck: his brother-in-law had almost died of an attack of shellfish poisoning the preceding August. Freud asserts that this knowledge was present in his patient's mind during the consultation with the fortune-teller, and that it was 'transferred from him to the supposed prophetess – by some unknown method which excluded the means of communication familiar to us. That is to say, we must draw the inference that there is such a thing as thought-transference. The fortuneteller's astrological activities would in that case have performed the function of *diverting* [my emphasis; Kant's word again] her own psychical forces and occupying them in a harmless way, so that she could become receptive and accessible to the effects upon her of her client's thoughts – so that she could become a true "medium" ' (SE, 18:184). Or so that she could become a true analyst or a true paranoid. And in the distance, given that Freud gained insight into thought-transference and paranoia at the same time, I hear this echo: 'You see Wilhelm, not only am I not afraid of the analogy between paranoia and psychoanalysis, I am no longer afraid of your accusation that I am a thought reader. Instead, I will attempt to give thought reading an energic explanation.' ᨠ Can philosophy be far off in this situation? This is the question I have repeatedly asked here. Now, 'Psychoanalysis and Telepathy' was presented to the 'Committee,' and then left unpublished. How much did or did not Freud disguise the information about the patients discussed in this article? We will probably never know. But in the text as we have it, Freud insists a great deal on the profession of the patient whose thought was so successfully transferred to the medium – and then transmitted to the analyst (who had recently gained new insight into paranoia). The patient had first consulted Freud for difficulties in his professional life, difficulties that were successfully resolved. He then returned to analysis with Freud, because of the interest psychoanalysis had for him in his field; he told Freud the story of the medium during this second phase of treatment. Moreover, Freud mentions the patient's university appointment as a guarantee of the veracity of his report. Of course you have guessed. He was a philosopher.

NOTES

1. Faraday's 1838 statement quoted in Abraham Pais, *Inward Bound* (New York: Oxford University Press, 1986), p.79. All references to Immanuel Kant, *The Conflict of the Faculties/Der Streit der Fakultäten,* trans. Mary J. Gregor (New York: Abaris Books, 1979) are in the text; I am presuming familiarity with its arguments throughout.

2. *The Standard Edition of the Complete Psychological Works of Sigmund Freud,* 23 vols., ed. James Strachey (London: Hogarth Press, 1953–61). All further references to this work, abbreviated SE, are indicated in the text by volume and page number.

3. A similar analysis of this paradox can be found in Philippe Lacoue-Labarthe, 'L'Oblitération,' in *Le Sujet de la philosophie* (Paris: Aubier-Flammarion, 1979), p.137.

4. Jacques Derrida, 'Mochlos; ou, le conflit des facultés,' in *Du droit à la philosophie* (Paris: Galilée, 1990).

5. Ibid., p.411. All translations from 'Mochlos' are my own.

6. Ibid., pp.412–14, *passim.*

7. Jacques Derrida, *The Post Card: From Socrates to Freud and Beyond,* trans. Alan Bass (Chicago: University of Chicago Press, 1987), pp.305, 339.

8. I am assuming some familiarity with the Freud-Fliess story here. Moreover, this is far from the first look at the theoretical and institutional implications of this story. For some essential references on this topic see Mikkel Borch-Jacobsen, *The Freudian Subject,* trans. Catherine Porter (Stanford, Calif.: Stanford University Press, 1988); Jacques Derrida, 'My Chances,' in *Taking Chances,* ed. J. Smith and W. Kerrigan (Baltimore: Johns Hopkins University Press, 1984); François Roustang, *Dire Mastery,* trans. Ned Lukacher (Baltimore: Johns Hopkins University Press, 1982); Michel Schneider,

*Voleurs de mots* (Paris: Gallimard, 1985); Frank Sulloway, *Freud: Biologist of the Mind* (New York: Basic Books, 1979); Peter Swales, 'Freud, Fliess and Fratricide: The Role of Fliess in Freud's Conception of Paranoia,' printed privately.

9. *The Complete Letters of Sigmund Freud to Wilhelm Fliess,* trans. and ed. Jeffrey M. Masson (Cambridge: Harvard University Press, 1984), p.447.

10. *The Freud/Jung Letters,* ed. William McGuire (Princeton: Princeton University Press, 1974), pp.380–81.

11. As quoted in Ernest Jones, *The Life and Work of Sigmund Freud,* 3 vols. (New York: Basic Books, 1955), 2:83.

12. Sulloway, in *Freud: Biologist of the Mind,* has expanded upon Strachey's delineation of the paradox in order to revise the usual account of Freud's and Breuer's differences over the specifically sexual etiology of hysteria.

13. The psychiatric and psychoanalytic description of the paranoid has long noted the typical idea of being influenced by apparatuses and their energies. The classic reference is Victor Tausk's article, ' "The Influencing Machine," ' *The Psychoanalytic Quarterly* 2 (1933): 519–56.

14. Borch-Jacobsen, *The Freudian Subject,* p.61; translation slightly modified.

15. Masson, ed., *Complete Letters of Sigmund Freud,* pp.106–9. Further references are given in the text.

16. Sulloway, *Freud: Biologist of the Mind;* pp.393–418; Laplanche, *Vie et mort en psychanalyse* (Paris: Flammarion, 1970), pp.175–212; Derrida, *The Post Card,* pp.275–410.

17. Jacques Lacan, *Ecrits,* trans. Alan Sheridan (New York: Norton, 1977), p.188.

18. Lacan, *De la psychose paranoiaque dans ses rapports avec la personnalité* (Paris: Seuil ['*Points*'], 1980), p.229.

19. Lacan, 'Sur quelques mecanismes névrotiques dans la jalousie, la paranoia et l'homosexualité,' *Revue Française de Psychanalyse* 3 (1932), 397.

20. Lacan, *Ecrits,* p.188. All further references are in the text.

21. Jones, *The Life and Work of Sigmund Freud,* 3:81–82.

**8**

Canons and Metonymies:

An Interview with Jacques Derrida

R R : *Not entirely by design, our symposium orbited around three poles of interest, three texts, and I would like to mention them here. The first two are Kant's* The Conflict of the Faculties, *and your own discussion, in 'Mochlos,' of that and other works, among them Heidegger's* Discourse of the Rectorate.[1] *We know the repercussions of Kant's discourse in Germany – how it gave rise to von Humboldt's plan for the University of Berlin, and to the writings of Schelling, Fichte, Schopenhauer, Nietzsche and Heidegger about our academic institutions. And we know that the German university became the model for a similar project in the United States. How did it happen, then, that the initial essay by Kant was largely overlooked? And did it suffer a similar eclipse in France?* ❧ *Our third pole is the work of Paul de Man in light of the discovery of his wartime writings.[2] Paul de Man, in the field of literature, reaffirmed for American academics the pertinence of German philosophy, of Kant and certainly of Heidegger. Do the wartime writings eclipse this contribution?*

J D : Your question turns, then, around an eclipse. The eclipse of a text. A text is not a star. In every way, it is never visible, never present. It's 'effectivity' (in itself already problematic, this word), its operation and the marks it leaves, are not reduced to the visibility of its phenomenal presence, its appearance. A text will never be reduced to its (visible, sensible) phenomenon. It is an ellipse, an ecliptic in itself. But its not being phenomenal does not make it essentially intelligible (or noumenal), or mean that it shelters some substantial presence behind its appearance. We are already with Kant, as you see, but also far from Kant when we start talking about politics and writing. So the eclipse you mentioned is a supplementary eclipse, within a general ecliptic of the text as such. This phenomenon of the supplement of the eclipse (a text hiding right up to the point of its essential dissimulation, or finding itself repressed, over-dissimulated, in the very withdrawal that initiates it) has, in fact, interested me to the point of obsession for a long time. But I also try to find a legitimate research topic there, pressing, even urgent. It joins the great questions of canonization. Why and how do the university, the editorial process, and memory in general practice their hierarchies, in terms of a body, a corpus, a problematic, a thematization, a language or an author? After all, what is this body? Why is such hegemony annihilated now and then without a remainder? For the figure of an eclipse is still governed by teleological optimism (already or still somehow Kantian). It assumes that any text, once occulted, minorized, abandoned, repressed or censored (and let us not forget that *The Conflict of the Faculties* is also a text about censorship) ought to reappear, if possible like a star! Justice has to be done! This optimism, which I have never shared, also inspires a politico-psychoanalytic concept of repression: what was repressed is stored in the unconscious of a culture whose memory never loses a thing. There is a political unconscious, no doubt, and also a politico-academic unconscious – we should take them into account, so as to analyze, so as to act – but there are ashes also: of oblivion, of total destruction, whose 'remains' in any case do not stay with us forever. ❧ Not even an eclipse, then! The body in question is not even deprived for a while of light – it is simply burned. This incineration, this finitude of memory corresponds to a possibility so radical that the very concept of finitude (already theological) is in danger of being irrelevant. Without it, perhaps, the violences of censorship and repression would not even be imaginable. So, too, for the violence marking every procedure of legitimation or canonization. Sometimes this violence is overtly political, and one could undoubtedly give examples, other than those now canonical or academic in their turn, of literatures, languages and discourses belonging to oppressed (or colonized) nations or classes, to women or blacks. To these massive and very obvious examples, we ought to add examples less visible, less direct, more paradoxical, more perverse, more overdetermined. ❧ Before growing indignant, as some have done, at the deconstructive and destabilizing analysis of certain canons, structures, procedures or events of canonization, we ought to consider all the devices and interests presiding over the establishment of 'assured values.' Analyzing or reinscribing this history of canonization in a broader, more diversified, more intelligible field is hardly to argue for amnesia or the destruction of traditional works. I might be tempted to think the contrary. From this point of view, deconstruction answers to a greater desire for memory, intelligibility and responsibility in the face of tradition. It is true that a redistribution of canonical values in fact leads, concretely, to difficult choices in the organizing of study and research. Whether or not we want to, we sometimes run the risk of reducing the range, force or intensity of research dedicated to what are justifiably celebrated as great classical works. We have to limit this risk, but also to look for the better ways of taking it. This concern, which I share with numerous colleagues, ought rightly to lead to deliberate reflection, to a more systematic and more responsible reflection – without reactive evasion – about the history of canons. Is not this reflection the better guide when practical decisions have to be made, when we have to decide what corpus to study, what research to authorize, what money to distribute and so on? I do not see, apart from such reflection, a better way to limit the risks I just mentioned while still opening up new fields of research. ❧ You asked me if *The Conflict of the Faculties* has experienced an eclipse in France similar to one in this country. Yes and no. An eclipse, yes, but a different one. The text is available in translation. Allusion is made to it now and then. But rather rarely and, to my knowledge, it was not previously read as a discourse on the university, on the history and structure of this institution or its relationships to the state or to other forms of political power inside or outside the university – on any of the issues, in sum, that we discussed in Tuscaloosa. In France this essay was considered of interest mainly for its links to [Kant's] *Religion within the Limits of Mere Reason,* for its remarks on the French Revolution and for various questions about Kantian architectonics. This is also legitimate, but masks a dimension of the book that I have attempted to recognize. In the United States, where I first delivered 'Mochlos' for a very specific academic occasion [the centennial of the founding of the Graduate School of Columbia University, 17 April 1980], the eclipse was very different. An old translation did exist, but the invisibility of the text was, so far as I can tell, almost complete. If we sought to analyze *The Conflict of the Faculties* today, we would have to attend as much to its 'content' as to the conditions of its tradition: for example, what philosophical, institutional, editorial or political reasons explain the difference between the French eclipse and the American eclipse? Why and how, according to what (French or American, Franco-American) trajectories does this eclipse today have a chance to end? These are just some examples of possible or necessary questions. ❧ I would like now to back up a bit. You have suggested that this interview be guided by three texts.

You have designated them with the proper names of authors – Kant, Heidegger, de Man. This is a good strategy. But in the course of an interview we cannot approach those writings with the rigor and philological patience they require. We are not about to propose a reading of them, least of all a micrological reading. I will displace the word 'micrology' just a bit to underline the following point: the strange three-headed corpus that you have marked off is composed of what everyone agrees to call 'little writings,' or minor texts: *The Conflict of the Faculties, The Discourse of the Rectorate,* and the newspaper articles or 'early writings,' as they say, of 1941–42. Without reading them 'in themselves,' as I have tried to do elsewhere, we can treat these writings as pathways or arrows on the territory of the conference you organized.[3] These writings take us back to the political or historical text where they are inscribed. Thus we have already broached the 'big' question of the text. When nothing of 'deconstruction' has yet been read, or when one does not want to have read it, or when one wants not to have read it, or when one has not wanted to read or know that one has read without reading (just so many temporal modalities of avoidance that I hesitate to call 'denials,' and which would also have to be analyzed micrologically in their turn), then what is held against 'deconstruction' thus reconstructed and held up to reproach is a 'textualism' that transforms everything 'real' into a book. Now you well know there is nothing to this, that the concept of text, once re-elaborated, leaves nothing outside itself, and is especially irreducible to the book or to writing. It does not exclude the referent or the real or history: quite the reverse, if one could say so. It is open there, it is opened there. I recall this briefly to underline the fact that we do not speak merely of writings 'small' or 'great,' canonical or otherwise, but of historico-political places, if you will, within which these writings are inscribed and exceeded. ✿ You suggested amnesia. With the reservation just noted – a reservation with the depth of an abyss, of a place without place for aleatory, unintelligible, in-significant forgettings – this exception aside, amnesia is never accidental. It signifies something; its phenomenon is not just negative. It is not just a loss of memory. A selective, hierarchizing operation organizes the inheritance. It even produces it. Amnesia does not merely happen to some inheritance already received, undergoing this intervention afterward. The inheritance is itself this thematizing violence of memory, this sifting thematization, this thesis filtering within the general sys-tem. As a theme or thesis of memory *pos-*

*ing* and proposing, putting and *promising* as much as receiving, it gives rise to academic anamneses and amnesias: to position, transposition, deposition, institution of memory, to a genealogy of inheritance. ❧ The concept of censorship is undoubtedly too narrow to cover this series of events. Within it there certainly can exist – and we must never neglect it – censorship in a strict sense, in the sense defined by Kant in his Preface to the first edition of *Religion Within the Limits of Mere Reason:* a criticism with force *(Gewalt)* at its disposal. Moreover, Kant justifies the recourse to such censorship.[4] But this concept of censorship – like the concept of censorship in general, even in its figurative sense – is still not enough to account for the selective and overdetermined genealogies we are talking about. It supposes, on the one hand, the exercise of a well-delimited power of state or church, legal agencies supposedly competent and officially legitimized, conscious *subjectivities* (or unconscious ones, 'censorship' in the figurative sense of the word), representations and responsibilities that can be attributed to such subjects, and censors and authors who can be named. It supposes, on the other hand, a philosophy of language, a concept of the work and a delimitation of the corpus that can be attributed to, or controlled by, such subjects. These subjects and objects must give rise to judgments. An act of censorship so defined would be a *judgment* sustained by force. Now the strange history we have been talking about, and which was, it seems to me, of interest during the conference, exceeds and disorganizes all these categories and axioms. That certain texts, for example, are marginalized or minorized, that they are unread, or no longer read, or little read, or badly read – this is not, or not always, due to the effect of judgments pronounced as such. We will never be able to speak seriously of these processes if we do not interrogate all that the concept of censorship assumes. This, be it said in passing, is why my remarks on the questions of 'subject' and 'spirit' in Heidegger are pertinent here; they concern the choices preliminary to any possible recasting of the problematic: with, without or against Heidegger. This holds as well for what I say about a new concept of responsibility in 'Mochlos.' ❧ The reasons why *The Conflict of the Faculties* retrieves its pertinence and virulence once again are as interesting – and certainly as little accidental – as the reasons for which it was kept in the shadows up to now. The history of this text attests, among other things, to the power relationships reigning in the university. War or conflict? You know that Kant distinguishes 'conflict' (which can become legal, giving rise to regulated arbitration within the university) from 'war,' which escapes this legality and its system of boundaries. Now it seems to me that we can no longer trust, we know that it was undoubtedly never possible, in fact, to trust to such a boundary between 'war' and 'conflict,' between the socio-political outsides and insides of an institution like the university. We can no longer master (to do so was doubtless never possible) or even *think* of mastering those forms of opposition, at once 'conflicts' and 'war,' with the concepts, boundaries and criteria once available to us. No longer capable of mastery or belief in mastery, we have difficulty defining our responsibilities. Along with all its implications (subjectivity of the individual subject, consciousness, intention, free will, representation, objectivity and so on), the concept of responsibility – which we inherited and cannot separate from the inheritance we have just been talking about – is no longer commensurate with what we have to think and do. Doubtless it never was. Knowing this and saying so is not to abdicate, is not to renounce responsibility; it is instead to appeal to a *surplus* of responsibility, to the responsibilities I talk about in 'Mochlos.' This surplus of responsibility – for me, the very experience of deconstruction – leads to interrogating, suspecting and displacing those tranquil assurances in whose name so many moralisms, today more than ever, organize their courts, their trials and their censures. So long as those assurances are not interrogated or put to the test of a vigilant deconstruction, these moralisms will signify above all else a repressive violence, dogmatism and irresponsibility: the very irresponsibility that claims to speak in the name of responsibility, the well-known immorality of edifying moralism. ❧ On the subject of this surplus of responsibility at the heart of deconstructive affirmation, I would like very quickly to add two specific points. ❧ On the one hand, because of this surplus, and because deconstruction does not obey the dogmatic clear conscience of the moralisms just mentioned, it is no surprise that it disturbs that clear conscience, and finds itself accused of 'irresponsibility' by those who wish to be undisturbed in their tranquil certitudes. A classic scene. When someone asks, 'Are you sure your morality or your politics are well founded? Are you sure they can be founded? Are you sure you see them clearly? Do you know where they come from? Do you see their limits? Do you think you can delimit them that way? And what if your complacency on this subject were immoral and irresponsible?' and so on, the first defensive and reactionary reflex is to accuse of ethico-political irresponsibility, even of 'nihilism,' the very one who comes like this to question and disturb the *doxa* in its slumber. ᛗ On the other hand, an essential surplus or excess of responsibility is somehow the 'normal' condition of responsibility. If it were not excessive, if it could assign limits to itself, appease itself, arrest itself or calculate its own proportions, then the meaning claimed for 'responsibilities' would include anything but the meaning of responsibility. It would confuse responsibility with a calculation of causalities and programs. Responsibility is infinite or it is not, excessive or null, forever disturbed or denied. So the surplus of responsibility that I recognize in deconstruction is only an 'excess' of responsibility itself. ᛗ I permit myself to insist on this point because this call to reelaborate the concept of responsibility is at the heart of the three texts devoted to those 'authors' (Kant, Heidegger, de Man) we have been talking about. These are the very first words of 'Mochlos' (see p.1) and the very first words of 'Paul de Man's War.'[5] And *Of Spirit* is organized not only around the question of Heidegger's responsibility (at the moment of *The Discourse of the Rectorate* and before and after it) but also around the meaning of questioning, of responding, of saying 'yes' in advance of any question.[6] These motifs communicate with those of affirmation and the 'yes, yes' to which I have devoted a number of texts.[7] Formalizing things in the extreme, my concern today would take the following form: the three texts of the three authors we have been discussing take a different approach (explicitly or implicitly) to what responsibility can or must be. We have a responsibility (as readers, interpreters, heirs) with respect to these approaches which are also assignments. How can this help us define and assume our responsibilities today, particularly in the university and on the uncertain frontiers between the university and the social, call it textual, field in its broadest generality? ᛗ All the values constructing the Kantian concept of responsibility (subject/object, self, conscious will, intention, representation, synthesis of the 'I think' and so on) are made to account for the possibility of a responsibility, but also to delimit it, to guard it against the excess or infinity that carries it, has to carry it, beyond itself. This infinite excess is necessary to the concept of responsibility. But it remains intolerable to the finite subject having to take on its determinate responsibilities while never able to measure itself against the infinite, bottomless demands of responsibility – against the question, that is, of the other, to which or before which responsibility has to answer every time, in a way that is universal and singular. It is in this situation that a terrible and always unsatisfactory choice is imposed – of strategy, negotiation, the lever: *Mochlos.*

RR: *An impossible title. Why?*

JD: This title, rather than another, I chose in the first place because it is a Greek word. At a time when this text could wrongly be considered hostile to a traditional concept of the university, even dangerous for the 'humanities' and their canons, I wanted, through the choice of this somewhat learned word, to reaffirm a taste for the classics, the desire and necessity of a certain memory. So *Mochlos* also signifies Mnemosyne, Clio, Mneme, Anamnesis. . . . You have no doubt noticed that 'deconstruction' is always simultaneously accused *both* of destroying the canons and the norms of classical culture (deconstruction, a new form of barbarity, in sum!), *and* of being unreadable, difficult, esoteric, elitist, and therefore 'reactionary,' since it overloads itself with historical, not to say historicist, culture, suffers from hypermnesia and overcodes its texts (deconstruction, the new form of a precious and neo-baroque hypersophistication, in sum!). These two accusations are contradictory and incompatible. Those who formulate them ought to think about them some more, and ask themselves more seriously what is going on here, since it is, anyway, typical, and is not happening for the first time in history. ❧ A second reason for the choice of this word *Mochlos:* deprived of an article and placed in a title, it resembles a proper name. And in this resemblance to 'someone,' it seemed to me as monstrous, gigantic and dangerous as a mean animal, a dog for example (in French a *molosse* is a big watch dog whose name comes from the Greek *molossos,* a dog from the land of Molossia); or that big Australian lizard, the 'Moloch,' an animal more than twenty centimeters long covered with spines; or that giant and mythical serpent called the Loch Ness monster. A fantastic expandable serpent: It resembles a *phallos,* doesn't it? The proper name of a giant and slightly monstrous, almost inhuman animal: This is what I understand in the hollow or the hole (*Loch*) or the lack (*los,* loss) of this name, *Mochlos.* So many metonymies or pseudonymies to sport with the proper name. An almost inhuman giant, we could say, but just like 'responsibility': if responsibility must always be excessive, incalculable, forever carrying beyond the measurable norms and the units of measurement of law and morality; if responsibility is something that responds only to the other within us, and can therefore never be reappropriated, resubjectivized or reconstituted autonomously – a heteronomy of this kind needs to keep some quality of the an-human. (I am not saying 'in-human.') No doubt the choice of this name, resembling a proper name though not one, corresponds within me to some other desire. Elsewhere I have tried to show that the proper name doubtless never exists in complete purity. Nor is the noun reappropriated. But this mixture of proper name and common noun may serve to signal that the responsibility we are talking about remains a singular one always. It undoubtedly passes through the common law, but each person must take it up in his or her own name. The assignment is always singular, which is not to say empirical, let alone subjective or subjectal. The 'who' of the responsibility in question is not necessarily a subject. ❧ It remains a fact that the principal accent falls on the common noun, meaning the concept of *mochlos*. I wanted to privilege the question of the trampoline or the strategic lever. In the university, as elsewhere, one must always deal with contradictory injunctions in the form of the 'double bind.'[8] Since we always have to assume responsibilities quickly, lest the action be endlessly delayed, the question of 'What to do?' or 'How to do it?' is always a strategic question, the question of something I call a 'negotiation'[9] between two contradictory imperatives, both of which exclude negotiation, and at least one of which presents itself as 'categorical' or 'unconditional.' Is there, in the face of such antinomies, a good stratagem? Is strategy not impossible? Does the concept of strategy hold when the question of the better outcome is the very thing that gives rise to the antinomy? 'Mochlos' is a question on the lever. What this text asks is not: what is, technically, the best lever? but rather: what is technique in this case? Is there a lever? Is there a better lever? ❧ The Western university, be it said in passing, is still, for a while at least, the place where questions of this kind can be posed, or more precisely, pronounced. At any rate the question is not excluded, any more than the person who poses it or tries to draw certain consequences from it. But let us not indulge in too many illusions: this tolerance can be explained by the fact that the question has not yet been posed truly, effectively, noisily enough, or because the effective consequences are not yet visible, understood, measured. But as soon as they become suspect or obscurely glimpsed, then of course signs of nervousness appear. . . .

R R : Mochlos, *then, is an instrument – an operator's device?*

J D : *Mochlos* recalls a word which Kant himself uses, *mochlium* or *hypo-mochlium*. He does so in a footnote (in a lowly and minor place) to this text which is itself considered minor (see pp.49–50). I wanted to draw attention to the 'lowest' level of this minority, not just to recall the problems of evaluation, hierarchization and canonization which we just discussed, but for three other reasons as well.

1. On the one hand, as I said in my lecture, the question posed in strategic terms is that of the left and the right. Kant's footnote concerns the difference between the left foot and the right foot (for soldiers! during war!). This footnote allows me to recall what Kant says elsewhere about the paradox of symmetrical objects and the difference between the two hands, whose orientation cannot be defined in purely conceptual or logical terms, but has instead to be defined as the function of a topology of the senses, and of the subjective position of the human body. I used this figure to suggest that the political opposition between right and left must, when it concerns a strategic lever, be handled with the greatest care, even with vigilance, with the greatest sensitivity precisely to paradoxes. You know, for example, that deconstruction is attacked by liberal conservatives or by the extreme right as a leftist or anarcho-revolutionary movement, at the very moment when some who call themselves 'leftist' see it as a conservative or restorationist movement disguised in radical clothing. And when we suggest that this left/right opposition does not perhaps function so simply, then the same people remind us that the gesture of doing away with the left/right opposition is traditionally a gesture of the right. They are correct about that, but it should also have dawned upon them that 'deconstructionists' are well acquainted with this objection and its program, especially if they are of a certain age, if they are not too somnolent and if, to top it all off, they are European. All of which implies that they have in mind something other than that well-known program. This is especially true since the basic strategy of deconstruction has never been simply to neutralize or surpass oppositions, but rather to commence by reversing a hegemony or an established hierarchy, a gesture that will always be 'leftist,' even if it sometimes has to be made against forces and powers which, calling themselves leftist, stand in the way of movement, finding refuge in a dogmatic and comfortably clear conscience.[10]

2. This footnote involves the problems of feet and shoes, of left and right feet, of pair and symbol, which allowed me to tie it into my very political writing on this subject in *The Truth in Painting*.[11] It is tied in particular to a scene which both is and is not very academic, between two Jewish professors who fled the Nazis; and it involves Heidegger as well, his peasant ideology, the question of the subject and a crowd of ghosts, some of whom came back from the death camps in their shoes, represented, I mean, insofar as phantoms, as shoes without bodies. . . .

3. This footnote is one of those autobiographical passages in Kant which has always interested me: he talks there about his insomnia, his old age, the weakness of his left side and so on. What happens when a philosopher (and moreover a professor of philosophy, a state functionary) says 'I,' and talks about his health? And when he associates the 'risk of falling' with a military question as posed for the foot-soldiers of his country?

R R : *I am struck, from another direction, by the discussion of the future, of 'promise,' in your recent writings on Heidegger, and particularly, in* De l'esprit, *of the figure of the flame – the spirit regarded now as a flame of promise. I need not review here the enormous* guerre, *the war concerning the text of Heidegger and the flame that is Heidegger, and the necessity in the United States of reading this flame of Heidegger today – especially with regard to those topics generally termed 'ideological.'*

J D : Yes. If I chose to speak of Heidegger at the Tuscaloosa conference and to speak of him in this little book, *Of Spirit: Heidegger and the Question,* as you have mentioned, it is for several reasons. First, I had already alluded to him in 'Mochlos,' in connection with the *Discourse of the Rectorate.* There I had even said that the whole of 'Mochlos' maintained a 'constant,' if 'oblique and indirect,' relationship with this 'sadly celebrated' text and sinister event, in other words, with Heidegger's Nazism, precisely in connection with responsibility (see pp.9–10). ❧ I had thus situated, like a promise, the necessity of dealing with this act and Heidegger's writing in this context. I have often done so in seminars and, from a certain point of view, in *Of Spirit*. Everything or almost everything in that book revolves around *The Discourse of the Rectorate*. Without being able to reconstitute the entire chain of the demonstration, I would recall here that there are still after all some Kantian elements in Heidegger's *Discourse:* for example the imperative or the duty of knowledge (the responsibility specific to the university) which, despite its coorigin with two others (those of civil and military service), retains the status of an absolute privilege. If you recall, however, that the *The Conflict of the Faculties* prescribes that professors, and professors of philosophy in particular, obey the power of the state in all things concerning action and even concerning discourse insofar as discourse is active (as distinct from theoretical judgments with respect to truth), then a slight transposition will tempt you to an analogy. Kant lets the King of Prussia, Friedrich Wilhelm II, call him to order and to his 'responsibility' *(Verantwortung)*. He humbly defends and justifies himself before the king as a 'teacher of the youth' and an 'educator of the people.' If he also defines the faculty of philosophy as the lower faculty, the faculty farthest from political power, he still hopes that one day the philosopher, without exercising power, will inspire it:

*Thus we may indeed eventually see the last becoming first (the lower faculty becoming the higher faculty),* not in the exercise of power *[my emphasis, and Kant, even with this reversal, remains true to the absolute distinction between knowledge and power]* but in giving counsel *[and counsel, as he sees it, is not power]* to the authority (the government) holding it, which would thereby find, in the freedom of the philosophy faculty and the insight it yields, a better way to achieve its ends than the mere exercise of its own absolute authority.[12]

Here as well, despite the ancient dream of the philosopher-king and the king-philosopher, the philosopher would continue to be a counselor serving the royal purposes. Did not Heidegger also dream of playing this paradoxical role during the Rectorate? ❧ But let us not push the analogy too far. For, inversely, Kant would have judged as scandalous this *Discourse of the Rectorate* and all it implies. It transgresses every rule imposed by *The Conflict of the Faculties*. The concept of truth it propounds is no longer the same. The reference to a singular people and to the German character of the university, the privilege accorded the German language in the *Introduction to Metaphysics* of 1935 (which, on this point, is closer to Hegel),[13] the rather disdainful allusions to a certain concept of academic freedom, all this is not only not very compatible with the spirit of *The Conflict of the Faculties,* but with the pacifist and cosmopolitan spirit of a certain *Aufklärung* that animates it. And there would be further complications, further nuances. We cannot review them all right now. Instead of rehashing published texts or some well-known analyses of the political dimensions of the event named *The Discourse of the Rectorate,* I would be tempted to formalize things as follows: *The Discourse of the Rectorate* represents a *limit.* Profoundly coherent with *Being and Time,* despite the lifting of the quotation marks around the word 'spirit' (I explain this in *Of Spirit*) it confirms something essential to a relatively traditional concept of the university. What remains traditional is the role assigned to knowledge, to a philosophical questioning and a kind of fundamental ontology that would come to oversee, organize and dominate ontological regions, disciplines or departments engaged in research. This gesture can remain consistent with the innovation of *Being and Time* while still confirming the traditional organization of the *universitas* (which could also be called 'modern' in Kant and Kant's aftermath). It confirms a hierarchical verticality that submits all knowledge and research not only to the authority of questioning but also, with the same stroke, to the authority of the ontological question and a fundamental ontology. Such would be the truth within the university and the truth of the university. Now here is the other side of the limit: After 1935 or so, Heidegger no longer contemplates this fundamental ontology, whose authority should have organized the entire structure of the university. One could even say, and I have tried to show this in *Of Spirit,* that questioning is no longer the most thoughtful part of his thought, nor is it the most speaking element of *Sprache.*[14] From this moment on, and to this extent at least, one could venture to say that Heidegger's thought no longer pertains in its essence to the university. It no longer corresponds to what we call the university and to what articulates the *universitas* with the political, even though Heidegger continues to be a professor who gives his texts (but here too we must move with care) a form that is still academic. I believe that Heidegger's entire itinerary can be interrogated as a drama of sorting things out with the university, in the deepest reaches of a concept inseparable from politics, and, on the other hand, with what we call German idealism. ❧ What therefore makes *The Discourse of the Rectorate* so troubling, so disquieting and so provocative is something more than a direct or indirect political involvement with the Nazi party. It is rather that it works on a crest, on the line of a limit: first, in remaining consonant with the most forceful and most inaugural part of *Being and Time;* second, in repeating certain moves from the most respectable self-reflexive discourse of the Western university (in particular, as we have seen, repeating at least a few axioms from *The Conflict of the*

*Faculties*); third, in taking up again the project of a science of being and a fundamental ontology; and finally, by articulating this project along with a politics, showing the intolerable countenance of a university whose essence, by means of this fundamental ontology, would be inseparable from such a politics, or at least from an essence of politics which has never been able to exclude this particular politics. A consequence: if you really want to analyze the possibility of that politics and to uproot it – for it is also a politics of the root which pretends at times to be a radical politics – you must do nothing less than deconstruct this kind of contract that binds the hierarchizing project of a fundamental ontology to the political structure of the university and to politics as such. This undoubtedly seems quite abstract; not all of us living in the *polis* or the *universitas* are aware that we count on the project of such a fundamental ontology. But who ever said that things happening in such places should always present themselves to the consciousness of citizens, professors and students? When it is a matter of becoming conscious so as to take action and assume responsibilities, then deconstruction in any case can help. &#x25ba; To go any further we would have to analyze the letter of *The Discourse of the Rectorate* more closely. I have tried doing so elsewhere, and this is too difficult to repeat in an improvised interview. I will content myself at this point with taking up what you said about the 'promise' and the 'come' *(viens)*. In 'Mochlos,' but also in 'The University in the Eyes of its Pupils,' I suggested that the transformation of the university then in progress required the founding, somehow, of a different, even if unwritten, constitution, of another charter for the university. This resounded as a kind of promise. Not simply a promise in the form of a decision but in the form of a *coming,* through which a forth*coming* announces itself. This is hard to figure out. The future is that from which we are provoked to take a responsibility, and to say, beyond a determining knowledge, 'come.' That which says 'come' is the forthcoming, the future. It is not a subject which says 'come.' It is not we. The 'subject' only comes into itself out of this 'come,' which comes from the forthcoming.[15] It is a little difficult to improvise here, but this is a matter precisely of thinking something unforseeable, which does not, therefore, give rise to improvisation; of responsibility to something as yet unseen, to a non-knowledge, to *that* non-knowledge which, utterly intolerant of obscurantism and ignorance, is never opposed to – gives, on the contrary, its chance to – the knowledge that must found the university. I am speaking of a new university, a new *Aufklärung* demanding far more of us than did the eighteenth century's or the one they recently talked about in Frankfurt.

R R : *Your own history as a critic of Heidegger's political thought is not widely known – or not, it seems, in the philosophical circles of Paris. There is an essay stating, with apparent certitude, that no deconstructive publication, apart from the latest writings of Ph. Lacoue-Labarthe, 'could be said to have pondered the uncanny and familiar strangeness of Heidegger's "politics," or to have tried to work out the issue of Heidegger's "Nazism," let alone of his silence on the extermination.' Elsewhere, in the same essay, it is said that 'the question of "Auschwitz," as Adorno calls it, is lacking in deconstruction – this lack being something that J. Derrida, insofar as he keeps to deconstruction, can neither absorb (relever) nor displace (lever).'[16] But quite apart from the institutional critiques of the past fifteen years ['Mochlos,' 'Géopsychanalyse,' Otobiographies, etc.],[17] have you not, in* De l'esprit *and 'Geschlecht,' directed your thoughts toward Auschwitz? Wasn't your address on Kafka at the Lyotard* décade *(Cerisy, 1982)[18] composed in large measure as a response to Lyotard's own address, 'Discussions, ou phraser "après Auschwitz",' delivered at the Derrida* décade *in 1980?[19]*

J D : Certain responses are already implied in your questions, and I will add nothing to these. Lengthy analyses would be necessary to account for phenomena that are not only French, certainly, but are also somewhat excessively too much so. ❧ So I will be very brief. Certainly 'Auschwitz' as you correctly state has never been 'very far from my thoughts.' It would be easy to show this, though I have no wish to do so. The thought of the incineration (*brûle-tout*) of the holocaust, of cinders, runs through all my texts, well before *Of Spirit* which speaks exclusively of this, and well before *Cinders* which includes the necessary references,[20] and well before *Shibboleth (for Paul Celan)* whose sole theme it is.[21] What is the thought of the trace, in fact, without which there would be no deconstruction? (And one never does 'keep to deconstruction.' Deconstruction is never concluded because it was never nihilistic, contrary to what they say in *Newsweek*, but rather affirmative and generative. And it is difficult for me to imagine seriously, without laughing, what 'keeping to deconstruction' could possibly mean!) The thought of the trace, without which there is no deconstruction, is a thought about cinders[22] and the advent of an event, a date, a memory. But I have no wish to demonstrate this here, the more so since, in effect, 'Auschwitz' has obsessed everything that I have ever been able to think, a fact that is not especially original. Least of all does it prove that I ever had anything original or certain to say about it. The question remains: what does it mean to think or speak about 'Auschwitz'? Must one enter a contest or a competition for some prize ('Who has "spoken of Auschwitz" best or first?')? At all times this kind of polemical bidding has seemed indecent to me, as much as the reproaches or lessons given to those who could not 'think' Auschwitz. The author of *Heidegger and 'the jews'* litigates the 'sufferings,' the 'resistances' and 'unthinkables' of almost everyone, or of those at any rate who have nothing to say about 'Auschwitz.' He recognizes, however, as though in passing, that as for Auschwitz, he 'does not explain it any more than does anyone else.' So why blame others? He lays this inexplicability of Auschwitz (which ought at the very least to invite brevity) to the account of '*Verdrängung,*' the 'originary repression,' of which it would serve, in sum, as an example or particular instance.[23] This can leave some perplexity, and says nothing at all about that singularity, if there is one, not to mention those quotation marks around some 'jews.' Who died at Auschwitz, the 'jews' or some Jews? ❧ All of this would be less troubling if those who speak about Auschwitz began by saying with some rigor *what* they are naming 'Auschwitz,' and *what* they think about it, if they think anything about it (anything more or other than the generality of a problematics of 'originary repression') and what it is that they call 'thinking' in this case. What is the referent of this proper name, Auschwitz? If, as I suspect, one uses this name metonymically, what is the justification for doing so? And what governs this terrible rhetoric? Within such a metonymy, why this name rather than those of all the other camps and mass exterminations? Why this heedless and also troublesome restriction? As paradoxical as it may seem, respect is due *equally* to *all* singularities.

R R : *A question, now, about Paul de Man. He read Heidegger, but was he ever, do you suppose, a 'Heideggerian'?*

J D : It is late, and this interview has already gone on for too long. Let me be even more brief. In order to connect immediately with what we have just been saying, I return to the fact that de Man, who wrote on Heidegger and Kant, was neither Kantian nor Heideggerian.[24] He explained himself on this point. It is one of the aspects of his work that interests me most. All the aporias he analyzed with respect to the constative/performative relationship, notably in Rousseau, pertain to Kant as well, and in particular, as I have tried to show, to the Kant of *The Conflict of the Faculties.* As for the tension which, from his first theoretical writings, marks de Man's relationship to Heidegger (one of opposition, rupture, paradox), it follows the pattern that I have tried to articulate in *Memoires.* The greatest difficulty is precisely the enigma of the promise *(versprechen, sich versprechen, verheissen).*[25] That the thought and story of de Man are so foreign, even antagonistic, to Heidegger is evidence ridiculing in advance every conflation recently attempted on this subject by the most obscene of articles, in particular those by Jon Wiener, and Tzvetan Todorov who, among other stupidities, dared to say that de Man was 'an influential propagator of Heideggerian philosophy.'[26] ✍ I have said what I thought I could and should about the writings of de Man during the war, when he was only twenty or twenty-two years old. Since our theme is set by the symposium you organized in Tuscaloosa, and therefore ought to concern the politics *of* the university, *within* the university, and *between* the university *and* civil society or the state, I shall limit myself to just a few final points.

1. As one might, alas, have predicted, the most compulsive, hateful and confused reactions were signed, in so many publications, not by journalists but by irresponsible professors in their stead. Often, in saying almost anything at all with not the slightest concern for justice or truth, they thought the moment had come to settle accounts: accounts either with de Man (his person, his intellectual figure, his influence in the university, or anything else they projected there), or with his friends, or with those they thought they could associate with him; or, as the titles and substance of all but a very few of these sloppy articles indicated, accounts with deconstruction as such. That deconstruction did not appear until more than a quarter-century after the 'early writings' of de Man, that any connection between the articles of 1941–42 and deconstruction is a flagrant absurdity, was not a problem for anyone given to slander. I think the essential has now been said on this subject. I insist on only one last point concerning the context of our symposium. What that accumulation of resentment has revealed, among other things, is a renewed 'conflict of the faculties': the resistance to what de Man and deconstruction in general brought to the university also concerns a certain crossing of the boundaries between disciplines, the introduction of the theoret-

ical and the philosophical into the study of literatures (de Man regularly taught and wrote on the great philosophers), the elaboration of an institutional criticism, a fresh look at the ideology of the profession, and a new logic of academic responsibility.

2. The accusation of *nihilism* has once more been brought against de Man (and deconstruction) in the press and elsewhere. I shall not try here to get to the bottom of this, to the bottom, that is, of a daunting philosophical problem that cannot be solved by a journalistic phrase, and which, besides, is never really addressed by those heavyweights and lightweights manipulating that clumsy accusation. I shall not try to show yet again how this accusation, aimed at de Man or deconstruction more generally, rests upon the most serious confusion. Within the ideologico-doxo-journalistic context where this confusion is produced, I merely point out that this accusation of 'nihilism' was also frequent, coded and judged convenient during the war, notably under the Occupation. It was hurled *by the pro-Nazi press* against all its adversaries, notably among intellectuals and writers.[27] I invite those who manipulate this accusation with such ease to think about that fact. The many intellectuals and teachers who came from Germany to take up residence in the United States after the war – not all of whom fled Nazism! – could attest to it as well. An enormous amount of historical work remains to be done on what might be called the American memory or 'crypt' of Nazism.

3. To conclude, I would like to thank you and congratulate you on the organization of the Tuscaloosa symposium: for everything it made possible and which has subsequently been made available in print, certainly, but also because a coincidence of dates and an affinity of themes allowed us to take the initiative on the writings of de Man in 1941–42. I believe more than ever that this initiative was just and necessary. It will not be forgotten. In the best of conditions, it afforded an opening to one of the most necessary debates of the decade, inside and around the university. It initiated discussions and fostered indispensable publications. Without losing a second. This reflection (on politics, philosophy, the academy and so on) will take a lot of time. It will cut, especially in the field of the American university, some deep furrows. I think in the end the transformations encouraged in this way will be positive, interesting and significant. It was therefore much better to undertake this task at the earliest

possible moment. Many signs encourage us, at the time we are speaking, to think that a first phase – we knew it was inevitable – is fortunately behind us, one of immediate exploitation: hysterical, thoughtless and irresponsible, persecuting, and sometimes explicitly xenophobic. And analyses, more informed and more careful, are now appearing or scheduled to appear. One day, I hope, it will again become possible to discuss, from the viewpoint of deconstructive strategies, the singular inflections that the immense work of de Man in the United States impressed upon what is called deconstruction. These are difficult and necessary questions. As you know, there certainly are differences between the many deconstructive approaches, necessary as all of these approaches can be, and as necessary as their differences also are. In the face of what I have just called the de Manian 'inflections' of deconstruction, I would certainly have work to do (the better to understand, formalize and so on) and questions to pose. Our differences would appear more clearly and quickly, and our debates would unfold in a more interesting way, if there were not so many who have a stake in preventing them and drowning them out with war cries against Deconstruction, all the while feigning belief in some homogeneous whole, some camp, some *bloc.* You ought to be thinking about a second conference, again in Tuscaloosa, perhaps in five years, for a retrospective analysis of what will by then have been filtered (kept, forgotten, selected, changed) in the interval. A kind of *Mochlos* Two? I no longer know for sure what I said about the name of *Mochlos* a while ago. I no longer know who or what could bear its name. But it is most closely associated now in my memory with the last meeting of the conference, Saturday evening, when we began to speak, in deepest Alabama, of certain articles published in *Le Soir* in Belgium by a very young man almost a half-century before. . . . We knew, even then, that this event would be more remarkable and more remarked in the United States of the 1990s than it was in the Belgium of the 1940s.

Irvine, California, 1 May 1988 – Translated by Richard Rand and Amy Wygant

NOTES

1. Immanuel Kant, *The Conflict of the Faculties/Der Streit der Fakultäten,* trans. Mary J. Gregor (New York: Abaris, 1979). Jacques Derrida, 'Mochlos; ou, le conflit des facultés,' *Philosophie* 2 (April 1984), 21–53. Subsequent page references are to the translation that constitutes the first chapter of this volume.

2. *Wartime Journalism, 1939–1943,* ed. Werner Hamacher, Neil Hertz, and Thomas Keenan (Lincoln: University of Nebraska Press, 1988).

3. In addition to 'Mochlos,' Derrida's readings of *The Conflict of the Faculties* include 'The Principle of Reason: The University in the Eyes of its Pupils,' *Diacritics* 13 (1983), 3–20, and *Graduate Faculty Philosophy Journal* 10 (1984), 5–29. See also 'Languages and Institutions of Philosophy,' *Recherches Sémiotiques Semiotic Inquiry* 4 (1984), 91–154. These texts are collected in *Institutions of Philosophy,* ed. Deborah Esch and Thomas Keenan (Cambridge: Harvard University Press, forthcoming). Heidegger's *Discourse of the Rectorate* is read in Derrida's *De l'Esprit: Heidegger et la question* (Paris: Galilée, 1987), trans. Geoffrey Bennington and Rachel Bowlby, *Of Spirit: Heidegger and the Question* (Chicago: University of Chicago Press, 1989). Texts on Paul de Man include Derrida, *Mémoires pour Paul de Man* (Paris: Galilée, 1988), trans. Cecile Lindsay, Jonathan Culler, and Eduardo Cadava, *Memoires: For Paul de Man* (New York: Columbia University Press, 1986); and Derrida, 'Like the Sound of the Sea Deep within a Shell: Paul de Man's War,' trans. Peggy Kamuf, *Critical Inquiry* 14 (1988), 590–652; reprinted in *Responses: On Paul de Man's Wartime Journalism* (Lincoln: University of Nebraska Press, 1989), pp.127–44.

4. See Derrida's 'Unoccupied Chair: Censorship, Mastership and Magistrality,' *Recherches Sémiotiques Semiotic Inquiry* 4 (1984), 123–39.

5. 'Unable to respond to the questions, to all the questions, I will ask myself instead *whether responding is possible* and what that would mean in such a situation. And I will risk in turn several questions *prior to* the definition of a *responsibility.* But is it not an act to assume in theory the concept of a responsibility? Is that not already to take a responsibility? One's own as well as the responsibility to which one believes one ought to summon others?' Derrida, 'Like the Sound of the Sea Deep within a Shell: Paul de Man's War,' p.590.

6. See Derrida, *De l'Esprit,* p.147, n.1; *Of Spirit,* pp.129–36.

7. Among others, Derrida, *Spurs: Nietzsche's Styles,* trans. Barbara Harlow (Chicago: University of Chicago Press, 1979); and *Ulysse gramophone: Deux mots pour Joyce* (Paris: Galilee, 1987).

8. The issue of the double bind in the university is treated by Derrida in 'Lettre préface: Les antinomies de la discipline philosophique,' *La Grève des philosophes, École et philosophie* (Paris: Osiris, 1986), pp.9–31.

9. See Derrida, *Negotiations,* ed. Deborah Esch and Thomas Keenan (Minneapolis: University of Minnesota Press, forthcoming).

10. In 1967, 1968, and 1971, three interviews appeared in which Derrida commented upon this basic strategy. They have been published as *Positions*, trans. Alan Bass (Chicago: University of Chicago Press, 1981).

11. Derrida, *The Truth in Painting*, trans. Geoff Bennington and Ian McLeod (Chicago: University of Chicago Press, 1987).

12. Kant, *The Conflict of the Faculties*, p.59.

13. See Derrida, *Glas* (Paris: Galilée, 1974), trans. John P. Leavey, Jr., and Richard Rand (Lincoln: University of Nebraska Press, 1986); and *De l'Esprit*, p.161; *Of Spirit*, p.99.

14. Derrida, *De l'Esprit*, p.147, n.1; *Of Spirit*, pp.129–36.

15. See Derrida, 'Il faut bien manger, ou le calcul du sujet: Entretien (avec J.-L. Nancy),' *Confrontations* 20 (1989), 91–114.

16. The reference is to Jean-François Lyotard, *Heidegger et 'les juifs'* (Paris: Galilée, 1988); Lyotard, *Heidegger and 'the jews,'* trans. Andreas Michel and Mark S. Roberts (Minneapolis: University of Minnesota Press, 1990).

17. Derrida, *Otobiographies, L'enseignement de Nietzsche et le politique du nom propre* (Paris: Galilée, 1984). 'Géopsychanalyse' appears in *Psyché, Inventions de l'autre* (Paris: Galilée, 1987), pp.327–52, as does 'Geschlecht,' 395–451.

18. See Derrida, 'Préjugés devant la loi,' appearing in the proceedings of the 1982 Cerisy colloquium, *La Faculté de juger* (Paris: Minuit, 1985), pp.87–139.

19. Lyotard's address appears in the proceedings of the 1980 Cerisy colloquium, *Les Fins de l'homme, à partir du travail de Jacques Derrida*, ed. Ph. Lacoue-Labarthe and J.-L. Nancy (Paris: Galilée, 1981), pp.283–310.

20. This polylogical meditation on the short sentence, 'Cinders are there' *('Il y a là cendre')*, which first appeared in *La Dissemination* (Paris: Seuil, 1972), pursues the theme of cinders through Derrida's texts. There is, for example, this: 'You just said that he could not have an "up to date" phrase for this cinder word. Yes, there is perhaps only one worth publishing, it would tell of the all-burning, otherwise called holocaust and the crematory oven, in German in all the Jewish languages of the world' (Jacques Derrida, *Cinders*, trans. Ned Lukacher [Nebraska: University of Nebraska Press, 1991], p.57).

21. Jacques Derrida, *Shibboleth* (Paris: Galilée, 1986), trans. Joshua Wilner in *Midrash and Literature*, ed. Geoffrey H. Hartman and Sanford Budick (New Haven, Conn.: Yale University Press, 1986).

22. 'I have the impression now that the best paradigm for the trace, for him, is not, as some have believed, and he as well, perhaps, the trail of the hunt, the fraying, the furrow in the sand, the wake in the sea, the love of the step for its imprint, but the cinder (what remains without remaining from the holocaust, from the all-burning, from the incineration, the incense)' (Derrida, *Cinders*, p.43).

23. Lyotard, *Heidegger and the 'jews,'* p.130.

24. See Paul de Man, 'Phenomenality and Materiality in Kant,' in Gary Shapiro and Alan Sica, eds., *Hermeneutics: Questions and Prospects* (Amherst: University of Massachusetts Press, 1984), pp.121–44; 'Heidegger's Exegeses of Hölderlin' in *Blindness and Insight* (Minneapolis: University of Minnesota Press, 1971), pp.246–66; 'Heidegger Reconsidered (1964)' in *Paul de Man: Critical Writings, 1953–1978*, ed. Lindsay Waters (Minneapolis: University of Minnesota Press, 1989), pp.64–75.

25. Jacques Derrida, *Mémoires*, 145–50.

26. Jon Wiener, 'Deconstructing de Man,' *The Nation*, 9 January 1988. Tzvetan Todorov, *Times Literary Supplement*, 17–23 June 1988.

27. See Pascal Fouché, *L'Edition française sous l'Occupation, 1940–1944* (Paris: Biblio. litt. franc. contemp., 1987), 1:92.

CONTRIBUTORS

**Timothy Bahti**, a professor of Comparative Literature at the University of Michigan, is the author of numerous essays on German and British Romanticism.

**Alan Bass**, a principal translator of works by Jacques Derrida, is a psychoanalyst practicing in New York City.

**Jacques Derrida** teaches at the École des Hautes Études au Sciences Sociales in Paris.

**Peggy Kamuf**, a translator and editor of Jacques Derrida's writings, and a specialist in eighteenth-century French literature, teaches at the University of Southern California.

**John Llewelyn**, an author of books on Jacques Derrida and Emmanuel Levinas, was until recently a professor of philosophy at the University of Edinburgh.

**Christie McDonald**, author of books on eighteenth- and twentieth-century French literature, teaches at l'Université de Montreal.

**Richard Rand**, a specialist in British Romanticism, teaches English at the University of Alabama.

**Amy Wygant**, a graduate student in French at Johns Hopkins University, is pursuing research in seventeenth-century theories of the opera.

**Robert Young**, a professor of English at Wadham College, Oxford University, is publishing a two-volume study of politics and literary theory in the twentieth century.